DEWEY

The Arguments of
the Philosophers

EDITOR: TED HONDERICH

Grote Professor of the Philosophy
of Mind and Logic, University College, London

The purpose of this series is to provide a contemporary assessment and
history of the entire course of philosophical thought. Each book
constitutes a detailed, critical introduction to the work of a philosopher
of major influence and significance.

Already published in the series

DEWEY

J. E. Tiles

London and New York

First published 1988
by Routledge
11 New Fetter Lane, London EC4P 4EE
Paperback edition first published 1990

Simultaneously published in the USA and Canada
by Routledge
a division of Routledge, Chapman and Hall, Inc.
29 West 35th Street, New York, NY 10001.

© 1988, 1990 J. E. Tiles

Phototypeset in Great Britain by
Input Typesetting Ltd, London in 10/12 Garamond
Printed in Great Britain by
T. J. Press, Padstow, Cornwall.

British Library Cataloguing in Publication Data
Tiles, J. E.
Dewey.—(The arguments of the philosophers)
1.   American philosophy. Dewey, John,
1859–1952.   Biographies
I.   Title   II.   Series
191.

Library of Congress Cataloging in Publication Data
Tiles, J. E.
Dewey/J. E. Tiles.   p.   cm. – (The Arguments of the
philosophers)
Bibliography: p.
Includes index:
1.   Dewey, John, 1859–1952.   I. Title.   II. Series.
B945.D44T55 1988
191--dc19

ISBN 0–415–05310–2

For my parents

Contents

CONTENTS

Preface

Someone relatively new to philosophy might expect from the series title to have here a book about the disputes in which John Dewey engaged with other philosophers. 'Arguments' in the present context, however, refers to a general way of articulating thoughts, that is by offering some as reasons for holding others. This certainly takes place in any dispute which is worth following, but it is also the form of articulation which philosophers use when they are not specifically addressing those who disagree with them. A philosopher uses argumentative articulations to convey a vision – or, if that sounds too pretentious, a general view – of human beings and of their relationships to one another and to their environment, especially of those respects in which such relationships are mediated by thought.

Now one might profitably look at how philosophers articulate their general views by examining records of the disputes in which they engaged. In the case of John Dewey these are numerous and readily available. The editors of Dewey's *Works*, for example, have thoughtfully included (as appendices to the various volumes) articles which Dewey singled out for criticism, as well as articles which attacked his views and to which he published replies. For debates which were all conducted within the past century, however, these documents are curiously remote and sometimes hard to follow; they do not on the whole illuminate Dewey's general views; they presuppose them. This phenomenon illustrates in a striking way that arguments do not on their own carry a sense of what is at stake, let alone carry conviction.

In Dewey's case this phenomenon is no doubt intensified by the fact that his views, which had a considerable following during his life, have fallen into relative neglect. This is not, as some have suggested, because his following was generated entirely by the strength of his personality and could not be sustained without it. Dewey had genuinely original views, a remarkably comprehensive and coherent vision, and is at the present time neglected because those who pursue the development of philosophy, particularly in English-speaking countries, have clung to intellectual habits and patterns of thought which Dewey worked to undermine.

It remains, nevertheless, possible for philosophers who think of themselves as belonging to the analytic tradition to profit from a familiarity with Dewey, if for no other reason than to gain a sharper, more self-conscious perception of some of their common assumptions. In Section I.b it is suggested that Dewey offers a picture of what contemporary philosophy would be like if, transformed as it has been under the influence of modern science, it had at the same time carried with it more of the legacy of the post-Kantian (or 'Hegelian') philosophy of the nineteenth century.

This book is an attempt to specify some of the most important features of that picture and how they bear on the way philosophy conducts argument. As a vehicle for this purpose it has sometimes seemed useful to illustrate by drawing on disputes in which Dewey participated, e.g. with Bertrand Russell or Arthur Lovejoy. But it has sometimes seemed more useful to confront Dewey's views with those of philosophers, such a Hume and Aristotle, who flourished long before he did, as well as with those philosophers who have written since his death, such as Thomas Nagel and Bernard Williams. These disputes are not rehearsed to determine who should be declared the victor, but to illustrate how difference in outlook leads to a difference in the way argument is conducted.

The principal features of Dewey's outlook arise from a method of proceeding, a habit of thought, which Dewey both recommended and practised, that of looking at a unified phenomenon, whether it be sentience or self-hood, consciousness or community, as the product of internal differentiation over time in some simpler unity. This habit of thought works directly contrary to that in contemporary thought, which leads it to reduce wholes to parts and to treat parts as prior in the order of understanding to the wholes which they form, to neglect context and to seek to examine things in isolation from one another, and to deny the relevance of temporal development and to view things ahistorically.

Dewey's habit of mind is that of one who hopes to understand living things and it manifests itself in the way he approaches all philosophical issues with conceptions, which he has developed in a biologically-based psychology, but one which is still sufficiently general to deserve to be called a 'philosophical' psychology. This orientation is so important that although the first chapter sets out some of the main lines of Dewey's divergence from the dominant trends in analytic philosophy by beginning with issues of truth and knowledge, Dewey's own doctrines on truth and knowledge need to wait until his approach to mental phenomena has been considered. This occupies the second, third and fourth chapters, beginning with an account of how Dewey's views developed out of his early idealism and going on in successive chapters to outline his accounts of sentience and his distinctive way of maintaining the doctrine that thought depends on the use of language.

The fifth and sixth chapters then return to truth and knowledge and to Dewey's claim that these have no life outside the context of the reflective procedures which we adopt to deal with problems which are essentially practical. Clearly in the light of this claim any distinctive doctrines which Dewey had on practical reason will bear on truth and knowledge. What will be seen in the seventh chapter to be crucial in this regard is what Dewey calls 'the thoroughly reciprocal character of means and ends'. This is the view that, as well as ends constraining means, the development of means makes possible the development of ends. This doctrine is not only the basis of Dewey's resistance to the separation of scientific inquiry from practical and social concerns, but also the basis of his moral psychology, which is directly at variance with that found in empiricism.

Dewey presses 'the thoroughly reciprocal character of means and ends' into a principle of social and aesthetic criticism, the foundation and application of which are treated in the eighth chapter. The ninth chapter considers how this principle bears on social and individual ideals. This chapter also considers how views on the nature of knowledge, which Dewey was seen to resist in the fifth and sixth chapters, are the principal obstacles to the acceptance of the way he characterizes our ideals and the way he proposes we should pursue their elaboration and refinement.

I believe these ideas deserve to be taken seriously and I have tried to interpret Dewey sympathetically. I have not had the space to mark where I depart from other interpreters, nor to engage in disputes with them. The last two chapters treat in the most general way Dewey's views on art, politics and education. Dewey contributed to debates in all these areas and is still well known for his contributions, particularly to the last of these. Again I have not had the space to consider these issues in detail.

In the second chapter I decided that the best way to explain the earliest of Dewey's distinctive doctrines was to follow his own suggestion and present them as the result of the impact of reading James's *Principles of Psychology*. I have otherwise not presented a developmental story, have not written an intellectual biography or tried to contribute to intellectual history as such. I have tried to make plain the main features of Dewey's vision. This vision is needed if his philosophical arguments are to be read with an appreciation of what is at stake, his treatise on art is to be read with an understanding of the contribution which thought is supposed to make to aesthetic experience, his educational theories are to be read with a grasp of what for Dewey is involved in gaining knowledge and in developing a self, and his political columns are to be read in the light of his conviction that human intelligence, if applied correctly, could resolve some of our most serious conflicts.

Acknowledgments

Anyone who studies Dewey with care will be grateful for the effort and thoroughness which has gone into the project of producing a definitive edition of his *Works*. Having the *Early, Middle* and *Later Works* available made it much easier to undertake this book, and I am also grateful to the staff of the University of Reading Library who found resources for a 'special purchase' of the *Works*.

Many people have been kind enough to read or listen to portions of this book as it went through various stages of development. I am grateful in particular for the written and spoken reactions of Jon Bostel, Karen Hutchinson and Kathrine Morris. Early drafts of various parts were read to philosophy seminars at the universities of Bradford and Warwick, to an Open University Summer School and to a politics department seminar at Reading University. Other portions formed the basis of classes taught over a number of years at Reading and a series of classes ('Peirce and Dewey on Truth') given at Oxford in Trinity Term 1987 with Cheryl Misak. I am grateful for all that I learned from my audiences on those occasions and in the case of the Oxford classes for what I learned from my collaborator. Cheryl also performed the invaluable service of reading a relatively finished draft of material not included in those classes. Her advice on what to emphasize and what to leave out helped to put a better shape on the whole of the book. My wife, Mary, exerted the same beneficial influence on even the earliest drafts, and also worked hard to keep my spirits up and my efforts from becoming lost in minutiae. There were times when as a result of not grappling with Dewey's texts she saw more quickly and more clearly what he was saying. I am grateful for all she put into this book.

For the paperback edition I have corrected some misprints and attempted to remove some infelicities, which Peter Hershock drew to my attention. I am grateful to him for undertaking the sort of careful reading which authors commonly find themselves unable to perform on their own published work.

I

Legacies

Section I.a: Dewey's place in the history of philosophy

Works which pass as 'history of philosophy' fall on a continuum between two poles, poles which are marked by the two main components of that phrase, 'history' and 'philosophy'. Outsiders, who are likely to understand more of the historian's enterprise than of the philosopher's, will expect something from the history of philosophy near to the first pole. That is they will expect to encounter a branch of intellectual history, narrative accounts of what people thought about certain matters and what difference this made to life and culture generally. (They may even hope to gain an understanding of what philosophy is through reading its history.) In this sense of the phrase John Dewey has a secure place in the history of (twentieth-century) philosophy.

Dewey was an academic philosopher; his occupation was that of teacher and scholar. He commanded the recognition of the academic profession early in his career (from 1886) and he continued actively to contribute to professional debate until shortly before his death in 1952.[1] His work was acknowledged even by his severest critics to be highly original. But Dewey was also a public philosopher in the sense that he exerted influence on American intellectual life directly – as well as indirectly through tne influence of people who had been his students. He lectured frequently to groups outside the university; he helped to organize, and participated in, a wide variety of lobbying activities. From the time of the First World War onward he wrote regularly on national and international issues in (non-academic) journals of current affairs. Long before his rise as a political pundit he had an influential voice in debates about educational policy.

On all these issues, educational as well as political, Dewey regarded his views, as well as his readiness to contribute to debate, as grounded in his philosophic outlook. This does not mean that his views were

1

derived by strict deductive steps from his philosophical principles. (One implication of his philosophic position is that this would be an inappropriate, if not absurd, expectation.) His views, rather, were formed by assessing circumstances in the light of his philosophic position and it is possible that on many points he failed properly to appreciate the situation, or misapplied his own principles. But no historian who wishes to evaluate Dewey's contribution to American public life in the first half of this century can treat these contributions in isolation from his philosophy. And while Dewey's thought was not the only or even the most important element of American thinking during this period, no intellectual historian of the period can afford to overlook it.

Dewey was a public philosopher in another sense as well. By the onset of the Great Depression (by which time he was a semi-retired emeritus professor at Columbia University), Dewey had come to be thought of as the pre-eminent living American philosopher. Educated people who could name no more than one living American philosopher would be most likely to name John Dewey. His position in this respect can be compared to that of his contemporary Bertrand Russell, who at about the same time came to be regarded as the pre-eminent living British philosopher. Russell, too, worked on behalf of progressive ideas in education and engaged in high-profile lobbying activities, e.g. on behalf of nuclear disarmament. But even without such activities the historian cannot overlook men who held for a number of decades such a place in the public consciousness.[2] Such facts are the phenomena which concern the historian of philosophy, regarded narrowly as an intellectual historian.

But the history of philosophy encompasses more than a faithful record of what philosophers have thought and what difference it has made to other people. At the opposite extreme the history of philosophy is a vehicle for doing philosophy. This may be done openly by taking the text of a 'great dead philosopher', identifying what is living matter and suggesting what dead wood should be pruned and discarded. This may also be done less openly by writing a commentary on the text and, under the guise of making the original accessible to a new age, developing it into something well beyond, but still under the aura of, its ancestor.

Akin to the use of the history of philosophy as a vehicle for new philosophy is its use as a vehicle for educating philosophers, for continuing and developing a tradition. A philosophic tradition maintains and adapts itself in ways which resemble an oral literary tradition. It tells and retells its stories, its myths, about its past. Philosophy does not live by argument alone; its students are given a historical perspective through which they assimilate the standards of rigour, and above all relevance, which are needed to grasp and use its arguments. The selection of material from the past, the identification of past errors and past

2

triumphs, in an important way shapes a tradition; and one way to alter the course of tradition is to alter its view of its own past.[3]

Approached from the philosophic pole of the continuum, Dewey's place in the history of philosophy is more problematic. There have been recent signs that those actively doing philosophy are coming to regard Dewey's work as a resource,[4] but for many years it appeared that Dewey's thought contained nothing on which, or with which, to build. There have been scholars and educational theorists who have studied Dewey, and the project of producing a definitive edition of his works bore its first fruit in 1969. But compared to the role in the analytic tradition of Frege (born only eleven years before Dewey) and Wittgenstein, Dewey appears to be neglected. Russell similarly fell some distance from favour; both men were out of fashion among academic philosophers well before they died. But if the mainstream of analytic thought left Russell behind, it flowed through and out of Russell's thought. In Dewey's case what flowed through his life and work and inspired his contemporaries seems, for the time being at least, to have run into the sand.

Richard Rorty has, however, suggested a more hopeful picture. Drawing his own conclusions from the tendencies of 'post-positivist analytic philosophy', Rorty found the results 'kept sounding like questions from Dewey' (Rorty, 1985, p. 39). If analytic philosophy passed through and out of Russell's thought, 'James and Dewey were . . . waiting at the end of the dialectical road which analytic philosophy traveled' (Rorty, 1982, p. viii).[5] It is true that under the influence of Quine and others, some of the criticisms which Dewey had made of Russell and Moore[6] have come to be commonplace. But these commonplace criticisms sound in other respects like Dewey's position only if they are fairly freely extrapolated. The extrapolation which attracts Rorty is the conclusion that a whole philosophic tradition going back to Descartes can be drawn to a close and discarded. This does indeed sound like what Dewey urged, but while Dewey hoped this would allow a new and more fruitful philosophy to grow in place of what he regarded as moribund, Rorty hopes that nothing will take its place.

For Rorty the project of discovering the foundations of knowledge (including, if possible, value judgments) is bound up with the project of articulating the methods of science, with attempts to provide illuminating accounts of concepts of experience and consciousness, with efforts to describe the most general characteristics of reality, and with claims on behalf of philosophy to possess an authoritative role in culture. All this is for Rorty 'Philosophy', and when it is discarded, we will be left only with 'philosophy', 'an attempt [in words which Rorty quotes from Wilfrid Sellars] to see how things in the broadest possible sense of the term hang together in the broadest possible sense of the term' (Rorty, 1982, p. xiv). Now Dewey held such broad vision in high esteem, but as one of several patrons of Rorty's 'end of Philosophy' campaign (Rorty also invokes the names of Wittgenstein and Heidegger), the historical Dewey is something of an embarrassment.

The point of having a broad vision was for Dewey to have a vantage point from which to criticize, judiciously and sensitively, existing cultural institutions. Such criticism was for him the distinctive role of philosophy and it could not be conducted properly without an understanding of the methods of science. To mount such criticism effectively, moreover, requires certain distortions in our conceptions of experience and of reality to be corrected, and it cannot be carried out without a sound grasp of the nature of the general goals of intellectual endeavour (such as 'truth') and how these goals are progressively refined as our methods for pursuing them develop. All this leaves intact a great deal of what Rorty stigmatizes as 'Philosophy', and moreover presents 'Philosophy' as instrumental to the proper conduct of 'philosophy'.

Rorty recognizes these features of the historical Dewey but is prone to treat them as occasions when Dewey succumbed to the diseases he was trying to cure (Rorty, 1982, p. 88). It is true that Dewey wavered over the best way to advance his views and on the surface appears to abandon the attempt to analyse notions such as 'truth' and 'experience'. But this is because the views he wanted to supplant clung tenaciously to the vocabulary which he used to attack them, blunting and thwarting his efforts. He eventually abandoned the word 'true' and its cognates in an obscure corner of his *Logic* (LTE) and adopted 'warranted assertibility' as a description of the goal of inquiry less prejudicial to what he was trying to say. This was a tactical retreat over a point of vocabulary, not the surrender of a traditional task of philosophy. Shortly before the end of his life, as he considered how best to present a new edition of *Experience and Nature*, Dewey proposed to retitle it '*Culture and Nature*'. The reason was not that he saw the futility of trying to treat 'experience' (in Rorty's orthography) 'Philosophically'. 'I would abandon the term "experience" because of my growing realization that the historical obstacles which prevented understanding of my use of "experience" are, for all practical purposes, insurmountable' (L1, p. 361).[7]

Confronted with Dewey's commitment to 'Philosophy' Rorty distances himself from Dewey the philosopher and moves toward Dewey the pundit. 'In his hedgehog-like capacity as a philosopher, as opposed to his foxy capacity as a columnist, he kept insisting that a new logic and a new metaphysics were required if moral and political thought were to be rejuvenated' (Rorty, 1985. p. 44). But this 'rhetoric' is to Rorty an obstacle to making the best use of Dewey's thought.

. . . a thinker's own self-image may not be usable by his heirs.

Making use of Dewey as an instrument for our present purposes seems to me hindered rather than helped by preserving Dewey's idea that there is something called 'philosophy' which needs to be revised and revitalized by new ideas in the rest of culture. (Ibid., p. 47).

Rorty is, of course, entitled to his own assessment of what is usable in Dewey's legacy, but he is in the end no more prepared to take seriously and develop the philosophic position for which Dewey argued than are those who remain firmly within the analytic tradition. He is no more able to see how Dewey's arguments might achieve what they set out to achieve than are those for whom pragmatism is 'an outdated philosophical movement' (Rorty, 1982, p. xvii).

Section I.b: What is needed to make use of Dewey's philosophy

It does not follow that a consideration of Dewey's arguments, even for those who are not able to see how they get underway, is a pointless exercise. But to see how familiarity with Dewey's thought might enrich even a tradition which has so far bypassed him requires an appreciation of the total eclipse, which took place in Britain and the United States in the first part of this century, of the post-Kantian or '(absolute) idealist' tradition. Both Russell and Dewey began their careers in a milieu shaped by this tradition. Russell broke so cleanly with it that it left virtually no traces on his subsequent thinking. Dewey, who was arguably more committed at the outset of his career (emotionally as well as intellectually)[8] to a form of Hegelianism, also broke with the tradition, but the transition was gradual and his early commitment left, as he acknowledged (L5, p. 154), a 'permanent deposit' in his thinking. Russell's philosophic development up to the point where he parted company with the thought of the later Wittgenstein, presents a microcosm of the development of the dominant philosophic tradition in Britain and America. Dewey's Hegelian deposit remained to present an obstacle even to locating him on a doxographic map. It is not so much that Dewey's was out of fashion as that he was out of sight.

It must be stressed that neither Dewey nor the nineteenth-century tradition, which he in his own way transformed, are wholly ignored by scholars in the English-speaking world. There is scholarship in both fields and by no means all of it is condemned to distorting and misreading its subject matter. But for the majority of active philosophers a veil has been drawn over these episodes. They are not mandatory parts of the story of how we came to be where we are: they are not obligatory locations on the map of possible positions. Idealism is Berkeley. It is as though Green, the Cairds, Bosanquet and the Haldanes never lived. Dewey's philosophy lies in a similar way behind a veil. 'Instrumentalism' is the name for a view of scientific theories that in one form relegates them from the embodiment of knowledge to devices for anticipating what is *really* known, viz. individual experiences. Small wonder it is forgotten that the name, which this positivist changeling bears, was originally applied by Dewey to a doctrine that implied that an experience taken in isolation cannot constitute knowledge.

Those whose philosophic outlook has been shaped by the movement which identifies itself as in one form or another conducting 'philosophic analysis' may well find that lifting the veil on these episodes only confirms the view that what lies behind it was error and nonsense, and such obviously benighted doctrines are best left in obscurity. But for the heirs of Frege, Wittgenstein or the Vienna Circle to fail to appreciate the doctrines against which their movement defined itself is to fail to appreciate important aspects of their own heritage. It is to risk mistaking the ruts worn by their own habits of thought for grooves laid down in the nature of things. However, to use the history of philosophy in this way, as a means of revealing more clearly how and what one thinks, requires openness and imagination both to perceive the issues from a different perspective and to find in the cognitive dissonance, which is set up by the effort of moving perspectives, traces of what constitutes one's original perspective.

For this purpose Dewey's philosophy may be both easier to use and more fruitful, for it is defined by its revolt against the same tradition and it moves in many respects in the same general direction taken by the analytic tradition, although always with important differences. Dewey was convinced that the rise of natural science has given us profound new knowledge of the natural world, but he held a different view of what that knowledge consists in. He agreed with latter-day empiricists in insisting that this knowledge had to be firmly grounded in experience, but he worked with a radically different concept of experience. He was convinced that man was a part of nature; he professed naturalism, which is in a sense physicalism, but on the basis of such a different conception of nature (*physis*) for it to be misleading to speak of him as a physicalist. He was a behaviourist, but too prepared to interpret behaviour to be classed with Watson or Skinner. He was a consequentialist in ethics but too critical of what constitutes utility to be a utilitarian.

Although individual scholars may live philosophically at the end of the nineteenth century, we cannot as a culture go back and start from there, any more than we can go back to the Italian Renaissance and resume its artistic traditions. Whatever we learn about ourselves from studying the end of the nineteenth century we do not learn it by confronting a live option. The development represented by Dewey, on the other hand, is a route Anglo-Saxon philosophy might have taken to near where it is now. It is a portrait of contemporary philosophy carrying different baggage from its past and brings into sharp relief what actually is being carried. But to use Dewey's thought in this way one has to be prepared to recognize the possibility of carrying a different set of assumptions and responding with a different set of intellectual habits, otherwise Dewey's thought will appear only as a distorted picture of something more familiar. This is why Dewey is hard to locate; to each of the competing factions, whose assumptions he does not share, he appears to be a member of the opposition, but one too clumsy to be worth taking seriously.

Consider the debate conducted in contemporary philosophy of science between realists and positivists. For the former the truth of scientific theory consists in a correspondence between its theoretical statements and a reality lying beyond experience; for the latter the truth of a theory consists in a correspondence between its observation statements and what we experience when we make observations. When pragmatists suggest that correspondence is a misleading notion to use when trying to give an account of what makes a good scientific theory, they sound to realists like confused positivists, for they insist that the role of theory is as an instrument to guide experimental and observational practice. But as they deny that we can make a sharp separation between our theoretical and observational claims they sound to positivists like muddled realists.

Rorty also sees this pattern behind the neglect of pragmatism. He considers the issue of whether there are any truths other than those for which the natural sciences take responsibility, viz. statements which correspond to 'facts about how spatio-temporal things work' (Rorty, 1982, p. xv). 'The empirical philosophy' or 'positivists' (in a more general sense than that used above) hold that there are not. 'The transcendental philosophy' or 'Platonists' hold that there are statements, e.g. about values, which correspond to facts and objects beyond space and time. When pragmatists suggest that correspondence is a misleading way to characterize what constitutes the acceptability either of a scientific or of a value claim, they sound to Platonists like positivists, for they are not prepared to secure their value claims to timeless 'Real entities'. But because they insist upon treating value claims as in no way intellectually inferior to scientific claims, and seek relatively stable patterns of social function on which to base such claims, they sound to positivists like Platonists.

According to Rorty, this opposition between Platonists and positivists 'crystallized in the nineteenth century' and he assigns Hegel and the British neo-Hegelian T. H. Green, one of Dewey's early philosophic heroes,[9] to the Platonist camp. 'To side with Hegel and Green was to think that some normative sentences about rationality and goodness correspond to something real, but invisible to natural science' (ibid.). One needs to read this with great care in order not to be misled, especially by the words 'correspond' and 'invisible'. Here an understanding of the assumptions and preoccupations of the nineteenth century is vital and is also an important element of what is needed if we are to make use of Dewey's philosophy to see our own more clearly.

Green belonged to a movement which saw itself as 'post-Kantian' in this sense: Kant had taught that it was an error for philosophy to pretend to transcend the bounds of experience: we can know only what is a possible object of experience. Kant himself then turned around and appealed at a crucial point to a 'noumenal' realm, to things-in-themselves, which were not possible objects of experience.[10] Post-Kantian philosophy was characterized by a resolve to apply Kant's doctrines, especially his injunction against transcending the bounds of experience, more rigorously than Kant himself had managed.

Green is thus able to start from 'certain accepted doctrines of modern philosophy', viz. 'knowledge is only of phenomena, not of anything unrelated to consciousness', and its 'relation to a subject is necessary to make an object' (Green, 1883, I i 10). 'The growth of knowledge on our part is regarded not as a process in which facts or objects, in themselves unrelated to thought, by some inexplicable means gradually produce intelligible counterparts of themselves in thought' (ibid., I i 36). It follows that if there are truths, which science is not competent to deliver, it is not because they involve a correspondence to something outside possible experience.

Green expected to share the 'accepted doctrines of modern philosophy' with his empiricist opponents. It was not taken for granted that truth had to involve correspondence, so that the issue was: 'What corresponds to what?' It was taken for granted that what is known must lie in experience and the issue was whether what the mind had to grasp in order to achieve knowledge was particular experiences or a unified structure within the multiplicity of particular experiences. Green held the latter. Natural science aspires to knowledge of nature and 'nature is the system of related appearances' (ibid.). The more we comprehend of this unified system as our scientific inquiries progress, the greater our knowledge. Experience, which we cannot relate systematically, represents at best partial knowledge. At the extreme, a sensation or feeling, which is experienced in isolation from everything else, has no epistemic value whatever.

Green's general position shares some features of the doctrines which were developed and advanced during the same decades, the 1860s and 1870s, by C. S. Peirce.[11] Green's position is anti-nominalist in the sense that the object of knowledge, *reality*, must have general features; the mind must grasp universals – *unities* comprehending *diversity*. The position is also teleological in the sense that truth is a state toward which we are working and our finite minds represent various rudimentary stages

8

of completion. Instead, however, of referring to this *telos* in the way Peirce did as 'the opinion which is fated ultimately to be agreed by all who investigate' (Peirce, 5.407), Green appealed to

the concrete whole . . . which may be described indifferently as eternal intelligence realised in the related facts of the world, or as a system of related facts rendered possible by such an intelligence, [and which] partially and gradually reproduces itself in us, communicating piecemeal, but in inseparable correlation, understanding and the facts understood, experience and the experienced world. (Green, 1883, I i 36)[12]

This 'eternal intelligence', God, represented to Green and to the young Dewey the end of our moral as well as our intellectual endeavours. As our knowledge can develop toward the ideal state actualized in the eternal intelligence (through our grasping the system that structures appearance), our 'selves' can develop toward the ideal state possessed by the Perfect Being through their acquiring the dispositions and motivations which are realized in that Being. This would be a process of fully realizing our 'selves'.

'The inseparable correlation' of knowing and thing known (in the passage quoted above) reflects the post-Kantian commitment to avoid any separation between the two which might reintroduce the unknowable, noumenal, thing-in-itself. Neither the object of thought, nor the ultimate reason for our thought having the character of knowledge (as opposed to fancy), was to lie outside of or be independent of possible experience. An object is part of the organization immanent in experience, which constitutes experience as objective. It may transcend the experience of any particular individual subject in the sense that 'piecemeal communication' of the necessary organization has not yet taken place, but it may not transcend experience as such. We do not, moreover, have knowledge because an object, which transcends experience, imposes itself casually upon our experience. Causality, Kant had taught, is a concept arising from the general form of the judgments which we make about experience and is part of what gives rise to that immanent order of experience which constitutes it as objective. It must not, however (Kant's apparent lapses notwithstanding), be applied to what are not possible objects of experience.

The upshot of this is idealism, but it is an idealism which differs in important respects from that of Berkeley. Berkeley was a thorough nominalist and could not take systematic relatedness seriously as the object of knowledge.[13] He placed the ultimate reason for our thought qualifying as knowledge in a causal relation to Being, God, which completely transcended experience. In an early article (1886), which he published as a partisan of Green's general approach, Dewey began by praising Berkeley for having adopted a method in harmony with what Green declared to be 'the accepted doctrines of modern philosophy'. That is to say Berkeley was right to have considered all real and imaginary things through their involvement in our self-conscious lives (E1, p. 123). But Dewey went on to make this observation:

> Berkeley, in effect, though not necessarily, as it seems to me, in intention, deserted the method in his reference of ideas to a purely transcendent spirit. Whether or not he conceived it as purely transcendent, yet at all events, he did not show its necessary immanence *in* our conscious experience. (E1, p. 124)

Even when Dewey was no longer prepared to refer all real and imaginary things to our self-conscious lives, he held onto the conviction that it is a mistake to treat the truth of our beliefs as residing in a correspondence between what we can bring into experience and something wholly outside it. When Russell broke with the idealists he returned to this view of truth and held it in such a way that it gave life and urgency to problems which were for Dewey unreal. To illustrate how what Dewey retained from his idealist legacy leads to cross-purposes with those who retained less, we will in the next section examine part of an exchange which took place between Dewey and Russell in and around 1915, when both were well beyond idealism. To start to see in Dewey's philosophy a sense of their own perspective, analytic philosophers would need to appreciate how Russell's problems can appear unreal to Dewey.

Section I.c: The external world

Within a decade of making his observation on the transcendent elements in Berkeley's philosophy Dewey had parted company with Green, and the development of his own distinctive position was well underway. Nature ceased to be an order possessed by an ideal experience; experience instead came to be one of many possible kinds of natural event. But Dewey remained as hostile as Green had been to the idea that experience in isolation from anything else has any epistemic value. In 1929 he wrote,

> To assume that anything can be known in isolation from its connections with other things is to identify knowing with merely having some object before perception or in feeling, and is thus to lose the key to the traits that distinguish an object as known. . . . The more connections and interactions we ascertain, the more we *know* the object in question. (L4, p. 213)

In accordance with this doctrine about what is involved in knowing something Dewey characterized the goal of intellectual effort as that of bringing systematic unity to experience. This was written into his definition of 'inquiry',[14] and it had been a constant theme before then. At the time of his exchange with Russell on the 'external world', he wrote of 'reflective inquiry as a phase of reorganizing activity . . . *that will confer upon* [the present situation] *the unification which it lacks*' (M8, p. 42). Fourteen years later he wrote, 'In the face of a problem, thought always seeks to unify things otherwise fragmentary and discrepant', (L1, p. 32). And two years after that, 'Thinking has the task of effecting unification in a single coherent whole. In this sense the goal of all thinking is the attaining of unity' (L6, p. 8).

As we will see in Section V.d below, this did not mean that thought is the pursuit of a single all-comprehensive unity, such as that embodied in Green's 'eternal intelligence'. Dewey's development involved the purge of all such absolutes. The purge began with a dissatisfaction over how Green's ideal of self-fulfilment was to be used as the basis for the guidance of concrete conduct (E3, p. 159). A parallel worry can be raised about the epistemological role of this 'Absolute', one which points to an important weakness in the way the Absolute Idealists sought to avoid Kant's capitulation to a transcendent perspective.

There is a sense indeed in which someone who subscribes to such unity, particularly if it is believed to be actualized in the mind of God, will be tempted to an account of truth which involves a correspondence with this ideal state. Any state of awareness will be a partial representation of the total system of nature, but if it were sufficiently adequate, so that it could be matched to a part of the total system without needing radical modification or reinterpretation, we could say it was to that extent true. And the temptation would be to treat truth as consisting in that sort of match. But if the burden of the analysis of 'truth' rests here, we have come dangerously close to the problem with which Descartes in his *Meditations* inaugurated modern philosophy. Truth – what we are trying to achieve in our efforts to know – is ultimately how God sees things. How can we be certain that our thought on some matter is ever sufficiently like God's view of things to count as anything other than massive illusion? What assurance have we that the natural world represented in our thoughts and in our perceptual experiences is anything more than the content of a dream?

One of the things which attracted the young Dewey to post-Kantian absolute idealism was that it dissolved this question by presenting our intellectual efforts as directed at something which we can recognize in our experience, namely its systematic unity. But as we have just seen, it was all too easy to restate the old problem in the new framework. What continued to motivate Dewey, as he grew out of his early involvement in neo-Hegelianism, was the belief that it was possible to avoid the fundamental dualisms that introduce a gulf betwen experience and its object (entailing the gulf between mind and body) and between moral life and its ideal. An achievement, intellectual or moral, had to be something one could find in the qualities of experience itself. Thus in mid-career he wrote, 'Truth . . . is just the name for an experienced relation among the things of experience' (M3, p. 126). It is true that in a relatively late work Dewey subscribed to Peirce's definition of truth in terms of the ultimate opinion of the community of inquirers.[15] But by this point 'truth' had become the name for something on the periphery of Dewey's concerns. The weight in Peirce's definition had to rest for Dewey on 'inquirers' and what they seek, which, as we have seen, is a unification of experience.

The development and character of Dewey's own distinctive position will occupy us in succeeding chapters, but it is worthwhile considering first an episode which illustrates the extent to which Dewey's background shaped what he came to see as the real problems of philosophy. In 1916 Dewey published a critique of Russell's treatment of the question of the 'existence of the external world' (M8, pp. 83ff.). The main thrust of that part of the argument which Dewey referred to as 'formal analysis', was that Russell was addressing a problem which could not be coherently stated, and hence needed no solution. This part of the argument owed very little to the development which Dewey's thinking had undergone in the intervening years; it was almost entirely the product of (what remained of) the outlook he had acquired at the outset of his career.

The two forms of the question which Russell preferred and on which Dewey focused were, 'Can we "know that objects of sense . . . exist at times when we are not perceiving them?" . . . Or, in another mode of statement: "Can the existence of anything other than our own hard data be inferred from the existence of those data?" ' (M8, p. 84). Russell preferred these formulations because of the difficulties over the concepts of self which would arise if he used a more familiar 'Can we know of the existence of any reality which is independent of ourselves?' (Russell, 1915, p. 62). Dewey's note on 'own' pointed out, however, that Russell's formulation had not entirely avoided the issue; 'Who are the "we," and what does "own" mean, and how is ownership established?' (M8, p. 84n). But Dewey concentrated his attention on Russell's use of the term 'sense' to describe the data, e.g. 'The hardest of hard data are of two sorts: the particular facts of sense, and the general truths of logic' (Russell, 1915, p. 60). 'Sense' invokes the physiological conditions of the experience and hence seems to require an immediate 'yes' answer to the question about whether we can infer the existence of things other than our own hard data. Yes, we can infer from the statement of the question that there are physiological organs and processes involved in the occurrence of the data.

Russell could easily have replied that the label 'sense' belongs to a

'soft' portion of the data, a portion which would require eventual elimination 'under the solvent influence of critical reflection', because under
that influence the dependence on physiological organs and process
becomes 'more or less doubtful' (ibid.) But Dewey insisted he was not
out merely to trip Russell up over careless language. A term such as
'sensory' is needed, Dewey believed, if 'even a preliminary disparaging
contrast between immediate objects and a world external to them' is to
be instituted (M8, p. 85). It is not that 'sensory' suggests 'physiological',
it is that the bare datum rigorously regarded as such does not raise, does
not provide scope for, any questions – about itself or about anything
else. There is not, for example, anything given in the bare datum which
provides material to ask about limitation in time or about reference to
other times. If one bare datum, red, is replaced by another, blue, 'There
is still no ground for a belief in the temporally limited duration of either
the red or the blue surface' (M8, p. 88). What the phrase 'object of sense'
betrays is the need for an object (a *sensed* object) which is at one time
red and another time blue.

Dewey recognized that Russell was seeking to avoid this conclusion
of traditional metaphysics, but what Russell offered in its place – an
experienced 'correlation of muscular and other bodily sensations with
changes in visual sensations' (M8, p. 89; Russell, 1915, p. 65) – was for
Dewey just as much the world which Russell was supposedly calling
into question. 'But in addition there appears the new term "correlation".
I cannot avoid the conclusion that this term involves an *explicit* acknowl-
edgement of the external world' (ibid.). Dewey's response here is that
of an intellectual descendent of Kant. Objectivity is a funtion of the
structure of experience; objects are objective things only as a consequence
of their place in that structure, 'particulars can be identified *as* particulars
only in a relational complex' (M8, p. 90). The 'external world' enters
with the structure of experience. If Russell allows in a little structure
that 'may not be a very big external world, but having begged a small
external world, I do not see why one should be too squeamish about
extending it over the edges' (ibid.).[16]

But Russell's question, surely, was not about whether experience had
a structure but whether there was anything beyond it. To which Dewey's
reply would be that an answer to such a question will have to be
represented *in* experience *as* possible experience. A question about the
totality of experience can only be a question about, or phrased in terms
of, the structure that obtains within it. Within the structure of experience
one experience is linked to another in such a way that we regard the
second as a cause of the first. To treat the whole of experience as a result
of the action of things outside it is to treat the whole by means of
concepts which can only be coherently applied within. A corresponding
error is to pare down experience to a core of hard data, bare isolated

13

presentations, and then ask if we can infer any objects beyond them. These data cannot constitute a possible total experience; to try to get into a position to ask the question requires destroying the foundation for asking it, 'the very attempt to state the problem involves a self-contradiction' (M8, p. 83).

Dewey's argument is not intended to reassure those who fear that future experience may well upset our most firmly established beliefs. That it may well do; but that is not the question which Russell is addressing. Even when we find we have to treat the system of related appearances in a fundamentally new way, the old way of treating the system (on which we previously based our 'anticipations and previsions' – see note 16) had successes, which we must reconcile with our new way of treating it. We will regard the old way as totally worthless only if we conceive the point of dealing with the system of appearances as lying in a correspondence to something beyond experience, rather than as achieving something within our experience.

Russell complained 'that Professor Dewey ignores all fundamental skepticism. To those who are troubled by the question: "Is knowledge possible at all?" he has nothing to say' (Russell, 1919, p. 243). But this is not fair; what Dewey had to say was that the question lacked foundation.[17] Russell proceeds as though all that require foundation are *beliefs*, the answers to questions. Questions are regarded as neither having nor needing foundations. Questions are psychological events having causes and histories, but not subject to justification and hence not entering into logical relations. They are, after all, the products of human activity, of the 'subject' of experience. They may usher in the objects of experience, but in the interests of knowledge we must concentrate solely on those objects and may safely ignore the ushers. Anyone who regards the meaningfulness of questions as independent of the procedures by which their answers are to be established, will find Dewey's criticisms of Russell largely beside the point.

Section I.d: Genesis and justification

Although Dewey's attempt to expose the contradictions in Russell's *problem* took up the greater part of his article, he did not regard it as sufficient to leave the matter there. In a critique of Lotze some years earlier he insisted, 'It is an idle task to expose contradictions unless we realize them in relation to the fundamental assumption which breeds them' (M2, p. 330). And having completed his 'dialectical' treatment, he approached Russell in a similar spirit. What 'actual questions' give rise to Russell's 'unreal problem'? What is being misconstrued? Dewey's attempt to get behind Russell's motivation exhibits further characteristics of his philosophical approach, which make it difficult for most of those who regard themselves as 'analytic philosophers' to treat his arguments with respect. Some of these characteristics have their source in Dewey's early philosophy, but they also reflect the influences which led to Dewey's mature position. By drawing attention to these characteristics this section will seek further to elucidate what divides Dewey from those who see themselves as belonging to the analytic tradition.

Dewey began the second part of his critique by suggesting there might be at work in Russell a mistaken impression that psychology supports the view that we 'construct' ordinary objects in space from 'patches of coloured extensity, sounds, kinaesthetic qualities, etc.' (M8, p. 94). But the idea that 'infancy begins with such highly discriminated particulars' (ibid.) was not only dubious in itself – involving the extremely improbable notion that the first quality of an experience corresponds to the functioning of a single (neuronic unit of a) sense organ (M8, p. 95) – but it had been challenged by eminent psychologists such as William James.

Dewey's argument at this point reflects the significant development which his thinking had undergone a quarter of a century earlier as a result of reading James's *Principles of Psychology*.[18] Central to this influence was James's notion that primitive experience was to be characterized not by discriminated particulars but as an inclusive and undifferentiated whole. Using a turn of phrase now famous, James had asserted, 'The baby, assailed by eyes, ears, nose, skin, and entrails at once, feels it all as one great blooming, buzzing, confusion' (James, 1890, I, 488).[19] Dewey somewhat more prosaically spelled out the consequences of this view of genetic psychology:

> . . . the original datum is large but confused. . . . That knowledge grows from a confusedly experienced external world to a world experienced as ordered and specified would then be the teaching of psychological science, but at no point would the mind be confronted with the problem of inferring a world. (M8, pp. 94–5)

The philosophical consequences of this alternative psychological account are that 'the world', a primitive universe (unity in diversity), is a *'logical'* primitive (M8, p. 90), a given which cannot be called into question. All that can be questioned is whether distinctions subsequently introduced are adequate, are justified by the extent to which they enable the suggestions or expectations contained even in the most rudimentary conscious experience (M8, p. 94) to bear themselves out. We cannot doubt the common-sense world; we can only doubt 'some received piece of "knowledge",' some received piece of *common sense*, [the] complex of beliefs about specific things and relations *in* the world' (M8, pp. 96–7).

Russell, however, repudiated the suggestion that his analytical approach of seeking to rest our belief in the existence of the external

15

world on the 'hard data' of 'sense objects' stood or fell as a psychological account of the origin of knowledge. His was a question of justification not genesis. Dewey had stressed that inferences constituting a conception of an 'external world' were themselves natural events present in 'the simplest form of anticipation and prevision'. (See note 16.) Russell replied, 'Certainly no one denies that inference is an empirical event, what is being examined is not its *occurrence* but its *validity*' (Russell, 1919, p. 252). Russell wanted to locate the most secure basis on which the 'most educated person' could make such inferences.

But in Dewey's eyes what Russell sought as *data* were among the more sophisticated *products* of the central movement of thought from the less differentiated to the more differentiated. Dewey thus could only look upon the attempt to seek the sort of 'hard data' which Russell sought as a foundation for knowledge, as bound to be ridden with contradictions as Russell both pretended to dispense with the thought processes by which his data were generated and was forced more or less explicitly to appeal to those processes. Nevertheless, confident that the logic of his question about the 'external world' was above reproach, Russell shrugged off the alleged contradiction and dismissed the appeal which Dewey made to the Jamesian conception of infant experience (as a 'large but confused' datum needing to undergo functional differentiation), saying that how the world is given to babies is irrelevant (ibid., p. 250). Dewey's approach, Russell argued, made assumptions about human beings and their environment, which amounted 'practically to a complete metaphysic' (ibid., p. 243). And he complained that 'Professor Dewey, almost wilfully as it seems, refuses to perceive the question I am discussing, and points out the irrelevance of what I say to all sorts of other questions' (ibid., p. 247).

Dewey's refusal to address Russell's preoccupations was indeed wilful. He held that a great deal of the philosophy of his time was addressed to the wrong questions. His call in 1917 for a 'Recovery of Philosophy' was a call to rethink the questions with which philosophy should concern itself. Is it not time that philosophers turned from the attempt to determine the comparative merits of various replies to the questions to a consideration of the claims of the questions (M10, p. 24)? This is not simply a matter of one man urging the pursuit of questions which do not interest another. Dewey regarded Russell's question not merely as idle or baseless, but as obstructive. It was the product of a method which precluded the relevance of certain other questions and thereby gave rise to incomplete and distorted images of ourselves and our intellectual capacities.

Russell's tactic was to present Dewey as interested in other questions, questions which might admit investigation by empirical science, but which were irrelevant to Russell's concerns. If succesful this tactic would insulate the assumptions which Russell made from having to confront competing alternatives. Disentangling questions is, to be sure, one of the most important techniques which a philosopher needs to learn and practice. Confused questions, questions posed at the wrong point, can permanently stall intellectual effort. Dewey was as sensitive to this as anyone; getting clear about one's problem is more than half the solution (LTE, pp. 108–9).

Whereas the tendency in Dewey's philosophy is to require all disciplines to develop theories and perspectives which interlock, Russell represents a tendency in analytic philosophy to erect distinct questions into autonomous subdisciplines which are not supposed to bear at all on one another. Questions of ontology are to be kept distinct from questions of epistemology, we are told. This does not mean simply that 'What sort of fundamental entities are there?' and 'What do we know?' are different kinds of questions. It means we are not to trouble those who make claims about the sorts of fundamental things there are with questions about how we might know their claims are correct. Questions of meaning are said to be distinct from questions of epistemology. This means that questions about how we might come to know the answer to a question has no bearing on whether it is a meaningful question. More than anything this tactic of erecting distinct questions into autonomous subdisciplines has blunted criticism of the idea that truth consists in a correspondence to a realm outside experience, and has obscured the extent to which assumptions about what is involved in knowing bear on what we take to be the nature of the thing known.[20]

Other questions we are to keep sharply separate are those which Russell sought to hold apart, questions of genesis and questions of justification (or in the philosophy of science, the context of discovery and the context of justification). Dewey was far from regarding justification as unimportant or from holding that our justification for using a concept or holding a belief was to be found in the events which lead up to our acquiring that concept or belief. Justification was his central preoccupation but it lay in how well the concept or belief enables us to deal with present and future problems. Now problems, and the means which we have for coping with them, are historical products; we will understand neither the problem we face, nor the resources we already possess, nor what modifications to those resources we require in order to meet the problem, unless we are prepared to link things to their origins. Problems do not arise in isolation but in historical contexts, and one must grasp the relevant features of the context to meet them. This is the source of Dewey's preoccupation with genetic considerations, but unless one appreciates this, Dewey's approach will appear to be ridden with what some are prone to call 'genetic fallacies'.[21]

Thus Dewey allowed that sense data could play a crucial role in testing

17

and justifying beliefs, but stressed, and continued in subsequent years to stress, that they are not 'primary . . . as historic originals' (L1, p. 246), as though genesis really was the issue. He acknowledged that 'sensa form a limit approached in careful analytic certification', and that science would in testing crucial cases find it 'necessary to touch the limit' (ibid.). In his critique of Russell he suggested that far from being elements which resist 'the solvent influence of critical reflection' (Russell, 1915, p. 60), sense data were (although not usable on their own) instruments for dissolving the individual and social habits which stood in the way of scientifically adequate beliefs about the world (M8, pp. 95–6). But in neither role was it appropriate to treat them as foundation stones for the edifice of knowledge.

Instead of proposing a better candidate for foundation stones, however, Dewey continually turned away from the foundation metaphor to stress how we actually set out from the 'coarser and more inclusive', and seek the ultimate and harder, which is 'sensory in character' (L1, p. 246), only when problems arise in the course of applying the softer and more proximate. It seems that Dewey's thought was just drawn inexorably to the patterns which characterize actual procedures. Yet he wanted to insist that such patterns had a bearing on the nature and legitimacy of our beliefs and practices. When accused in 1911 of mounting a critique 'from the standpoint of genesis' (M6, p. 483) because he had stressed 'the active process of getting knowledge' (M6, pp. 139f.), he insisted that his was a 'formal standpoint' (M6, p. 143). He saw his preoccupation with coming to know as making a contribution to the question of what it is to know, and indeed what motivated him was much deeper than simply an interest in how things came to be the way they are.

Defences which Dewey offered of 'inquiry into origins' did not always help his cause or make clear how such inquiries might bear on other questions. In 1902 he argued that the genetic method was continuous with the experimental method in science (M2, p. 4). The argument was based on the idea that experiment is an attempt to generate under controlled conditions the phenomena to be studied. 'What experimentation does is to let us see into water in the process of making. Through generating water we single out the precise and sole conditions which have to be fulfilled that water may present itself as an experienced fact' (M2, p. 5). But experimental procedure is not necessarily directed toward the production of what is to be studied; we stand to learn from any transformation which we can control. The electrolytic analysis of water into hydrogen and oxygen is as significant as the more difficult task of synthesizing it out of these elements.

Other themes which appear along with this somewhat embarrassing argument give a better idea of what Dewey was driving at, and over the years these themes emerged into greater prominence. One was the identification of 'the materialistic fallacy', viz. the belief that effects can be reduced to their causes, or that 'the earlier fact somehow sets the standard of reality and of worth for the entire series' (M2, p. 10).[22] Another theme that reappears is that raising genetic questions reflects a concern with context.

> [Empiricism] regards the idea simply as a complex state which is to be explained by resolving it into its elementary constituents. By its logic, both the complex and the elements are isolated from an historic context. The genetic method determines the worth or significance of the belief by considering the place that it occupied in a developing series. . . . (M2, p. 31)

The point was repeated a few years later when Dewey decided he could advance his position as a form of empiricism – 'Immediate Empiricism'.

> What is criticized now as 'geneticism' (if I may coin the word) and now as 'pragmatism' is, in truth, just the fact that the empiricist does take account of the experienced 'drift, occasion and contexture' of things experienced – to use Hobbes's phrase. (M3, p. 162, n. 8)

Eventually lack of concern with context emerged in Dewey's view as the most significant source of all that he opposed. There is a link between the way Dewey came to diagnose the errors of those who opposed him and the rationale he felt for a concern with questions of origin. Tracing the development which Dewey's diagnosis underwent reveals not only that rationale but also what is perhaps the most fundamental of the differences which divide Dewey from the analytic tradition. This task will be taken up in the next section and will round out this preliminary survey of the distance between Dewey's philosophy and that commonly practised in English-speaking countries today.

Section I.e: Methods and fallacies

Proposing new names for 'fallacies' and identifying them in the approach of one's opponents was a fairly common rhetorical ploy in the first half of this century.[23] Dewey was as prone to this habit as any (witness: the 'materialistic fallacy' mentioned above), and late in his career he attempted to identify '*the* philosophic fallacy' (L1, p. 34), the single greatest obstacle to seeing things as Dewey saw them. The phrase and the project followed a pattern set by James in the *Principles of Psychology* of identifying 'the psychologist's fallacy'. According to James, an individual makes this mistake when he confuses his 'own standpoint with that of the mental fact about which he is making a report' (James, 1890, I, p. 196). It is the uncritical assumption that an animal's or a child's experience of something must have the structure and qualities of that of

19

an adult human being. It is a natural assumption to make. If another creature inhabits the same locality as ourselves and appears to have the same basic perceptual apparatus as we have, we take it for granted that what is salient to us is salient to that creature.

Dewey agreed readily that this assumption could not and should not be made.[24] As his thought developed, his reasons for this were strengthened. He came to see attention as the exercise of a flexible set of habits of selecting from the multitude of influences bearing on the peripheral nervous system at any one time; and these habits were in turn seen as integral to habits of behavioural response, so that what is salient to a creature in perception is a function of that creature's repertoire of behavioural responses. But as Dewey began to develop this line of thought in his famous 1896 article on the reflex arc concept[25] he also began to see the psychologist's fallacy as a product of ignoring the historical dimension.

> The fallacy that arises when this is done is virtually the psychological or historical fallacy. A set of considerations which hold good only because of a completed process is read into the content of the process which conditions this completed result. A state of things characterizing an outcome is regarded as a true description of the events which led up to this outcome. . . . (E5, p. 105)

Dewey is here putting the psychologist's mistake in a wider context and generalizing it. Certain things become salient only after a creature acquires a pattern of behaviour which renders it prone to pick them out. To assume a child, who has yet to acquire the necessary patterns of behaviour (but may eventually), already experiences the same perceptual saliency as an adult, is to read the end product back into an earlier stage of development.

Our later reflection on episodes of our experience will introduce distinctions into our representations of that experience. It would be a similar mistake to assume that those distinctions were fully present in the original experience. In an unpublished paper read in 1912, which clearly looked back to the period when he wrote on the reflex arc, Dewey identified this as 'a retrospective fallacy'. 'Looking back there is the sad event *and* the saddened me; the fearsome bear *and* my fright; the encouraging symptoms *and* my elated hopefulness, but the original situation came with no such duplicity' (M7, p. 37).

In *Experience and Nature* Dewey named this pattern '*the* philosophic fallacy' and characterized it as 'the conversion of eventual functions into antecedent existence' (L1, p. 34; but cp. M14, pp. 122–3). He identified this pattern of fallacious thinking in the way philosophers treat matter, life and mind as separate kinds of Being. This doctrine 'springs as so many philosophic errors have sprung, from a substantiation of eventual functions. The fallacy converts consequences of interaction of events into causes of the occurrence of these consequences' (L1, p. 200). In other words, what prevents life and mind from being treated as phenomena which emerge in nature is the assumption that what is present in the outcome must be present at the outset, and since life is not necessarily present in matter, nor mind in life, these must have an independent status apart from matter or life.[26]

The phrase 'eventual function' in *Experience and Nature* is a clear signal of the tack Dewey is pursuing. When he insists, 'Personality, selfhood, subjectivity are eventual functions that emerge with complexly organized interactions, organic and social. Personal individuality has its basis and conditions in simpler events' (L1, p. 162),[27] it is clear that he will accuse those who assume individual human beings are constituted as conscious rational beings prior to, or independently of, their entering into social relations, of committing '*the* philosophic fallacy'. Just characterizing the position of one's opponents as the product of fallacious thinking, of course, is not a sound refutation. But those who hold that social organization is reducible to the particular acts of individual human beings ('methodological individualists') are prone to argue that, as (adult) human beings can live outside society, and human beliefs and desires can be understood in isolation from social context, we can safely disregard social relations when studying the thought and behaviour of individual human beings. And Dewey's reply will be that any biologist who argues on behalf of vitalism by claiming that living organisms can be studied without reference to the material environment from which they emerge and which sustain them, is clearly arguing fallaciously. Here we see how an impulse to abstract and consider certain phenomena apart from, and as independent of, a wider context is associated with a resistance to seeing things from a developmental or genetic perspective.

Dewey did not let the matter rest after he wrote *Experience and Nature*. In an article 'Context and Thought', published two years after the second edition of *Experience and Nature*, he made another attempt to characterize 'the most pervasive fallacy of philosophic thinking', this time as having its roots in 'neglect of context' (L6, p. 5). It is not difficult to see this as a generalization of his characterization of the fallacy identified in *Experience and Nature*, for there the complaint is in effect that those who commit the fallacy obscure part of the context necessary for understanding. Some of the applications Dewey made of his new characterization move along familiar lines. In one form, neglect of context gives rise to 'the analytic fallacy'. We divide up a phenomenon for the purposes of interpretation and control; if we then neglect the context of our purposes, we come to take the elements, which we isolate, as existences independent of our analysis and of each other; and we find ourselves 'terminating in a doctrine of atomic particularism' (L6, p. 7).

In 1896 this would have been reading into a situation, antecedent to the process of analysis, features which only hold good of the completed process. In 1912 it was specifically the mistake of reading the sharp distinctions, which are introduced by careful analysis and control of the conditions of observations (so that which of several possible 'sensa' appear will settle a question for us), into experience in general (including that which gave rise to our question). In *Experience and Nature* this would have been converting eventual function (what emerge as the significant elements in the light of our special purposes) into antecedent existences.

'Neglect of context' is a useful generalization of what in Dewey's view is mistaken in the various doctrines he repudiated, not only because it relates his complaint less specifically to temporal context, but also because it enabled him to tie in the account of thought and its necessary social context which he had developed over the years.[28]

> There is no thinking which does not present itself on a background
> of tradition, and tradition has an intellectual quality that
> differentiates it from blind custom. Traditions are ways of
> interpretation and of observation, of valuation, of everything
> explicitly thought of. They are the circumambient atmosphere which
> thought must breathe; no one ever had an idea except as he inhaled
> some of this atmosphere. (L6, p. 12)

'Context' is a much better word than 'genesis' to focus the issues between Dewey and his opponents for a further reason. It speaks of a different attitude to the parts and wholes found in reality and of a correspondingly different method. Dewey always starts with the inclusive and the connected, and considers the process of differentiation. His opponents assume the task is to assemble wholes out of isolated elements. This is why Dewey was attracted to James's description of infant experience; it is based upon the idea of progressive differentiation within an organic whole. Our knowledge of the 'external world' is not something put together out of self-contained independent particulars. It is something which begins as a whole, large in terms of what it includes (which is everything) but small in terms of the differences, detail, complexity and relations of significance which it incorporates.[29] Seen in this light it is not Dewey's appeal to 'the original datum, large but confused' which is irrelevant, it is Russell's fixation on a narrow range of the discrimination found at a later stage in the development of that complexity which is irrelevant.

For Dewey's opponents[30] what is *given* in experience is particulars and the function of thought is to build complexes while remaining true to the given parts. For Dewey what is given, 'the original datum, is always a qualitative whole' (L5, p. 250). 'All thought in every subject begins with just such an unanalysed whole' (L5, p. 249), and the function of thought is to *select*; 'There is selectivity (and rejection) found in every operation of thought' (L6, p. 14).[31] Consequently there have to be behind every instance of thought two vital factors constituting context, *background*:

> Surrounding, bathing, saturating, the things of which we are
> explicitly aware is some inclusive situation which does not enter
> into the direct material of reflection. It does not come into question:
> it is taken for granted with respect to the particular question that is
> occupying the field of thinking. (L6, pp. 11–12)

and *selective interest*:

> Every particular case of thinking is what it is because of some
> attitude, some basis if you will; and no general theory can be framed
> which is not based upon what happens in particular cases. This
> attitude is no immediate part of what is consciously reflected upon,
> but it determines the selection of this rather than that subject matter.
> (L6, p. 14)

Dewey, as Russell acknowledged, did not subscribe to the 'artificially archaistic view which . . . [holds] that the large confused data spoken of by James . . . have more capacity for revealing truth than is to be found in scientific observations' (Russell, 1919, p. 236). Dewey indeed would have agreed unreservedly with the claim that 'greater discrimination and more analytic observation yield more knowledge . . . we know more about an object which we have inspected closely, with attention to parts and diffentiation, than about an object of which we have only what is called a "general impression" ' (ibid., pp. 235–6). His reservations would all have fallen upon the fact that Russell leaves it at that, neglecting the *process* of differentiation, its starting point, its conditions, its functions - in the end neglecting the whole and the contribution made by what we have yet to examine. Both knowledge and reality were, as a result of this neglect, represented by Russell as wholes logically posterior to their parts.

Analytic philosophy has moved away from the thorough-going atomistic approach which Russell favoured. But it has not (yet) arrived at the sort of holistic method which Dewey favoured and and did his best to practise. The wholes, to which Davidson (see Davidson, 1980, 1984) and those influenced by him have drawn our attention are totalities of beliefs, desires and linguistic dispositions possessed by adult human beings. Such totalities are not considered from the developmental perspective which inquires into the movement from less to greater differentiation; moreover the general logical framework with which these wholes have to be treated, Tarski's theory of truth, is atomistically structured. Thus the interpret-

23

ation of linguistic behaviour involves postulating semantic elements, which are capable of giving rise to a set of sentences each of which is logically independent of every other. Finally, it is assumed that interpretation can be carried out by taking linguistic behaviour as having the single function of representing the world in indicative sentences.

Dewey by contrast applied his holistic method not to all-inclusive totalities but to modest portions of experience down to single reflex actions, always bearing in mind that there were larger, more inclusive wholes providing a wider context. He applied his method from a developmental perspective, in which increased functional differentiation was the crucial movement. And like Wittgenstein, he treated language as having a multitude of functions, insisting for his part as one of his central doctrines that the function of representing was subordinate to the general function of adjusting practice to cope with the natural and social environment.[32]

At all times he tried to avoid abstracting functions, abstracting particular patterns of representation or abstracting particular distinctions within such patterns and projecting them as all-important. In fact, the principal methodological error from his perspective is to abstract from experience and set up that abstraction as all that needs to be considered. In this respect Dewey's most mature thinking reflects an outlook which he exhibited in his earliest published writings. The answer, which Dewey gave to 'physical evolutionists' and 'so called empirical psychologists' in one of his earliest published articles, could equally have been addressed to Russell and would still apply to some of the most recent developments in analytic philosophy:

> The vice of the procedure of both is at bottom precisely the same – the abstracting of some one element from the organism which gives it meaning, and setting it up as absolute. . . . The only wonder is that men should still bow in spirit before this creation of their own abstracting thought, and reverence it as the cause and ground of all reality and knowledge. (E1, p. 162)

II

Sensation, Emotion and Reflex Action

We have seen that Dewey's philosophy is characterized by a disregard for the problems generated by attempts to treat truth in terms of correspondence, and by a holist perspective which prizes genetic accounts, particularly those which reveal progressive functional differentiation within an organically structured whole. These are among the principal features which render Dewey's doctrines and arguments opaque to those who have had their philosophic expectations shaped by the analytic tradition. A further, but not unrelated feature is Dewey's preoccupation with what appear to be pyschological questions.

Elizabeth Anscombe once recommended that we should cease to do moral philosophy 'until we have an adequate philosophy of psychology in which we are conspicuously lacking' (Anscombe, 1958, p. 26). Dewey's philosophy is that of a man for whom all branches of philosophy answer to views which belong to philosophical psychology. Dewey, however, never recommended suspending activity elsewhere in philosophy until issues of philosophical psychology were settled. Although his views of the phenomena of human thought altered in important respects, he was always confident enough of his prevailing position to address issues elsewhere. But what he had to say came consistently from this direction. For example, his views on the nature of inquiry and its products, knowledge and truth (or 'warranted assertibility') arise from a natural history of consciousness, which he began to develop in the mid–1890s, and which will be considered in Sections II.c, II.d and II.e.

For this reason this chapter and the two which follow will concentrate on Dewey's doctrines regarding consciousness, sentience and mind; matters regarding truth and knowledge will be taken up again beginning with Chapter V. The present chapter will follow the upheaval in Dewey's philosophy which was triggered by his reading of James's *Principles of Psychology*, and the first appearance of Dewey's own distinctive doctrines. Chapter III will consider the views regarding sentience and experienced qualities which grew out of this early upheaval. Chapter IV will examine the results of a slower transformation which took place in Dewey's thought as he brought social context to bear on human thought and experience.

The use of sociological and psychological material in developing his position is, we have noted, a further aspect which sets Dewey's approach apart from that dominant in analytical tradition at the present time. For that tradition follows Frege in insisting that logical and psychological (including social-psychological) questions must be sharply distinguished, insists the latter have no bearing on the former, and does its best to pursue the former even when considering the phenomena of mind and society. Questions which occupied Dewey about the conditions which give rise to thought, how we actually do think or how we might better invest our intellectual efforts are not logical questions and do not bear on logical issues. From Dewey's standpoint this and the other sharp boundaries which analytic philosophy erects are ways of insulating faulty doctrines from proper criticism,[1] ways of begging questions in favour of certain conceptions of thought and its activity, the mind and its relation to its objects. The point (once again[2]) is not that logical and psychological questions do not need to be distinguished; it is that answers which do not interlock, answers which involve distortions in the conceptions used in other fields, are not to be left standing in the name of disciplinary autonomy.

At a relatively late stage in his career Dewey allowed that psychology as a discipline had no more of a special relationship to philosophy than any other branch of science (L5, p. 158). However, if conducted properly, if purged of the view that mind can only be a 'subjective' phenomenon, it could do more than other disciplines to stimulate the right sort of philosophy:

> The newer objective psychology supplies the easiest way,
> pedagogically if not in the abstract, by which to reach a fruitful
> conception of thought and its work, and thus to better our logical
> theories – provided thought and logic have anything to do with one
> another. (L5, p. 158)

The preoccupation of traditional philosophy with mathematics, on the other hand, had only led to 'an exaggerated anxiety about formal certainty' (ibid.).

The denial of any special relationship between philosophy and psychology might look like a retreat from the position advanced in Dewey's earliest published writings, when he urged that philosophy should be conducted from 'the psychological standpoint', that psychology indeed offered philosophy the method it had long sought. In fact, these articles were published in 1886 just prior to the emergence of psychology as a discipline in its own right.[3] Dewey was not arguing for a special relationship between philosophy and a branch of science, but that the central subdiscipline of philosophy should be that which deals with the phenomena of the human mind. This is not far from what Dewey was recommending in 1930, except that in 1886 'the psychological standpoint' meant for Dewey the principle 'that existence means existence for consciousness' (E1, p. 129), and it was from this metaphysical position that he was to retreat within the next decade.

The stimulus to change came from reading James, but one should not hold to an exaggerated impression of how much James changed the way Dewey thought. Reading the *Principles* may have contributed to an intellectual landslide, but only because it removed a blockage in the path leading in the general direction in which Dewey's thought had been straining. One can see this direction in the 1886 articles which Dewey published in *Mind* (E1, pp. 122–67), urging idealists as well as others to adopt 'The Psychological Standpoint' and treat 'Psychology as Philosophic Method'. There Dewey sought to undermine the distinction between psychology as an empirical science and the kind of transcendental philosophy of psychology, which lay at the foundation of post-Kantian idealism and in which idealist philosophers explicated the sort of intellectual activity, supposed by them to make experience and knowledge of the Absolute possible.

Empirical psychology, to be a science, would, he argued, have to treat consciousness from an objective and universal standpoint; this is precisely that which transcendental psychology adopts. On the other hand, transcendental psychology cannot remain aloof from empirical psychology. The Absolute Object of knowledge[4] is an easy concept to attain in a vague and nebulous form, but knowledge of it means not a vague and nebulous awareness, but a grasp of as much of its detail, its distinctions and the interrelations of its parts as possible. Progress consists in getting more of the enormity and complexity which pervades the universe into our (finite) thoughts. For this we require the special sciences; there is no high road to the Absolute. Now the phenomena of human consciousness belong to the total system of nature, but also represent the whole in 'concentrated form',[5] and thus provide our best hold on the principles governing the Absolute. So the special science of human consciousness is in a unique position among the special sciences to make a contribution to our knowledge of the Absolute.

It might seem strange for an idealist to argue on behalf of the relevance of empirical science to knowledge of the Absolute, but it is quite consistent to argue *a priori* for the need for the system of related facts as a necessary condition of experience, and still take a very cautious view of what can be achieved by *a priori* reasoning when it comes to any specific principle governing the system of related facts.[6] To proceed to elaborate the Absolute by *a priori* deductive steps was what Dewey at this stage understood as the 'method of logic', which his 'method of psychology' was intended to supplant (E1, pp. 163ff.). Dewey's motivation in advancing an idealist outlook tied in this way to empirical methods was probably complex. He clearly saw in the standpoint he was adopting the elimination of a residual element of dualism in post-Kantian philosophy.[7] He was also, perhaps, concerned that idealist philosophy should not be held in contempt by men of science, and equally concerned that the new science of man should not adopt a materialistic outlook.

What Dewey had in mind when he recommended psychology as a method for philosophy had been set out two years earlier in 'The New Psychology' (E1, pp. 48–60), an article written for a less specialized journal. In this Dewey not only recommended the new laboratory techniques for exploring physiological psychology, he included tools appropriate to social and historical sciences and proclaimed the need to study language, folklore and myth, primitive culture, social customs, practical morality, ethical ideas, government and the state (E1, p. 57): 'history in its broadest aspect is itself a psychological problem' (E1, p. 58). (We see here, already, an openness to the relevance of social phenomena to articulation of philosophical theories.)

What Dewey described in general terms as the 'method of psychology' is also interesting in the light of what we have already seen as distinctive of Dewey's approach. Psychology cannot account for the origin of knowledge or consciousness itself (E1, p. 129). It can only show 'how consciousness or knowledge has differentiated itself into various forms' (E1, p. 130). In thus making out the origins of particular forms, the psychologist brings to light the elements of knowledge and through showing the place which these elements hold in experience, 'he is showing their special adequacy or validity', and at the same time 'explicating the nature of consciousness or experience' (ibid.). This is where Dewey saw laboratory and (especially social-) anthropological work done by individual branches of 'the new psychology' as making contributions of detail to a wide-ranging enterprise that in its totality coincides with the ambitions of (under at least one interpretation of it) philosophy.

> The business of the psychologist is to give a genetic account of the various elements within this consciousness, and thereby fix their place, determine their validity, and at the same time show definitely what the real and eternal nature of this consciousness is. (Ibid.)

All this sounds thoroughly Hegelian, and the relevance of the investigation of social institutions to the phenomena was acknowledged by

Dewey to be specifically Hegelian.[8] But subsequent developments in Dewey's thought are less surprising if one bears in mind his own testimony that Hegelianism satisfied a pre-existent demand for unification, within organically articulated structures. If Dewey's recollection is anything to go by the demand probably first took shape when as an undergraduate he was impressed by his physiology textbook, T. H. Huxley's *Lessons in Elementary Physiology*. Dewey later had the impression that the presentation there of the human organism as an interdependent and interrelated unity, 'created a kind of type or model of a view of things to which material in any field ought to conform' (L5, p. 147). Coming to Hegel from this direction it is not surprising that Dewey had a tolerant, even welcoming attitude to physiological psychology. However mechanistically its theories and results might be presented, Dewey had a model of how to view them as revealing organic unity. If a complex conceived of as put together from independent pieces always seems to have an adventitious unity, the conception of each part as having an identity bound up with the whole (so that it would not be what it is were it not a part of the whole) points to an essential unity.

What was it then in James's *Principles* which gave Dewey's thought a new direction? It was precisely the application of this pattern to experience. But was not experience, consciousness, supposed to be such an organic unity? It was indeed, but only ideally, supposed to be. Consider the similarity between the role which the Absolute is supposed to play in our thought and the role of the 'original datum . . . large but confused'. The latter is precisely what the Absolute Object must be to a finite mind, large but confused. Progress consists in putting into finite thought more of the distinctions, detail, complexity and relations of significance which the Absolute Object possesses.

But until he read James, Dewey does not seem to have regarded this as a process of differentiation within the experience of an individual, for his conception of finite consciousness was infected by an assumption which Kantian and post-Kantian philosophers had inherited from Hume. This was the assumption that the givens of experience, what the mind receives through its faculty of (passive) receptivity, come in discrete parcels, and *all* connection and relatedness is the result of the synthetic activity of our intellectual faculties. Green, for example, held that 'related appearances are impossible apart from the action of an intelligence' (Green, 1883, I i 36).

It was not assumed that there was any experience which had this discrete character, rather it was assumed that what would have this character was the limit reached by thinking of the synthetic activity of mind as reduced to nothing – in other words, to pure subjectivity. (For this synthetic activity was what constituted experience as 'of an objective world'.) This was the nature of the raw material delivered to the mind and on which it exercised its synthetic activities. As Dewey saw it twenty years after the publication of his articles in *Mind*:

> The logic of the case seems to be that Neo-Kantian idealism gets its status against empiricism by first accepting the Humian [*sic*] idea of experience, while the express import of its positive contribution is to show the *non-existence* (not merely the cognitive invalidity) of anything describable as mere states of subjective consciousness. (M3, p. 137)

Why the post-Kantian tradition did not manage to shake off this assumption is difficult to say. Somewhere, perhaps, a mechanical model of physiological processes worked to keep this assumption in place, but in the mid-1880s Dewey operated under its influence, and partly as a consequence of this, the textbook of psychology which he wrote failed to illuminate his idealist philosophy with the results of empirical psychology, and failed to display in results of empirical psychology that interdependent and interrelated unity which he so prized.

In the first edition of the *Psychology* Dewey distinguished two meanings of the term 'sensation', 'an event in mental life or . . . the significance of this event' (E2, p. lxi).[9] The former, the occurrence of an excitation, could 'occur without any relation to anything else'. An excitation 'as a new event in consciousness' could come 'abruptly and without connection with other experience'. Not so the quality, the characteristics by which it is recognized. These require 'comparison and association. The significance of the sensation cannot be known excepting through activity of intelligence, bringing it into complex relations' (ibid.).

In revisions which Dewey made to his textbook after reading James's *Principles* this passage was replaced by one declaring the opinion that sensations are independent mental states and the 'theory that sensations are a series of discrete mental states, numerically and qualitatively separate from one another – atoms out of which the mental life is built . . .' (E2, p. 34), to be errors. 'These separate ideas of color and sound, of the sounds of a piano and of a rattling cart, are developed states of adult life' (ibid.). And Dewey added his own image of the original continuum: if we are tempted to think of sensations as bricks out of which a house is made, we must recall 'that bricks are manufactured articles, for which we must go back to some original homogenous bed of clay' (E2, p. 35).

What the exposure of this residual piece of the mechanistic conception of experience meant was that it was no longer necessary for intelligence to carry the whole burden of supplying experience with whatever unity it had. It became possible to locate important sources of that unity in the physiological basis of sensation. Connections between the various qualities of our feelings are themselves also *felt*. It followed that if important parts of experience are not the product of the activity of intelligence, important parts of experience are not immediately accessible to consciousness. Not only are there existences which are not 'for consciousness', there are aspects of experience which are not 'for consciousness'.

Exposing this residual mechanistic assumption and suggesting a different basis for the unity of experience were not the only ways in which James's *Principles* helped Dewey to develop the kind of outlook which he had been straining toward. The next section will add to this picture of how the landslide came about and what effects it had.

Section II.b: Residues of dualism

To appreciate more fully the influence which James had on Dewey and the way it helped Dewey to arrive at his own distinctive position, it is necessary to appreciate an important respect in which Dewey's *Psychology* failed to live up to the aspirations of his early philosophic outlook. The central motivation of Dewey's early philosophical psychology was to avoid treating the subject and object of experience in isolation from one another: 'consciousness is precisely the unity of subject and object' (E1, p. 131). In Dewey's *Psychology* every activity of mind or state of consciousness was said (E2, pp. 18–26) to have a subjective side, aspect or element and an objective side, aspect or element. On its subjective side, consciousness is feeling; feeling is the aspect of consciousness which is different in different minds and thus reflects consciousness as it is realized in individuals. Every conscious state also involves an element, its content, which is accessible to all conscious beings and hence is universal, an object of knowledge. Even a very private hallucination has a content, more or less vague, which is in principle communicable. It is precisely to the extent that feelings are found 'clustering around objects and events', connected with objects as their causes, localized in parts of the organism, that 'they cease to be vague and indefinable' (E2, p. 22).

If an individual consciousness required nothing more than a rearrangement of its contents, or an internal logical development, for its feelings to come to 'cluster around objects and events' in a way which more nearly matched that of the highest form of consciousness, then this talk of 'sides' or 'aspects' would leave nature and consciousness in a tight unity. But this would require a greater commitment to *a prioristic* methods for developing human knowledge than Dewey possessed. Dewey, however, as we saw in the previous section, believed in the importance of an empirical/causal dimension in the development of finite consciousness. But he found it difficult to avoid describing this in a way which reinstated a form of dualism.

31

From an idealist perspective the empirical element in the growth of consciousness appears like this: nature is the system of related facts as it appears in the highest form of consciousness. Among the objects related in this system are finite minds, partial realizations of the total system. Not all developments which bring these finite minds closer (by however little) to realizing the total system are the products of internal (*a prioristic*) developments. Some arise (*a posteriori*) from changes in the system of nature, specifically the relationships obtaining between such finite minds (as located in nature) and the rest of the system of nature. In concrete terms a change in the body (particularly in its sense organs) may well occasion a change in the adequacy with which the mind realizes the total system. The problem is how to relate a change in the relations that constitute the system of nature as a whole (to which the body belongs) to a change in the partial representation (which constitutes the finite mind).

The materialist-reductionist would keep the two from drifting apart by a strict identification of body and mind, but this option was never attractive to Dewey, and at this stage materialism is the direct opposite of his policy of relating everything to consciousness. Yet all his stress on how feeling and object are just two ways of looking at one thing (consciousness) does nothing to mediate this problematic relationship. The change in the body, the physiological event, is indeed objective, but not the objective side of the event, which for Dewey holds subject and object together. The object which is *for* consciousness might, for example, be the ceiling of the Sistine Chapel. The (objective, natural) event which brings awareness of this object to consciousness will involve the modification of light falling on pigments and the resulting modification of optical nerves when the light strikes the eye. But in the typical case the object of awareness will not include pigments, light and nerves. To confuse the two would be to violate the psychological standpoint which requires dealing 'with things as *known* things' (E2, p. 41). Materialism is the attempt to impose such concepts on the description of the psychical events constituting consciousness, but in the first place this is to impose quantifiable concepts where only qualitative concepts are appropriate (E2, p. 40), and in the second place to use what is psychological, i.e pigments, light, nerves, *as known* (these are 'psychological' because we can only appeal to such things as we conceive them, not as they are in themselves) in pretending to explain the psychological in what purport to be non-psychological terms (E2, p. 41).

Dewey is thus at this stage in his career not able (and not very willing either) to identify the events in consciousness which initiate the empirical growth of knowledge, viz. sensations, with the changes in the system of nature which give rise to them. 'There is no identity between the sensation as a state of consciousness and the mechanical motion which

32

precedes it' (E2, p. 40). As a consequence, although he does not acknowledge it, he is forced to double up the system of nature in a way which
is dualist in all but name. On the one hand there are physiological
changes, on the other there are psychical changes. The two are not
identical; the former cannot, 'properly speaking', be said to cause the
latter (E2, p. 42). Rather, 'upon the occasion' of the former change
taking place, the mind or soul acts 'upon itself producing within itself a
new, original, and unique activity which we know as sensation' (E2, p.
43). It can be said only that the physiological changes act as stimuli to
this spontaneous activity of the soul, although in thus responding the soul
is not free, but rather subject to its own order of causality: 'it is not
left to the soul voluntarily to determine whether and how it will act, but,
by a mechanism of its own, it responds to the stimulus in a definite and
invarible way' (ibid.). The only difference between these separate mental
and physical orders of causation and those found in Cartesian philosophy is that in Dewey's development they have a decidedly lower profile.

The source of this (mildly scandalous) lapse into dualism lies in certain
weaknesses in the way Dewey conceives of the unity of subject and
object. There are, we have seen, supposed to be two sides to consciousness, manifested in feeling and knowledge. These are not sides of a
conscious *thing*, but of *unified* (hence the appropriateness of the count
nouns 'soul', 'mind', 'self'), conscious *activity*. 'Self is, as we have so
often seen, *activity*. It is not something *which* acts; it is activity' (E2,
p. 216). The expression of this activity manifests what is known as will
(E2, p. 19) and it is will which unites – 'comprehends' (E2, p. 23),
'connects' (E2, p. 25), 'is the relation between' (E2, p. 24) – the subjective
and the objective.[10]

Will, as we ordinarily think of it, refers to the way a self imposes (or
strives to impose) on things. What is initially subjective, a desire or plan
(registered in what Dewey calls 'feeling'), is rendered actual (objective
in the sense of accessible to other selves, hence knowable). This familiar
sense does not, however, exhaust 'will' for Dewey. He refers to this as
'out-going will' (E2, p. 24) and later on as 'will in the narrow sense of
the word' (E2, p. 299). The reason for needing a wider sense of the word
is that by itself this familiar narrow sense does not touch those events
in which, instead of self imposing on things, things impose on the self,
so that what is objective comes to have a subjective realization, the
subject's knowledge. To incorporate this under 'will' Dewey invokes a
wider sense in which 'will' is 'synonymous with all psychical activity
having a mental and not merely a physiological stimulus' (ibid.). What
is included in this wider notion, which is not included in the narrower,
'incoming will' (E2, p. 24) is 'attention . . . the activity of will as it
connects a universal content with an individual subject' (E2, p. 299).

What Dewey avoids by this manoeuvre is a notion of feeling as (or as

33

the accompaniment of) pure passivity. A paragraph introduced in 1891 (cp. E2, p. 240 and p. lxxii) seems to capitulate to this notion of pure passivity by distinguishing '*mere* feeling and developed feeling – *interest*'. But in fact, 'mere' or 'bare' feeling is an abstraction (not something which can exist on its own) arrived at by considering the concrete feeling 'apart from its connections'. Dewey would thus insist that every feeling considered as the subjective aspect of consciousness is the realization of a state in which the object or content is regarded with *interest*, i.e. as having value or importance.

Some eight years later, as the framework of his mature philosophy was beginning to emerge as a result of the impetus given to it by James's *Principles*, Dewey looked back on the doctrine 'that feeling is the internalizing of activity or will' and identified it as an 'old idealistic conception of feeling'. He acknowledged that in his own *Psychology* it had been 'laid down, quite schematically' and that before encountering, particularly, James's theory of emotion it had been a conception 'blank and unmediated' (E4, p. 171, n. 19). The idea that will, activity, striving is what characterizes self and provides the unity of consciousness – at least the idea in the abstract – evidently had a powerful appeal for Dewey. But the contrivance which held this abstract idea in place in the *Psychology* was not altogether convincing. The act of will which underpinned the intellectual functions of mind, 'attention' (with its corresponding feeling of 'interest') performed a role rather like the acts of the mind, whereby the soul produced (conscious) sensations on the occasion of appropriate modifications in the sense organs. Both seem like *ad hoc* arrangements to keep the mind looking busy.

Part of the problem was that it did not strike Dewey as plausible to subordinate intellectual activity entirely to 'outgoing' (narrow sense) will. He no doubt would have accepted that will in the familiar narrow sense gives rise to the attention and interest which in turn ends in a universal content being connected with an individual subject, but the tenor of the development of his book gives knowledge-generating activity an independence from, if not a precedence over, the activity of outgoing will. Knowledge is treated first and occupies over half the bulk of the book. Will is treated last and receives less than a third of the space devoted to knowledge.[11]

Now the portions of James's *Principles* which Dewey mentions as particularly influential are those dealing with 'discrimination, abstraction, conception, generalization' (L5, p. 158).[12] These are topics covered in the knowledge section of Dewey's *Psychology*, but unlike Dewey, James makes them explicitly subordinate to what Dewey referred to as 'outgoing will'. James, for example, agrees verbally with Dewey that conception always takes place for the sake of some subjective *interest*, but he regards a concept as 'really nothing but a teleological instrument'.

'*This whole function of conceiving, of fixing, and holding fast to meanings, has no significance apart from the fact that the conceiver is a creature with partial purposes and private ends*' (James, 1890, I, p. 482). This is the key psychological principle lying behind James's pragmatism[13] and it attracted Dewey to the extent that he was, when James proclaimed the new movement (and until he came to feel the term had outlived its usefulness), happy to follow James in professing pragmatism. Even when he wanted to emphasize the distinctiveness of his own development of this idea, Dewey called his position 'instrumentalism'.

This idea was pilloried for the apparent implication that thinking is always done for, and its adequacy measured by, its employment in obtaining some limited satisfaction. This is by no means a necessary consequence, and Dewey, for his part, frequently stressed that knowledge could come to be sought for its own sake and its adequacy measured by the breadth of purposes it could serve. The implications which Dewey saw in James's principle were that intellectual activities were not (initially at least) independent of the activities of will narrowly conceived and that consciousness did not have within it an independent knowledge component which could be treated in isolation from the system of purposes which constituted the will of the conscious being. Both of these were in harmony with the role assigned to will (mind as active) in Dewey's *Psychology*, for he was clearly trying to avoid treating intellectual functions as involving a mind doing nothing other than responding passively to the imprint of nature's causal influences.

But the activity he had previously assigned to the intellectual function of mind, attention, is too easy to see as a *mere* psychological preliminary, an opening of the mind perhaps, not an integral part of its coming to know. If, however, the very concepts in which its knowledge is expressed are fashioned to serve its 'partial purposes and private ends', 'will' in an undeniably strict sense is the foundation of all consciousness. This does not mean that the universal aspect of knowledge needs to be abandoned. It is still possible to transcend partial purposes and private ends by incorporating many such into more complete purposes and more public ends. The intellectual development of thought is still, as the idealist presented it, from a less toward a more comprehensive (universal) standpoint, and retains the distinctly ethical flavour of what idealism claimed constituted intellectual (including scientific) progress.

Section II.c: James's theory of emotion

Had Dewey done no more than follow James in subordinating intellectual activity thoroughly to 'outgoing will' the result would have been no less 'schematic', 'blank and unmediated' (E4, p. 171n) than the position advanced in the *Psychology*. Nor would it have touched the unsatisfactory state in which Dewey had left the relationship between physiological events and conscious sensations. What took place on Dewey's part was a rethinking (in terms of certain basic psychological concepts and phenomena) of the abstractions, which attracted him, and on which James's lively and concrete discussions had shed new light.

This culminated in the publication in 1896 of an article on the reflex arc concept, an article which has become something of a classic in the history of psychology. To understand fully its implications it is important to appreciate how in articles published in 1894–5 Dewey developed James's theory of emotion. For the famous reflex arc article brings to a head a line of thought which begins to take shape in Dewey's treatment of emotion. Accordingly this and the next section will deal with that treatment of emotion, and the reflex arc concept will be taken up in Section II.e.

The theory of emotions which is presented in Chapter XXV of James's work (1890, II) stands in opposition to an account which James attributes to 'common sense', but which is also clearly embraced by Cartesianism and classical empiricism. According to this account, a mental perception (of, for example, a loss, an insult or a mortal danger) excites emotions (of grief, anger or fear) which in turn give rise to actions (weeping, striking or running away). James insisted[14] that the correct account was that the perception excites by a 'pre-organized mechanism', *'bodily changes . . . so indefinitely numerous and subtle that the entire organism may be called a sounding board*, which every change of consciousness, however slight, may make reverberate' (James, 1890, II, p. 450), and it is the perception of these changes which is the experience of emotion. *Crudely*: things cause us to weep, strike and tremble and 'we feel sorry because we cry, angry because we strike, afraid because we tremble' (ibid.).

Many, even of those who looked beyond this summary statement which James marked as 'crude', saw in his theory only a materialist reduction, or an epiphenomenalist treatment of emotional experience. Dewey, however,[15] saw the possibility of translating 'into terms of concrete phenomena' the 'old idealist conception of feeling' as 'internalizing of activity or will'. The idea that one's *body* is affected via a 'pre-organized mechanism' by what one perceives did not worry Dewey; the point was not to find a vindication for some form of Berkelian immaterialism, but to defend a conception of mind as active in all its manifestations. The bodily response governed by such a 'pre-organized mechanism' could well express a form, if not of will, at least of desire. If the sight of a dangerous object (a bear) is to lead to rapid and effective efforts to avoid it, massive changes in physiology (blood flow, hormonal chemistry, etc.) have to be triggered automatically, and these changes can be regarded as in part constituting what it is to fear, i.e. *desire* to be well out of reach of, the bear.

From an evolutionary perspective this makes good sense. An animal alerted by a slight disturbance alters its posture and metabolism ready to flee, all on the basis of what is no more than reflex action. Mechanical, yes, but this is not incompatible with, indeed it can only be fully understood in terms of, the 'purpose' (*telos*) around which the whole activity of the animal is organized: survival (for at least long enough to reproduce viable offspring: cp. E4, p. 162). It perhaps needs to be stressed that although Darwin's theory of natural selection altered the significance of the concept of natural teleology, it by no means eliminated it from biological explanation. Rather the reverse: organs and processes are now to be explained, where they can, by reference to 'adaptive value'. Developments in the organism and its behaviour can be assessed relative to the general *telos* of maintaining the existence of the species. There may be no sufficient reason (no divine purpose) for there being a species of precisely that sort, but by virtue of being classed as a living example of a biological species, one can refer the organs and activities of a thing to the general purpose (*telos*) of 'survival'.

This is not to say that Darwin himself was always perfectly clear about the explanatory requirements of his own theory. In 1873 Darwin published a book, *The Expression of Emotion in Man and Animals*. The central principle, to which he referred his attempts to explain the phenomena, was known as that of 'serviceable associated habits'.[16] What the habits of expression (e.g. clenching the fist, laughing, shrugging) served was said to be the associated feelings (of anger, mirth, puzzlement). Looking at the way Darwin set up his problem in the light of James's theory, Dewey noted not only a conflict between James's theory and Darwin's assumption that the feeling is prior to the expression (E4, pp. 152–3), but also a failure by Darwin to conform to the demands of his own theory. There cannot be organs (muscles, nerves and patterns of response) which serve primarily the purposes of expression; the *movement* which we take as expression must be useful in 'serving life' (E4, pp. 153–4). The movement as a whole need not have adaptive value; it may fail to integrate with other patterns and the whole conflicting system lead to a breakdown, to thoroughly non-adaptive 'idiopathic discharge' (e.g. spasm or hysteria). But however the theory is elaborated, Darwin's 'movements useful in expressing an emotion' must be read as 'useful as parts of an act which is useful as movement' (E4, p. 159).

James, Dewey noted, had cited Darwin's theory without remarking on the inconsistency between Darwin's assumption, that emotion is prior to organic response, and his own theory. Dewey's *Psychology* had also served up Darwin's theory without critical comment (E2, pp. 305–7), but there was nothing in Dewey's text in open conflict with Darwin's assumption and at least part of Dewey's thinking was in harmony with it. That emotion should be regarded as prior to forms of bodily activity was wholly consistent with the way Dewey tended to treat the activities constituting the self as autonomous and separate from the natural world. On the occasion of a physiological change in the sensory organs, recall, the soul acted on itself to produce a conscious sensation. Dewey's incipient occasionalism did not, however, affect the reverse relation; at least his language is strongly suggestive of causal influence.[17] It was a number of such tacit but deeply rooted assumptions about the self which were blocking the development of other of Dewey's ideas.

James for his part held openly a set of similar assumptions. He professed a 'thorough-going dualism' (James, 1890, I, p. 218) and wrote of a 'pre-established harmony' between 'Object and Subject' (ibid., p. 220). As Dewey demonstrated in a later (1942) examination of the 'vanishing subject' in James's *Principles* (PM, pp. 396–409), there were already strong currents threatening to sweep this dualism away. But these currents were not tugging at the way James treated emotional experience. His theory simply altered its role within a dualistic frame-work; instead of functioning as a mental cause (motivating factor) it was assigned the role of mental effect (perceived sensation). In the 'common-sense' series of stimulus, feeling, behaviour, James simply reversed the role of the last two terms. Dewey was, however, responding to the non-dualistic currents in James's *Principles*, i.e. to what he later identified (L5, p. 157) as a revival of an Aristotelian biological conception of *psyche*, and as a result saw James's theory in a quite different light.

With a somewhat cumbersome deference to James, Dewey suggested a number of respects in which James's way of stating his theory could be improved. The central point was to avoid altogether the impression that the occasion of an emotional experience is split up into three separate parts and that the question is to establish the correct order between such parts (E4, p. 174). What James failed to do was to make clear how the *feeling* of emotion, e.g. anger, was related to 'the whole condition of *being* angry' (E4, p. 172). The crude statement stressed the wrong thing, it suggested that we *feel* (e.g. sorry) because of an activity of the body (crying): rather it should take its bearings from the question of what it is to *be* sorry (E4, p. 171). James had been 'wholly successful' in replying to critics who inferred from his crude statement that all laughter ought to 'give the mirthful emotion, all vomiting that of disgust, etc.' (E4, p. 161). The feeling is not tied to isolated bodily modifications, but to the complex of changes which the entire organism undergoes as it reverber-ates like a 'sounding board'. Thus trembling from cold or fatigue will not feel like trembling from rage or fear (E4, p. 160). But while more nervous 'discharges' elsewhere in the body may *make* the difference between the latter and the former, merely saying this does not adequately account for the difference (E4, p. 161).

These polite suggestions about what needs to be done to convey the theory more effectively are in fact clearing the ground for a radically different approach. What accounts for the qualitative differences in the various occasions on which people may find themselves trembling, is not merely that the emotional experiences involving trembling also involve additional 'discharge' elsewhere in the body, but that they possess an organization which lets them 'report the meaning or value of past co-ordinations'. That is to say (in Dewey's language) that the 'normal emotion . . . has an *object*' (ibid.) (while in pathological cases the various ways a body is disposed to respond do not coordinate with one another).

That an emotion has an object reflects not that it is aroused or caused by something, as in the 'common-sense' theory, but rather that it is the focus of the coordination of a complex variety of habitual responses. The difference in feeling is accounted for by the presence of an object and by the differences in attitude *toward* that object. 'Attitude' in Dewey's technical vocabulary means 'motor and organic discharges' (E4, p. 169) in the first stages of a pattern of response (E4, p. 183), and the feeling is simply the subjective aspect of that total attitude. The feeling is not a separate thing, but an abstraction from the complex concrete response.

What provides the focus of a coordination of active responses, what gives direction to an attitude, is an object in the sense of *objective*. Whether a coordination is successful or otherwise is measured against its 'object' in this sense. It follows that the object of the event, which constitutes the whole condition of, for example, *being* angry or afraid, cannot be regarded as something independent of that condition. The object like the feeling is simply an aspect of the condition (E4, p. 176).

> Emotion in its entirety is a mode of behavior which is purposive, or
> has an intellectual content, and which also reflects itself into feeling
> or Affects, as the subjective valuation of that which is objectively
> expressed in the idea or purpose. (E4, pp. 170–1)

Seeing the object of an emotion in these terms, as reflecting the unity of a variety of responses, is perhaps easier for someone emerging from a Kantian framework, where an object contributes, via its role in the forms of judgment, to the unity of the manifold of appearances. The manifold, the multiplicity, is not for Dewey subjective presentations but organic responses. The activity, which for Dewey results in the unity of the manifold, is not, as it was for Kant, mere judgment but the purpose or *telos* which informs the total pattern of behaviour. Nevertheless the notion of object continues as in Kant to stand inside, reflecting the unity of experience, rather than standing outside as something which imposes itself on experience.

Section II.d: Object and inhibition

Dewey thus takes over James's suggestion that rather than being the effect of the *mind's* response to an external stimulus, an 'expression' of emotion is a reaction of the body 'due to [either] inherited instinct or individually acquired habit' (E4, p. 178). But under the influence of the sort of account which he first applied to subject and object, to feeling and intellectual content (wherein they appear as sides, aspects or elements of consciousness), this suggestion leads in a different direction. 'Following the lead of this idea, we are easily brought to the conclusion that *the mode of behavior is the primary thing, and that the idea and the emotional excitation are constituted at one and the same time*' (E4, p. 174). It is no longer consciousness which holds subject and object together; it is 'the mode of [concrete] behavior' which performs this role.

As one might expect, shifting in this way the foundation of the unity, with which Dewey had so long been preoccupied, opened up access to an account of sense perception which both reflected an active subject and avoided an *ad hoc* lapse into dualism. James had already provided the paradigm. The body responds physiologically to the bear ('beating heart, trembling and running legs, sinking in stomach, looseness of bowels, etc.' (E4, p. 175)). It does not do this independently of being visually affected by the bear, but the mistake to avoid is that of making the visual response independent of, and prior to, the rest of the body's responses. The 'instinctive reaction' to which James appealed ('instinct' of course may be supplemented, overruled or intensified by acquired habit) includes that of selecting from the 'big, buzzing, blooming confusion' (E4, p. 179) what is vitally important. Importance reflects interest, which is manifested at a biological level by the nascent will known as the 'will to survive', specifically the desire to avoid what threatens death or injury. The bear as an object of perception is constituted by the same principles which constitutes it as an object of fear.

It follows, obviously, that in the situation where a bear is seen and feared the experience is a single coordinated reaction of various organs of the body, the content of which may be described with equal validity as 'that terrible bear' or 'Oh how frightened I am' (E4, p. 176). But while this approach makes it easy to see how will – now in the guise of a Darwinized biological 'purpose' (or *telos*) – lies at the basis of all perceptual experience, it still has to address the question of how perceptual experience can be free of such motive involvement. Or, because that way of putting it begs the question against Dewey, how a variety of motive responses can contain a common element, the bear. A bear behind bars inspires no fear, perhaps only fascination with its (caged) strength. Equally a bear under general anaesthetic may inspire an impulse to stroke its fur. Or a bear in a circus may inspire amusement at its clumsy antics

(E4, p. 180). All these are different responses and, from the way Dewey has employed the notion of object, different objects.

The answer to this challenge lies in the extent to which coordination of all the elements of a response may be problematic. James's theory is built on instinctive or acquired reflex responses and, although his discussion of these responses (James, 1890, I, Chapter II) allows for the possibility that they may interfere with one another, the tendency, especially in the discussion of emotion, is to speak in terms of a single response of which there are many ('indefinitely numerous and subtle') components. Dewey is more preoccupied with the way these components may interfere with, even override, one another, leaving some incomplete but still able to make a functional contribution to the total response.

> It is, indeed, a question of primary impulsive tendencies, but of these tendencies as conflicting with one another and therefore mutually checking, at least temporarily, one another. Acts, which in past times have been *complete* activities, now present themselves as contemporaneous phases of one activity. (E4, p. 182)

An animal whose behaviour has any significant complexity is not responding to a single feature of its environment but to a variety of such features each triggering physiological and behavioural responses, which would tend to serve in appropriate circumstances to increase the animal's chance of survival. This is why the notion of 'attitude' ('that which was a complete activity once, but is no longer so' (E4, p. 183)) is central to Dewey's analysis.

The answer to the question about the object, which is common to the variety of responses to encountering a bear, comes from these consider-ations, but one must not overlook the point that the prior question is, why of all 'the multitude of possible objects' was 'just *this* object' singled out from the environment. 'Discrimination, not integration, is the real problem' (E4, p. 179). And the answer to the prior question is, 'The predominating motor response supplies the conditions for its objectifi-cation, or selection' (ibid.). Then in the case of an animal, such as a human, which is capable of a variety of competing responses, this domi-nant response must be taken as emerging from a variety of responses, each of which could in slightly different circumstances override the others. The bear may remain ferocious (i.e. the person is frightened in its presence) even when caged or tranquillized. The motor response of running away in blind terror may not predominate, it may well be overriden, but it will remain in the form of an attitude which is felt, while the response which does predominate, gazing in awe or amuse-ment, stroking its fur, carries through. 'The consciousness of our mode of behavior as affording data for other possible actions constitutes the bear as an objective or ideal content' (E4, p. 180).[18]

41

At this point Dewey simultaneously takes the theory of emotion an important step beyond James and his own project, of a theory of feeling and cognition tied to volitional elements, an important step closer to fruition. 'It follows', he immediately goes on to say, 'that all emotion or excitation, involves inhibition' (ibid.).[19] By inhibition, he insists (E4, p. 182), he does not mean 'complete suppression'; he is referring rather to the notion by which he analysed emotion, 'the reduction of movements and stimulus originally useful into attitudes' (E4, p. 168), and to the incorporation of these attitudes in the resulting total response. This is not a feature of James's account but something which, according to Dewey, 'the James theory not only permits but demands' (E4, p. 182). If there is no tension set up by the triggering of competing responses, the whole episode is simply a discharge of habitual response; one activity leads smoothly to another; no excitement occurs. Stroking a tranquillized bear on the first occasion is almost bound to be a highly charged experience. Whether further experiences retain that high charge of excitement depends on how vividly one continues to feel the possibility that the bear might not after all be dormant.

The contrast to where James left the *feeling* of emotion is striking. We are according to his theory supposed to feel our body's responses. The more vigorous the response, i.e. the harder we are sobbing, lashing out, running away, the more intense should be the grief, anger or fear. In fact giving oneself over to vigorous active response is more often not accompanied by intense feeling of emotion. Rather it is when such channels of response are blocked, either by external circumstances or by some internal form of repression, that the feeling is most intense.

> There is one phase of organic activity which constitutes the bear as object; there is another which would attack it, or run away from it, or stand one's ground before it. If these two coordinate *without friction*, or if one immediately displaces the other, there is no emotional seizure. If they co-exist, both pulling apart as complete in themselves and pulling together as part of a new whole, there is great emotional excitement. (E4, pp. 182–3)

The principle extends to organic responses on the borderline of emotional experience. Nausea, for example, is neither the cause nor the feeling resulting from vomiting, but rather the feeling as the impulse to vomit is resisted.

It follows that an animal, which does not find its patterns of response in conflict, does not experience emotions. A carnivore attacking and tearing apart its prey is not experiencing anger or any other emotion.

> The animal of our ancestor so far as it was given up without restraint to the full activity undoubtedly had a feeling of activity; but just

because the activity was undivided, it was not 'emotion'; it was not 'at,' or 'towards' an object held in tension against itself. (E4, p. 183)

There are two wide-ranging consequences of this for Dewey's outlook. One is the recognition of a level of feeling which does not involve consciousness in any cognitive sense of the term. It is not just that unrestrained activity lacks any 'quale', which it is appropriate to think of as emotional; it lacks any structure, any object affording 'data for other possible actions', which it would be appropriate to think of as an object of cognition. Unrestrained animal activity 'undoubtedly' possesses its own feeling, its own subjective aspect, says Dewey, but the way this differs from the emotional feeling of a higher animal or human can only be glimpsed by comparing the feeling of some totally familiar habitual activity with that of a situation calling insistently for a number of incompatible responses. Unrestrained animal activity also has an intellectual aspect which stands to the intellectual aspect of human experience in much the same relation as these more and less complex feelings stand, and moreover the two aspects (feeling and intellectual) are far less separable. We are too readily tempted to read our own experience onto that of animals, but this is to commit what James labelled 'the psychologist's fallacy', i.e. of confusing our own standpoint with that of the 'mental fact' we are considering.

We have here an early form of one of the most characteristic doctrines of Dewey's mature philosophy, the insistence on feelings which occur, which are 'had', without being 'known' (L1, p. 198). The animal whose instinctive or habitual responses, once triggered, follow on smoothly without conflict or tension, has feelings which are simply the subjective aspect of the activities in which it engages. This includes the human animal, even though its responses to its environment have a greater proportion of patterns acquired by habituation. For the most part humans adjust themselves smoothly by carrying through and aborting a multitude of responses to variations in their environment, and thus have a vast range of feelings which they do not know.

Dewey condemned as 'intellectualism' (L1, pp. 28f.) the assumption that all experience is a mode of knowledge and with the error of intellectualism went a 'spectator, search-light notion of consciousness' (L1, p. 235), which assumes that all consciousness is transparent, all its contents manifest to the conscious mind. In place of this, Dewey advocated thinking of consciousness as having a focus shading off into a fringe of subconscious experience, a fringe reflecting 'all the habits [a civilised adult] has acquired, that is to say the organic modifications he has undergone' (L1, p. 228).

The term 'fringe' was applied by James to a 'part of the *object cognized* . . . to designate the influence of a faint brain process upon our thought' (James, 1890, I, p. 258). Already in the 1894–5 discussion of emotions Dewey was interpreting the 'fringe' in terms of what he regarded as 'the primary thing . . . the mode of behaviour'. 'A priori it is difficult to see what the "fringe" can be save the feeling of the running accompaniment of aborted acts, having their value now only as signs or cues, but originally complete in themselves' (E4, p. 178, n. 29). The word 'fringe', Dewey later cautioned, 'suggests something too external to meet the facts of the case'. What he was talking about 'suffuses, interpenetrates, colors what is now and here uppermost' (L1, p. 231). It represents elements felt, 'had', but not known, not known because not signifying, but nevertheless giving 'sense, feeling, as distinct from signification' to elements which signify.[20]

In *Experience and Nature* (L1, especially Chapter V) language played a crucial role in introducing the elements into experience which signify (belong to experience as cognitive) as well as are *had* in their 'qualitative immediacy'. In the 1890s Dewey did not make as much of the contribution of language. He did, however, rethink a number of crucial conceptual relationships and thereby determined the kind of role language would come to play. Hitherto Dewey had treated experience and consciousness as coextensive. With feeling now tied to active bodily response, experience followed feeling in covering cases where it would be inappropriate to speak of consciousness. Consciousness in turn came to be associated with circumstances where the adjustment of response to stimulus was problematic, requiring a resolution of tensions and conflicting tendencies, rather than a smooth completion of an instinctive or habitual pattern, and the conditions necessary for an experience to carry an emotional charge turned out also to be involved in the exercise of nascent intelligence and essential for constituting an experience as conscious.[21]

This is the most central of the ideas which Dewey developed in the process of rethinking his philosophical psychology in the 1890s. Knowing in the sense of conscious awareness was identified with the tension which arises when there is a conflict between dispositions that need to be coordinated. Knowing in the sense of a re-usable intellectual achievement was identified with the contribution which the re-coordination of behavioural dispositions makes to the resolution of future (actual and potential) coordination problems. Inquiry was identified as a reflective way of attempting this re-coordination under the pressure of a 'problematic situation'. Truth (later 'warranted assertibility') was identified with the product of successful inquiries. All intellectual endeavour became thus in a general sense a contribution to the carrying out of a practical project.

Section II.e: The reflex arc concept

This central idea emerged clearly in Dewey's well-known 1896 article on the reflex arc concept. The previous two sections have prepared the ground for a consideration of this article for, as will appear, much of what Dewey has to say in criticism of the way psychologists were using the reflex arc concept in his day was already implicit in his treatment of the modes of behaviour constituting emotional experience.

Dewey complains that as it is used the pattern of stimulus-response misrepresents an 'organic unity' and fails to indicate 'the single concrete whole' of which the terms 'stimulus' and 'response' designate merely 'functioning factors'. This reflects a concern recognizable in Dewey's earliest philosophic efforts. What Dewey says about the unity underlying the sensory and motor responses generalizes, as we will see, his account of how an instinctive or habitual mode of behaviour constitutes a bear as a fearful object, at the same time as it gives rise to the 'expressions' of fear. And his claim that stimulus and response do not represent 'distinctions of existence' (are not what Hume would have called 'independent existences') but are 'teleological distinctions, that is distinctions of function' (E5, p. 104),[22] echoes a claim made in the articles on emotion that the distinction between the intellectual and emotional aspects of an experience is only a functional distinction (E4, p. 177). What the treatment of the reflex arc adds to that of the emotions, apart from an examination of the central concept underlying the latter treatment, is an orientation toward the phenomena of growth, toward learning.

The reflex arc concept had attracted physiologically oriented experimental psychologists because it offered a way of representing the link between external influences and behavioural response without the mediation of some psychic entity or experience not accessible to experimental observation. The most elementary of the patterns of response to which the concept applied (knee-jerk, eye blink, withdrawal of hand before pain is registered) provide the best illustrations of these advantages, but the concept was not taken to apply strictly to responses governed by the 'lower' parts of the brain or central nervous system. James argued that the same muscles were represented at different levels of the central nervous hierarchy and a stimulus setting off a reflex loop through one level could equally well set off an overriding or modifying loop through a different level (James, 1890, I, p. 19). Ideas, conceived as modifications of a mental substance or spiritual entity mediating sensory inputs and behavioural outputs, could be eliminated, or at least shunted off to one side of the phenomena needing to be explained. The explanation would proceed instead to resolve the complexity of animal and human behaviour into structures of reflex arc. Even before the experimental identification of the precise nerve paths could be undertaken the reflex arc offered a useful conceptual tool, and as we have seen was employed as such in the treatment of emotions offered in turn by James and Dewey.

But what had happened, alleged Dewey (E5, p. 96), was that the old dualism of body and mind had been replaced by a new dualism of peripheral and central structures and functions. The metaphysically hybrid chain of *sensations, thought* and *act* had been replaced by a 'patchwork of disjoint parts, a mechanical conjunction of unallied processes' (E5, p. 97), viz. *sensory stimulus, central activity* and *motor discharge*. Dewey's discussion revolved around an illustration of a baby reaching for a candle flame and withdrawing its fingers in distress, which occurs, complete with graphics, in James's work (1890, I, pp. 24–6). The usual analysis of this event as the sequence of light (stimulus), grasping (response), burning (stimulus), withdrawal (response) is too rough, Dewey argues, for 'psychological adequacy' (E5, p. 97). The sequence does not begin with a sensory stimulus but with a sensory-motor coordination, an *act*, seeing, which involves coordination of movements of body, hand and eye muscles. These are responses constituting the light as a thing to be focused upon and they all contribute to 'the quality of what is experienced'. The sensations arising in the retina and elsewhere as well as the overt movements and adjustments 'lie inside not outside the act' of seeing (E5, p. 98).

If one considers the earlier step, the stimulus initiating the act of seeing, it is still not appropriate to treat it as the light intruding all by itself on the child's eye (as though it were like light striking the edge of the visual field and triggering the head-turning reflex that will survive into adulthood). Stimuli are not outside objects kick-starting an otherwise dormant organism. Even the response to a sudden loud noise depends on the activity going on when the noise occurs (E5, p. 100). What an outside influence does is to bring about a redistribution in the dominance of various organs in the coordination existing at the time. The result of the redistribution will depend on the habits, innate or acquired, which channel the consequences of the disturbance along certain lines rather than others.[23]

The act of seeing gives rise to an act of grasping because there already exists a habit coordinating the two acts and uniting them into a more comprehensive act. This pattern of coordination has its roots in an innate reflex, a 'natural curiosity', which is on the same level as, and contributes to, the so-called 'will to survive' (for eventually the mature human will survive through handling and manipulating). But by this time this innate reflex has been modified, reinforced and refined by previous occasions when grasping at what stands out, at what it is easy to follow with the eyes, has yielded further interesting and satisfying experience. The grasping activity does not simply replace the seeing activity, rather the eye, head, body coordination enlarges to incorporate the movement of the hand, which it must do if the hand is to reach its target, the light. Seeing develops under the patterns of habitual response into 'seeing-for-reaching-purposes' (ibid.).[24]

Now burning a hand stimulates (via another innate reflex of obvious adaptive value) a withdrawing movement of the hand. The movements of grasping-for-light and withdrawing-from-burning are accidentally related in the sense that occasions of the two do not always occur together. But the child is observed to 'learn' from this experience. If it did not, it would repeat the distressing episode on future occasions. And if the child is to learn, the seeing-for-reaching-purposes has to be an act comprehensive enough for the withdrawing-from-burning to enter *into* and transform the value of the seeing-for-reaching-purposes pattern. It is clear, then, what psychological facts are left out of the bare schema, *seeing, reaching, burning, withdrawing*: 'The seeing in a word serves to control the reaching, and is in turn interpreted by the burning' (E5, p. 99).

Dewey had stressed the importance of this back reference of outcome to original impulse in a treatment of moral psychology published in a text book, *The Study of Ethics* (E4, pp. 219–326), in the same year as the first of his articles on emotion. There he had applied the term 'mediation' to this effect and connected it to the growth of consciousness. It is in referring results back to the original impulse that the child becomes conscious that the results follow, and the impulse thereby acquires a 'meaning', 'significance', 'import'. 'The impulse is idealized' (E4, p. 237). It is true that the outcome of the reflexes of an organism must somehow return and alter the initial stages of the pattern, must form 'virtually a circuit, a continual reconstruction' (E5, p. 99),[25] if the organism is to profit from the outcome. But how this takes place may be too mechanical to make talk of consciousness of the result even remotely plausible. Thus although the result is the meaning, significance or import of an action, it is difficult to say the action is 'interpreted' by the subject as it would be by a mature human being observing the subject. Nevertheless, animals of very moderate complexity have their patterns of behaviour deformed and reformed by satisfying and distressing outcomes. 'Mediation' covers this effect without putting too much illicit second intention[26] into the account.

The article on the reflex arc concept two years later has a more complete account to give at this point, but the foundation of moral psychology which Dewey was proposing in *The Study of Ethics* had the essential piece ready and waiting to be put in the right place. Darwinian teleology requires that 'The various impulses of the individual are not a loose bundle of tendencies existing side by side. Because they have been evolved in relation to the one or more inclusive activity of maintaining

47

life, they are interconnected' (E4, p. 236). In lower animals this coordination is innately predetermined and in higher animals its flexibility is still very limited. For humans, particularly for immature members of the species, 'only the very general lines are laid down', leaving room for variation and novelty 'almost without limit'. 'The *definite* coordination of acts is thus, with man, not a *datum* but a *problem*' (ibid.).

What the discussion of the reflex arc added to this was an account of what it is for a problem to arise over coordinating reflex actions once impulses have been interpreted ('mediated') by a variety of outcomes. Consider a subsequent occasion on which the child is confronted by a bright object. On a number of previous occasions of reaching for it, the child has 'had a delightful exercise'; on at least one previous occasion, a disaster. The child thus confronts the new bright object, uncertain how to respond, and for Dewey, who had previously insisted that the response constitutes the character of the perception of the object, '*the response is not only uncertain, but the stimulus is equally uncertain; one is uncertain only in so far as the other is*' (E5, p. 106). The problem of how to complete the coordination is also the problem of discovering the right stimulus in the seeing activity.

In this case the structure of the whole episode has to be treated as having a further fold in the fabric woven of reflexes. The bright-object-seeing initiates activities which are inhibited by other 'attitudes'. The response when it comes, either reaching or backing off, is not to the seeing activity directly but to 'possible movement as "stimulus"' (E5, p. 107). The bright-object-seeing is stimulus to a conflict which is in turn constituted as the possible-movement-stimulus. The bright object, through being the intersection of conflicting responses, becomes, like the bear, constituted as 'an objective or ideal content' (E4, p. 180). It is 'at precisely this juncture that the distinction of sensation as stimulus and motion as response arises' (E5, p. 106). The experience will under Dewey's account of emotion have an emotional charge, for '*the idea and the emotional excitation are constituted at one and the same time; . . . indeed, they represent the tension of stimulus and response within the co-ordination which makes up the mode of behavior*' (E4, p. 174).

The emotional excitation is just the subjective side of an experience, where by virtue of conflict the original stimulus and final response are held apart. And by virtue of the same conflict, the original stimulus is constituted as an ideal object (i.e. one representing possibilities) by the same principle that the bear was constituted as a fearful object. 'Just here the act as objective stimulus becomes transformed into sensation as possible, as conscious, stimulus. Just here also, motion as conscious response emerges' (E5, p. 107).

III

The Emergence of
Mind and Qualities

Section III.a: The status of qualities

At various points in Dewey's discussion of emotion and of sensation in the context of reflex action, he wrote of the 'qualities' of experience. It is important to appreciate just how far Dewey's conception of 'quality' is from traditional conceptions, which treat them as among the objects of experience; for the difference in Dewey's conception is the key to the way he applied the ideas developed in his critique of the reflex arc concept to the mind/body problem. This chapter will examine how qualities are to be conceived, if they are not to be treated as objects, and how this involves a repudiation of widely held views on the nature of subjectivity and privacy. The first section will begin this task by considering an important unpublished paper ('What are States of Mind?' M7, pp. 31–43) in which Dewey lays out his characteristic doctrines in terms of ideas developed in the articles on emotions and on the reflex arc.

When the term gained suffcient currency Dewey was happy to acknowledge his approach as 'an "emergent" theory of mind' (L1, p. 207). Now one can offer up a theory under this banner which amounts to little more than dualism back from the laundry: life gradually evolved more and more complex forms until at some stage animals appeared which have minds in which conscious states succeed one another. What has emerged, as the content of these states, are qualities accessible to each individual alone. These 'secondary' qualities[1] (e.g. colours, tones, odours, etc.) adorn the objects, which through their primary qualities are accessible to all, and which constitute the whole of physical reality. Although the secondary qualities are not part of the fabric of the natural world, they have emerged for human beings with sufficient regularity and predictability for it to be possible to communicate about them and for this reason they were for a long time mistaken for a part of physical reality.

There also emerged (the story continues) on a much less predictable basis, and associated more regularly with the behaviour of humans than with the behaviour of non-conscious objects, 'tertiary' qualities. These add emotional tones to the 'gay-coloured vesture' with which humans are wont to clothe a world, which when 'undraped' appears in the austere primary qualities that are the concern of science.[2] Since the emergent secondary and tertiary qualities (see note 1) are not the concern of natural science, they do not belong to physical reality and the creatures which apprehend them do not do so by virtue of being purely natural beings. What happens in their eyes, nerves, etc., can be described purely in terms of primary qualities, while the secondary and tertiary qualities reveal the existence of an inner eye which gives each creature with a mind a view of these qualities accessible to no others. Even if what has emerged (mental states) are not treated as the properties of a substance distinct from the substances of physical reality, reality nevertheless has a dual structure.

In Dewey's theory, by contrast, what emerges when parts of physical reality acquire the right sort of complexity – when physical events 'come into more extensive and delicate relationships of interaction' (L1, p. 204) – are qualities of those events. Imprecise ways of talking, however, or a failure to understand properly modes of speech which are perfectly in order may generate bafflement and superstition about these qualities, and so care needs to be taken. In an unpublished paper delivered sixteen years after the publication of the article on the reflex arc, Dewey rested part of his analysis on popular usage and logical grammar.

'The preposition "of" in "states of mind" denotes an objective, not a possessive genetive' (M7, p. 31). The grammatical contrast here seems to be between 'milk of a cow' and 'milk of magnesia' or 'hair of goats' and 'herd of goats'. In other words, 'mental' and 'psychical' characterize qualities which are not possessions of a mind, but qualities which determine what a given behavioural disposition is. 'A state of mind is an essentially emotional attitude or disposition, this attitude or disposition being characteristic of certain conditions of organic agents' (M7, p. 33). The claim about the dispositional nature of an emotion is supported by appeal to colloquial English which uses adjectives reporting emotions, as well as phrases like 'state of nerves', to assess, and warn others about, the behaviour to be expected from a person (M7, p. 33; cp. p. 36 n. 4).

But it will come as no surprise, in the light of the previous chapter, that Dewey's claim to advance this as a completely general account of mental states, covering 'sensation, idea, image and volition' (ibid.), rests not on linguistic analysis but on what he reckons to be able to make of James's theory of emotion. James had, Dewey claimed, spoken of the 'organic resonances and reverberations' as constituting 'the "mind-stuff" of an emotion',[3] but these are the stuff of which every state of mind is constituted. Of course, not every state of mind is identified as 'emotional' because that term tends to be reserved for dispositions involving extreme or unusual manifestations, particularly in the circulatory and respiratory organs and the viscera. But we do speak of calm emotions, a state of tranquillity, being in a placid mood. The claim is that every event with a 'psychical quality' has to be constituted by a physiological event which has the structure displayed by more striking emotions such as fear and anger.

The generality of this claim, its application to sensations, ideas, images, volitions, etc., rests on the premise of Dewey's 'emergent' theory of mind. This is that psychical states emerged when certain events came into extensive and delicate relations of interaction, specifically the events in which an organsim adjusts to what is happening in its environment so as to maintain its own integrity and the continued existence of its species. When, according to Dewey, the organic unity of these events comprises a certain complex situation, one which qualifies at certain points of its development as constituting an emotional attitude, then elements of sensation, volition, etc., can be identified as functional parts of the unified response. Other so-called mental states (perhaps, for example, ideas or images) may well require an organic response of even greater complexity before they can be identified as functional parts, but the complexity constituting the total response as emotional will still be present and the generality of the claim unaffected.

What elaborations are needed in order to encompass qualities such as red, which are not obviously linked to emotional states, will be set out in Sections III.c and III.d, but this much can be said in advance of considering that treatment: The way Dewey would prevent the bare awareness of a sensation (say of a secondary quality like *red*) from appearing as an obvious counter-example to the claim that a state of mind is an emotional disposition, would be to claim that such an example is tantamount to an attempt to think of an organ existing in isolation from the organism. Someone who claims to have experienced such a thing is looking back on the experience and abstracting from a complex in which primary, secondary and tertiary qualities were 'indissolubly blended or fused' (M7, p. 37). If one claims that as species can lose organs or functions through evolution, so all the functions other than, say, an isolated sensation or volition might drop out (for a time at least) of human experience, it will be replied that while organs and functions can be lost, the organism cannot, as it were, atrophy and leave an isolated organ or function (e.g. an organism consisting entirely of a foot, which does nothing but walk). To treat sensation or volition as something which could constitute the whole of a state of mind is to reject the basis of Dewey's 'emergent' theory. An *adjustment* is a complex event in which there is a response *within* the organism to something *outside* the organism, a response directed *toward* a certain end. What constitutes it

51

as emotional is a certain tension within the various events that make up the adjustment and only so constituted are the elements of sensation (e.g. of red), motion, volition, etc., functionally distinguishable.

What characterizes Dewey's analysis of the term 'state of mind' is an insistence that the phenomena of mind must not be considered in isolation from the context, from the whole, in which they arise. The same characteristic governs what he says about 'the quales out of which [James] holds the emotion as conscious fact to be built' (M7, p. 36). These are nothing other than the qualities *of* the organic reaction. 'Fear, anger, curiosity, hope, love, elation, abasement are characteristic episodes in the vibrating career of success and failure of a living thing: as consciously psychical, they are the material of an individual organism's apprehension of its own characteristic attitudes' (M7, pp. 36–7). What one must be careful to avoid is thinking of the presence of qualities in feeling on the model of conscious awareness of an object, and hence, because they are said to be qualities of the organic reaction, as awareness of the states or processes of one's body as an object (of cognition). Falling into the confusion which tempts at this point is the source, for Dewey, of most of the prevalent superstitions about the relation between mind and body.

The organic reaction is an adjustment, a relation between what we distinguish within a situation as the inside and the outside of the organism. If the qualities of which the conscious fact are 'built' are qualities of the reaction, they are not qualities of any state or process of the body alone, but of a relation between the inside and the outside of the organism. The quality, consequently, is 'a quality of the situation of experience' (M7, p. 38).[4] What follows immediately from this way of locating qualities is that secondary and tertiary, as well as primary, qualities are objective in two related senses. They are first of all qualities of (events which take place in) physical reality: 'qualities characteristic of sentiency are qualities *of* cosmic events' (L1, p. 204). Secondly, we have every right to treat them as the qualities of the objects represented in our experiences. 'The qualities never were "in" the organism: they always were qualities of interactions in which both extra-organic things and organisms partake. . . . Hence they are as much qualities of the things engaged as of the organism' (L1, pp. 198–9).

To be the objective properties of something in the environment, qualities do not need to be wholly independent of the organism, whose experiences they enter. Relations were regarded by Dewey as part of what constitutes an object as the thing it is. This had been central to his definition of objectivity since the earliest part of his career, and he continued to regard relations as bestowing objective properties on whatever they related.[5] Arguments offered against the objectivity or physical reality of secondary and tertiary qualities appear, on the other hand, to rest implicitly, if not explicitly, on the premise that the relations into which an object enters do not contribute to its real objective properties.

In a book on the philosophy of Descartes published within the last decade, Bernard Williams argues that 'there is every reason to think' that a conception of the material world as it is understood by natural science, and of the world as it really is, should leave out secondary qualities (Williams, 1978, p. 241). Dewey would agree with Williams that the conception of the material world as it is understood by science *does properly* leave out secondary qualities. This is not because, as Williams implies, it is the aim of science to represent the (whole of the) natural world as it really is. Science like every other intellectual activity is selective. Its project is to produce compehensive intellectual representations of our natural environment, which can be used for predicition and control. In carrying this out it represents phenomena in terms of the qualities of things which most reliably indicate their behaviour under the greatest variety of circumstance and which most readily allow us to give unified explanations of their behaviour (L1, pp. 201–6). The qualities which Locke designated 'primary' were in the science of the seventeenth century the leading candidates for that role, and as science progressed our concepts of the qualities which play that role were refined or replaced with others, and these will in their turn be refined or replaced. Williams likewise sees the source of the primary qualities as 'the best scientific conceptions we now have or can hope for' (Williams, 1978, p. 239).

The argument which Williams offers for thinking that what now appear on lists of secondary or tertiary qualities will not appear on any list of primary qualities, or in the conception of the world as it really is, would, however, be rejected by Dewey as specious. The argument is that even a vague grasp of the physiological processes involved in the perception of colour shows us why the same things appear different colours to different people and why the same things seem coloured to members of one species and monochrome to members of other species. This understanding leaves behind the idea that objects really have one colour rather than another.

Dewey confronted the 'almost endless instances' of 'so-called relativity in perception' (M10, p. 29) with the obvious point that the differences in circumstance which give rise to differences in the way things appear are perfectly objective. If the same thing looks like a flat circle to one observer and a somewhat distorted elliptical surface to another it should be possible to set up two cameras to yield photographs of these apparent results. 'Photographs are as genuinely physical existences as the original sphere: and they exhibit the two geometrical forms' (M10, p. 30). To the argument that some species of animals have monochrome vision and others perceive colours, Dewey could reply in the same vein. This no more proves that colour is not a quality of things as they really are than the fact that a microphone or a photometer do not (while a Geiger counter does) respond to ionizing radiation proves that ionizing radiation is not part of the world as it really is. If the real objective properties of things were those which appeared the same in all circumstances, there would be no role for instruments in scientific observation. Indeed the principle that to be really F (green, spherical, frightening) a thing has to appear F in all circumstances and in all its relations is intrinsically implausible.[6]

Williams's appeal to physiology suggests that the feature of the relations which introduces the crucial differences in appearance may be inside, not outside, the nervous system of the perceiver. Some people are colour-blind, others distinguish red from green without difficulty. But physiology is an objective science. It must regard two people whose colour perception differs in this way as a technician regards two Geiger counters, one of which registers radiation where the other does not; one has a discoverable internal physical property which constitutes a malfunction or at least explains the difference in performance.

If Williams's argument does not rest on treating the *physical* relations into which things enter as not objective and not bestowing objective properties on things, then he must be appealing implicitly to what is known as the logical privacy of an experience. Dewey does not deny 'that "consciousness" in the sense of psychic existence is private, inner, fleeting and individualized' (M7, p. 37). This arises within his analysis of mental states and their qualities because the organic reactions which constitute them are not just *at* or *from* or *with* a change in an animal's environment, but are changes *within* that particular organism (ibid.). Logical privacy arises because of the logical fact that just one organism undergoes those changes and no other, so they and their qualities are had by no other organism. The subjective/objective 'side', 'aspect' or 'element' strategy[7] has come to rest on the traffic which takes place between an organism and its environment, as the former works to maintain itself and perpetuate its genetic structure in that environment.

But there remains a powerful feeling that this strategy, even deployed in a biological context, does not succeed in locating satisfactorily the private, subjective side of experience. There still seem to be things, qualities, which humans experience but which are not the qualities of material objects or events. This feeling lies behind the plausibility of the direction of Williams's argument even as it moves over ground that will not support it. In the final section of this chapter Dewey's resistance to this powerful feeling will be confronted by a recent expression of it due to Thomas Nagel.

The root of this feeling lies, if Dewey is right, in the temptation to treat the presence of a quality in feeling on the model of the conscious awareness of an object. Before confronting Nagel, the intervening sections will use tools provided by Dewey to dig further at this root. Section III.b will consider the qualities present in sentient experience which lacks the conditions necessary for it to contain objects. Section III.c will set out the nature of those conditions (but the claim that they include a linguistic/social context will be postponed until Chapter IV). Section III.d will contrast the qualities of a purely sentient experience with those present in an experience possessing enough structure to contain objects.

Section III.b: Life and sentiency

Dewey claims that the qualities present in our experience are the qualities of our organic responses, i.e. of the adjustments we make in order to maintain certain relationships between ourselves and our environment. If this claim fails to carry conviction it is because of the prior conviction that the organic adjustments are one thing and what we experience is another, not necessarily the same, thing. And this prior conviction arises from treating our relationship to the (felt) qualities of our experience in terms of the paradigm of looking at a patch of, for example, what we recognize to be the colour red. The red as experienced is one thing and what is going on between our bodies and the world is another. This paradigm and the way it governs our thinking about the qualities of feeling results in what Dewey regards as the error of 'intellectualism'.[8] The error is two-fold. On the one hand we are encouraged to operate with an incomplete (abstracted) picture of what it is to have this experience as seeing and recognizing, and on the other hand it imposes on all experience, specifically sentient experience, a structure which is present only in sophisticated (cognitive) developments of sentience.

To appreciate how one could come to view the familiar paradigm as a systematic misrepresentation, it is necessary to look at the elaborations which Dewey introduced into his 'emergent' theory of mind in the three decades which followed his studies of the emotions and the reflex arc concept. Consciousness continued as in the reflex arc study to emerge from situations of tension, of uncertainty over how to respond; it remained identified with the process of remaking organic habits (L1, p. 239). but Dewey came to regard those organic habits involved in social interaction as giving rise to a level of experience (which means a level of interaction between events in the natural world) significantly above that of habits involving only sentience. 'Consciousness' could, he allowed, be applied on both these levels to 'anoetic' sentiency, as well as to 'noetic' (or 'cognitive') awareness.[9] (He declined at one stage to legislate against using one word, 'consciousness', for two such different affairs (L1, p. 226), but within ten pages defined 'consciousness' in terms of what takes place on the cognitive level.)

In distinguishing experience, and with it nature, into a hierarchy of 'plateaus' (L1, p. 208) each of which incorporates the functions and relations of those below it, and is such that it cannot be understood in isolation from the level (or levels) below it, Dewey follows in the tradition of Aristotle's hierarchy of souls (*psychai*) as forms of natural bodies.[10] The two-fold error of 'intellectualism' is thus the attempt to treat a phenomenon occurring on the third (noetic) plateau in isolation from the plateau (containing 'anoetic sentiency') immediately below, and imposing on the second level, a structure found only on the third level. The result is that the distinctive contribution of the second level drops out of sight altogether and there results the modern form of the mind/body problem: how can two such different affairs as mechanical interaction and cognition possibly be related so as to influence each other? As so much of Dewey's philosophy revolves around the importance of the neglected second level, we must look carefully at its relations to the other two levels when considering how the (felt) experience of red should be related to the recognition of something as red.

The first of Dewey's three general 'plateaus' is that of inanimate nature, 'the scene of narrower and more external interactions' (L1, p. 208) which are adequately described in the mathematical-mechanical concepts of physics. The proper use of these concepts is not incompatible with – indeed they may give precision to – what are thought of as more colourful (if not coloured) phrases. Things on this level, 'atoms and molecules show a selective bias in their indifferences, affinities and repulsions, when exposed to other events' (L1, p. 162). One can on this level distinguish the *need* of a body as 'a concrete state of events', a condition of tension in the distribution of energies, which in turn effects distinctive changes such that the connection with the environment is altered (L1, pp. 194f.). In themselves, therefore, the life processes of a plant do not differ from the physico-chemical activity of inanimate bodies (ibid.).

What distinguishes the second plateau, life, is 'the *way* physico-chemical energies are interconnected and operate' (ibid.). An animate body responds in such a way as to 'maintain a temporal pattern of activity . . . to utilize conserved consequences of past activities so as to adapt subsequent changes to the needs of the integral system to which they belong' (L1, p. 195). What characterizes life is not merely activity contributing to homeostasis but also to, as Dewey puts it, a 'history'. There are no properties on this plateau which are not the products of the way things on the physical plateau have come to be organized. Iron continues to display the same selective biases it previously did, but within an organized body these same biases serve to maintain the activities characteristic of that body (viz. respiration and all that it in turn supports).

There will, of course, be 'subplateaus' within each of the three 'plateaus' which Dewey mentions. Within the physical plateau, for example, chemical properties emerge when conditions permit sub-atomic particles to be organized into the familiar chemical elements. Within the level of life the basis of the difference between sentient and non-sentient organisms lies, according to Dewey, in the way parts of complicated organisms come to be organized so as to maintain themselves while contributing to the maintenance of the whole organism. At the same time the organism as a whole provides the conditions under which the parts can maintain themselves and make their contribution to the whole. The capacity for feeling, whether or not it is actualized, exists whenever there is 'The pervasive operative presence of the whole in the part and of the part in the whole' (L, p. 197).

This is not a relationship which obtains merely in virtue of the structure of material parts and wholes. The organization Dewey is talking about is an organization of processes, of activities; 'the organism is not just a structure; it is a characteristic way of interactivity which is not simultaneous, all at once, but serial. It is a way impossible without structures for its mechanism, but it differs from structure as walking differs from legs or breathing from lungs' (L1, p. 222). Moreover, these are activities which throughout involve the environment. The model of a stimulus acting upon the organism from outside and resulting in a change in its internal configuration is not an adequate picture. An outside influence may of course disturb the structure which is the *sine qua non* of that particular organism, but this is not as such a stimulus. (An organism which receives damage does not thereby receive a stimulus.) An influence is constituted as a stimulus by the susceptibility which the organism has (by virtue of the organization of its processes) to alter its activities on behalf of some results rather than others and subsequently to alter its susceptibilities to influences from the environment. This constitutes these selective susceptibilities as 'discriminations' and the biases of its responses as 'interest' (L1, p. 197).

Dewey's stress on organization means that he has no need of the panpsychism espoused by Peirce (ENF, p. 208).[11] Feeling does not have to be present in some form or other at all levels of interaction. And because the organization is not tied to any specific material realization, a nervous system is not for Dewey a necessary condition for the presence of feeling. He leaves open, therefore, the question of whether plants and lower animals realize feeling, and (wisely) refrains from offering any condition as minimally sufficient for the actualization of 'susceptibility – the capacity for feeling' (L1, p. 197).

He seems confident, however, that a sufficient (if not minimally sufficient) condition obtains if an animal is able to respond to what lies at a spatial distance from it. For this means it must respond to what (potentially) lies in the future, at least so far as the events, which will involve contact with its periphery, are concerned. To respond in this way to what lies in the future involves a differentiation of its organized activities into 'the preparatory or anticipatory and the fulfilling or consummatory' (ibid.). There is here a presence of the whole in the part (a phase cannot be anticipatory except as a part of some larger temporal whole) and of the part in the whole along a temporal dimension; and this may be why Dewey feels confident that animals which move from place to place and have (as he puts it) 'distance receptors' (ibid.) actually feel.

The fact that this leaves open the possibility that feeling exists at a lower level of organization and that no sharp line can be drawn is not a worry to Dewey, who has come to stress 'the continuity of the historic process', and insists on avoiding views which introduce into it anything which amounts to a breach (L1, p. 209). The claim is that a certain level of a certain kind of complexity, of unity in diversity within events – viz. 'the pervasive operative presence . . .' – is feeling. Feeling thus represents the unity of experience which Kant and the neo-Kantians made the responsibility of cognitive activity, but which Dewey located on a lower level in the unity of organic activity.[12] Moreover each of the multitude of different ways in which this unity is realized has its own quality and these qualities distinguish different feelings.

> Complex and active animals *have*, therefore, feelings which vary abundantly in quality, corresponding to distinctive directions and phases – initiating, mediating, fulfilling or frustrating – of activities, bound up in distinctive connections with environmental affairs.
> They *have* them, but do not know they have them. (L1, p. 198)

The temptation is to treat felt qualities as objects of knowledge or of some form of cognitive awareness. The temptation is, if anything, strengthened by the word 'quality', which etymologicaly is a general name for answers to questions of the form 'What is it like?' This is a form of question which can be answered on the basis of cognitive aware-ness and its answer can constitute a form of knowledge. The colour scarlet is, as Locke's man blind from birth said (Locke, 1690, III iv 11), like the sound of a trumpet; it stands out, it catches the attention, it enters in a similar way into pomp and pageantry.

The ridicule which the classical empiricists poured on this judgment arises from assuming that the man was trying to convey the very experi-ence of the colour, an effort made all the more ridiculous by his evidently not having had the experience himself. From Dewey's standpoint the classical empiricists were mistaken in treating knowledge as consisting in the *having* of an experience (rather than in the ability to relate the experience to other experiences) and communication as consisting in the re-creation (or in prompting an audience to re-create) an experience.

Knowledge or cognitive awareness arises within (emerges from) non-cognitive feeling by virtue of a further level or organization. And while it greatly expands the felt qualities in experience, it always presupposes a context of that felt experience which is not represented cognitively. Locke's blind man did possess a kind of knowledge (cognitive grasp) of quality while lacking the experience of it, although his knowledge was, of course, supported by experience within other sensory modes.

Section III.c: Meaning and time

The matter is further complcated, and the temptation to confusion further strengthened, by the fact that the felt qualities usually discussed are those which, according to Dewey, depend on discourse for their discrimination and identification within experience. Dewey is convinced that:

> Without language, the qualities of organic action that are feelings are pains, pleasures, odours, colors, noises, only potentially and proleptically. . . . The notion that sensory affections discriminate and identify themselves, apart from discourse, as being colors and sounds, etc, and thus *ipso facto* constitute certain elementary modes of knowledge, even though it be only knowledge of their own existence is inherently . . . absurd . . . (L1, pp. 198–9)

The basis of this conviction seems to be the function (unification) within which Dewey has located the emergence of feeling. If feeling is the actualization of 'the pervasive operative presence', then feeling incorporates all the organic activities involved. What the activities involving the eye contribute to feeling merges with what is contributed by the other sense organs ('extero-ceptors') and internal organs (through the 'proprioceptors' (L1, p. 198) contribute. We are constantly making minute adjustments to maintain our balance or control the physical activities in which we are engaged. If the feeling, the feed-back-and-forth from these activities, which permits their coordination is interfered with by experiment or as a result of disease, 'we cannot stand or control our posture and movements,' L1, p. 227). All this contributes to what an animal feels. The problem which the experience of qualities presents is not (*à la* Kant) how do the experiences of such qualities become integrated into a unitary experience, but what leads to their discrimination within a unitary experience?[13]

Even before the details of Dewey's answer to this problem are examined, it is clear that the qualities of feeling which first emerge on the second plateau (before they are taken up into the third plateau, viz. of mind) will be qualities which pervade the whole of an organized set of responses. At the lowest levels they will typically be 'vague and massive uneasiness, comfort, vigor and exhaustion' (L1, p. 210). They will be describable in these terms because of the temporal structure, anticipatory and consummatory, assumed to be present when actualized feeling can be spoken of with confidence. There have to be phases like, 'Comfort and discomfort, fatigue or exhilaration', which 'implicitly sum up a history' (ibid.), if the pattern present in the anticipatory phase is to be conserved or reformed.[14] Likewise there would have to be phases of vigour when, say, a previously conserved pattern is elicited by a strong stimulus, or uneasiness when a stimulus elicits a pattern which has previously yielded an unsatisfactory/unsatisfying consummation.

Although animals may increase the scope and delicacy of the patterns of their responses, the qualities of their feelings will not necessarily acquire the internal complexity which is characteristic of the third plateau. What marks the presence of mind (intellect) in a situation is a 'double feature of meaning, namely signification and sense' (L1, p. 200). This distinction will be treated in some detail in the next section, here we can only make a beginning by saying that Dewey identified sense as 'the meaning of the *whole* situation as apprehended' (ibid.), and he explained that signification involves using a quality as a sign of something so that it may serve as a 'clew' to the sense of a situation. In order to begin to see what this amounts to it may help to place in contrast the different roles which qualitative elements have, first on the level of sentience and then on the level where mind is present.

Imagine a bull aroused by the intrusion into his field of a person wearing a red jacket. The red of the jacket contributes to the quality of the bull's feelings as he turns on it, lowers his head and gathers momentum. It contributes along with a myriad of other elements which help the bull to maintain his balance and coordinate his movements, and it can be said to be a dominant element to the extent that it is at or near the focus of the visual activity which leads the coordination. It does not, however, function as the *sign* of anything. It is simply a feature which makes it relatively easy to maintain the arousal of the bull's impulse to drive intruders out of his territory. The impulse is not specific to red; it is part and parcel of a general pattern which includes attacking other bulls, and other human intruders dressed more sombrely (although they may pass more closely without being noticed).

To grasp in terms of human experience the claim which is being made about the appropriate way to regard the bull's level of response to the colour red, consider Dewey's example (L1, p. 200) of a person made uneasy by the colour red and prone to faint, where it may be (mis)taken for blood. The faint may overcome the person before any images of gore reach the mind, just as the realization of the hitherto unsuspected presence of a person in the room may touch one's stomach before one registers whether it is someone strange or familiar. The level, in other words, is of the responses which constitute what James called 'coarser' emotions.

An instance of the quality red used as a sign is when the red of a light signifies the need to bring a locomotive to a stop (L1, p. 200). One feature of the difference between the train driver's *use* of red and the bull's response to an environmental situation, in which red is present, is that in the former case the quality can be detached from the response. The bull can be distracted (so that the red jacket ceases to be the focus of its sentient activities); it can also be drugged into indifference, but it cannot import counter-indications into its experience. The red is not a *sign* of a threat because nothing could count as overriding the supposed relationship between sign and threat; nothing within the immmediate situation would make the bull accept the red jacket as not an intruder to be challenged. The train driver can take the red light as a signal to stop and then import counter-indications; more circumstances are perceived and firmly suggest that this is not a proper signal light.

Dewey makes this point (L1, p. 140) in connection with a flock of hens which run to the farmer when they hear the rattle of grain in the pan, and then, as the farmer raises his arm to throw the grain, they respond in alarm and scatter, only to return when the movement ceases. They do not discount the stimulus to flee the farmer's sudden movement as just a further indication that they are about to be fed. This is not, although Dewey does not make this entirely clear, just a remark on how difficult it is to dampen a certain reflex in hens by the conditioning of familiarity. The point is not that *the connection* between stimulus and response cannot be broken, but that it cannot be overridden and remain possibly as a contribution to a wider pattern of responses.

An account of a primitive form of the overriding of a connection between stimulus and response appeared, as we have seen, in the article on the reflex arc concept. Competing patterns of response were held in tension and as a consequence of a certain qualitative element of the situation stood out; not because it was a dominant quality within a unified response, but because it stood at the intersection of competing patterns of response. We have a similar situation in the case of a train driver who has become uncertain whether the red light he is approaching is a signal, and is looking for further indications or counter-indications. In the case of the once burned and now uncertain baby, the resolution of the tension may only consist in the formation of discriminatory responses, a division in the stimuli to which it will respond by reaching. This is not (yet) a case of the relation of sign and thing signified. Nor is it a case of 'candle flame will bring distress, *but* it may be safely explored by poking with a piece of paper . . .' (see L1, p. 221). It is merely an adjustment to the range of stimuli to which the child will respond. Nevertheless, the *divided response* is part of the foundation of the relation of sign and thing signified.

> Only when behavior is divided within itself, do some of its factors have a subject-matter which stands for present tendencies and for their requirements or indications and implications, while other factors stand for absent and remote objects which, in unifying and organizing activity, complete the meaning of what is given at hand. (L1, p. 221)

The crucial division in behaviour which gives rise to a new unity and a fundamentally new qualitative structure is between present tendencies in reponse, 'contact activities', and absent and remote objects, 'distant things'. In the feelings of animals, which are capable of sensing what lies at a distance (potential contact in the future) and hence for whom responses form a *series* as opposed to a *succession* (L1, p. 206), consummatory experiences sum up, as we have seen, preparatory or anticipatory activities (L1, p. 197). When, moreover, a series incorporates the inhibitions or reinforcements (although Dewey's stress is on the former) of responses to further stimuli so as to attain the comsummatory activities, the stimuli (from 'contact activities') become *instrumental* to the consummatory.

> Thereby the original status of contact and distance activities is reversed. When activity is directed by distant things, contact activities must be inhibited or held in. They become instrumental; they function only as far as is needed to direct the distance conditioned activities. The result is nothing less than revolutionary. Organic activity is liberated from subjection to what is closest at hand in space and time. (L1, p. 206)

In effect what happens is that internal complexity (internal differentiation of structure) is added to the bare schema anticipation/consummation. There are now, intervening between the first and final activities, inhibited responses (and presumably also some reinforced responses in the sense of a lower threshold for their stimuli). The initial activity thereby 'gains the *meaning* of the subsequent activity', while the 'concluding term conserves within itself the meaning of the entire preparatory process' (ibid.).

Inhibition of one pattern of activity by another is what in the account of emotion was the crucial condition for emotional qualities to be felt in an experience, and there is likewise bound to be a subjective aspect to the unity constituted by the tension between 'contact' and 'distance conditioned' activities. This is probably (the text is not explicit on this point) what Dewey refers to at several places as 'temporal quality', the neglect of which he denounces as the root of many philosophical perplexities.[15]

In the critique of the reflex arc concept inhibition was crucial for the isolation of sensory activities (stimuli) within a pattern of response – in other words, for the beginning of objectification. What distinguishes the present pattern of inhibition (and thereby earns it the title of 'revolutionary') is that the tensions between responses do not merely arise at a single juncture in time, so that the resolution may consist simply in a refinement of sensitivity. They form a structure extending over time and thereby link together things distributed over space. 'What is done in response to things nearby is so tied to what is done in response to what is far away, that a higher organism acts with reference to a spread-out environment as a single situation' (L1, p. 213). Sensory activities and the qualities which dominate them are not merely isolated from responses because they stand in relation to more than one possible response. They also come to be joined together. The meaning, which the initial activity gains through 'subsequent activity moving toward a consequence', furthers the process of objectification. 'Objects are events with meanings' (L1, p. 240).

When considering the once burned baby for whom bright and shining again qualifies the focus of its visual activity, we might be tempted to describe its problem as determining the *meaning* of or 'interpreting' what it sees. This would be for Dewey at best a loose way of speaking.[16] One reason it is loose is that the child is not in the process of adjusting its responses to an outcome sufficiently distant in time. The quality over which it hesitates is at the focus of two responses (reaching or holding back) which will immediately embody the consummation. The red light over which the train driver hesitates is at the focus of two responses (braking or continuing) which are not fused with the possible consummations of the episode (danger, safety with and without a pointless delay). Meanings for Dewey are the ways things are used and interpreted, 'intrpretation being always an imputation of potentiality for some consequence' (L1, p. 147). Use and interpretation both involve a separation (which is not present in the case of the baby), in one case of instrument and end, in the other case of thing interpreted and potential consequence.

Another reason this would be a loose way of speaking is that 'Meanings do not come into being without language' (L1, p. 226) and the baby represents a prelinguistic stage. Fuller examination of this claim will have to wait until the next chapter, but something of its rationale can be indicated by placing in contrast the material foundation of the sort of series in which animals without culture (from chickens to cattle) are imprisoned, with that of the liberating sort of series which involves distance conditioned activities. Distressing consummations will warp, break up and lead to the reformation of even a chicken's habits. But the chicken's activities remain near the level of the bare anticipation/ consummation schema because it reforms largely at the level of coordinated organic response constituting simple stimulus triggered habits. The hen never discounts the sudden movements of the farmer's arm because its behavioural patterns never incorporate (encourage or inhibit) the simple pattern of shying from sudden movement.

The number of such simple responses which must be coordinated, the number of distractions which must be ignored, and the number of sub-operations which must be (flexibly) carried out in any straightforward act of human communication or manipulation reveals the organization required.[17] An analogy may help to make clear the sort of difference Dewey sees as involved here. Animals consisting of a single cell exist as independent organisms (as organisms they display internal differentiation of function). Multicelled organisms arose, when in the process of repro-duction divided cells failed to develop into independent organisms and instead developed differentiated functions within organized groups of cells. If a simple behavioural response is compared to a single cell and the complexity of human responses to multicelled organisms, this offers a hold on the levels between which, for Dewey, meaning, mind and intelligence emerge. And his complaint against prevailing accounts of mental and behavioural phenomena is that they treat the events in ques-tion like a biologist who treats a kidney cell as if it were an amoeba.

The claim, which Dewey repeats again and again, that the emergence of mental phenomena requires a social context, 'shared consummations' (L1, p. 147), 'association, communication, participation' (L1, p. 208) for its actualization (L1, p. 207), is plausible, if it is plausible to think that behavioural patterns of this complexity are only preserved and allowed to develop in a context of the sort we describe as a culture. The stress on language and discourse, at any rate, should be read in the light of Dewey's explicit announcement in the *Logic* that he would take 'Language in its widest sense . . . [as] the medium in which culture exists and through which it is transmitted' (LTE, p. 20).[18]

The consequences of this way of approaching the concept of mind are both radical and wide-reaching, and will be taken up in the next chapter. Our concern in this chapter is with the way this third plateau remains supported by that of life and sentience immediately below it, and with the way this bears on how we should regard the qualities of feeling or sensation in our experience. This in turn is bound up with the distinction which, according to Dewey, 'comes about' at this 'juncture of events' (L1, p. 207), that between sense and signification.

Section III.d: Sense and signification

We have noted, as a start toward explaining this distinction, that sense is the meaning of a whole situation. When Dewey says that it is 'felt or directly had' (L1, p. 200) he seems to be placing it in a class alongside feelings such as those having the qualities of the anticipatory and fulfilling or frustrating activities of animals. When he says it 'is distinct from feeling, for it has a recognized reference' (ibid.), this points to the difference made by the fact that sense is present only where habits of response are sufficiently complex to be 'distance conditioned'. The sense of a situation is not merely anticipatory, but of an outcome made definite by the pattern of inhibitions and reinforcements which extend toward the outcome. The sense of a situation is not merely consummatory, there is 'conserved' within it the early phases of this complex series. Sense is a peculiarly complex feeling, performing the role originally assigned to feeling, that of reflecting the subjective aspect of the unity of an organism's responses.

The complexity involved in sense, as opposed to *mere* feeing, arises through holding responses in a temporal pattern of tensions; and the activities at the foci of these tensions acquire not only a special prominence within the qualitative whole of the situation, they acquire as an integral part of their quality the consequences of their prior fulfilments. 'They have *significance* with respect to their consequences' (L1, p. 207). The distinction between sense and signification, in other words is a distinction between whole and functional parts. Its use to mark the presence of 'mind, intellect' reflects Dewey's conception of mind as based on the new level of organic unities (of complex habits) which have emerged in behaviour.

The precise nature of this function designated 'significance', Dewey suggests (L1, p. 200), is best revealed by the way it contributes to a *unified* sense. A situation may be perplexing, uncertain; it may contain elements, each of which has a significance incompatible with that of others. (This very conflict points to something which holds the elements together so that they can stand in conflict, viz. a unity and direction to activity prior to the entry of the conflicting elements.) The train driver's first impulse on seeing a red light is to bring his locomotive to a halt, but the red light is not quite what a signal should be and the train driver looks for further signs which will make what he sees fall into place: as, for example, an emergency signal, or just the tail light of a car parked in an odd but innocuous place on an overpass.

This is like the now experienced child once again with the features bright and shining qualifying the focus of its visual activity. But the train driver's response is not merely a matter of having to import into his visual activity a greater degree of discrimination. What he must do is discern further features (whether they be size, shape, hue of the light, or circumstances surrounding it) linked to further potential consequences (e.g. the impossibility of hitting a car on an overpass). The problematic situation for the train driver is resolved, in other words, by importing more signs, elements with significance, into the situation, until it acquires a unified sense.

In an article written not long after *Experience and Nature*, 'Qualitative Thought' (L5, pp. 243–62), Dewey placed the notion of a 'situation' in contrast to that of 'object'. 'Situation'[19] is the word Dewey uses to refer to all that is involved in a transaction between an organism and its environment. A situation is unified by a pervasive quality. This is the quality felt or directly *had* by the organism, whose unity of response constitutes the transaction. 'By object is meant some element in the complex whole that is defined in abstraction from the whole of which it is a distinction' (L5, p. 246). Sense/signification is the situation/object distinction in its subjective aspect, and this use of 'object' is consistent with the definition of 'objects' in *Experience and Nature* as 'events *with* meanings' (L1, pp. 241, 244).

It follows that here is an important difference between the way qualities may enter into an experience on the second and on the third of Dewey's 'plateaus'. Take first of all the tertiary qualities associated with emotions. Such qualities reflect how experiences are constituted as unities: '. . . a tertiary quality qualifies *all* the contents to which it applies in thorough-going fashion' (LTE, p. 69). 'When for example, anger exists, it is the pervading tone, color and quality of persons, things and circumstances, or of a situation. When angry we are not aware of anger, but of these objects in their immediate and unique qualities' (L5, p. 248).

The tertiary quality here does not have the role of object (we are not aware of anger *as an object*), rather it unifies a situation from which objects may be taken by a process of abstraction. Its presence is immediate; it is felt, directly *had*. If, however, the situation, which is unified by being qualified in this way, occurs in a more comprehensive situation, anger may be abstracted out of the more comprehensive situation and function as an object. A person may not merely become angry, and for a moment this emotional quality pervade the whole of his situation, he may within the next instant perceive this quality in terms of its manifestations and consequences. His pulse rate has risen along with his voice; he is placing in jeopardy an important business contract.

This is not to imply that an outburst potentially damaging to the prospective contract will be checked, but if it is not, it will still not have the quality of an unreflective outburst. Recollected, it will be a case of 'I just could not help myself . . .' or 'I felt the contract was not worth the principle . . .'. This does not happen without the quality undergoing a transformation. It cannot be felt in the same way because the situation, the way he is interacting with his environment, has changed, it is now qualified differently. But while what is felt undergoes a transformation, it neither becomes something entirely different nor is its presence as a qualitative element in experience exhausted by its role as an object. It remains a felt, immediately had, quality of a dispositional pattern of behaviour (a pattern which, however, may well now be in the process of being either inhibited or sanctioned, or even reinforced as 'righteous indignation'). It is not in its being known or recognized[20] that it enters experience. It enters as the peculiar way organic activities are unified, the 'what-like' or quality of a whole situation, and is transformed by being known.

What pass under the Lockean classification as secondary qualities require a slightly different account. Red, warm, rough, fragrant, cacophonous, do not ever qualify the whole of a situation. Even when they dominate a situation so thoroughly as to exclude the qualities of other sensory activities they remain elements of a situation which also involves some *response* to the quality of the sensory activity, an attempt to escape, an impulse to linger and prolong the sensory activity, a settling down in comfort, etc. They are felt, but not in isolation from other qualities, and only achieve a relative degree of isolation when they become the focus of conflicting or mutually inhibiting responses. They too can become objects within the complex kind of experience which emerges as the third 'plateau', although it is in Dewey's view a myth fostered by empiricism that they are the most prominent and hence the first qualitative elements to come into this role.

> It requires but slight observation of mental growth of a child to note that organically conditioned qualities, including those special sense-organs, are discriminated only as they are employed to designate objects; red, for instance, as the property of a dress or toy. (L1, p. 199)

Once again the objectification of the quality – this time not that of a whole situation, but of an element previously submerged in the quality of the whole situation – transforms the quality. The way of feeling is transformed with the way of responding. It is no longer just a quality of, say, the focus of visual activity fused with those of muscular response. The quality acquires significance; the visual activities it qualifies are now linked to a range of distance conditioned activities and inhibitions. Like anger, it is absorbed in more complex felt qualities of response, where it receives a prominence through the activities organized around its presence but at the same time is transformed by links between these activities and their consummations. It does not first come into experience in this way entering via what Dewey regards as knowledge. It enters experience as a contribution to something not known and continues to make a contribution to that which in every situation, no matter what objects it incorporates, 'cannot be stated or made explicit' (L5, p. 247).

It was suggested at the beginning of Section III.b that because we treat 'the experience of organic responses' on the model of recognizing something as red, we find it hard to escape the conviction that organic responses are one thing and our experience, feeling, of them is another. Thus when Dewey claims that the qualities of sentiency are 'qualities of interactions in which both extra-organic things and organisms partake' (L1, p. 200), the claim seems to miss something important. The nature of our confusion – which is what it appears to be from Dewey's perspective – can be clarified if we consider some untypical cases. Imagine someone who has been fortunate never to be provoked to anger, but who recognizes the signs of anger in others. This person is rather like Locke's blind man who had a hold on what 'scarlet' means. Should we say that what either of these people lacks is knowledge of an *object*?

The first has simply never *had* her responses brought together in the way that qualifies as anger, and this can be expressed naturally by saying that she has never *been* angry or felt *angry*. For to be or feel angry is to have a pervasive operative presence of a whole attitude in many parts: increased heartbeat along with other bodily disturbances; impulses to strike out verbally and physically; perception of someone, and anything associated with that person, as hateful; a desire to see that person injured or put down. And it is to have the presence of such parts in the whole.[21] To feel this way, to have an experience of this quality is not necessarily to become aware of (the object) anger. A person may *feel*, may *be*, angry and not know it (M7, p. 40). But what makes this difficult to see is that in a typical case an adult will be both angry and know she is angry. That is why the phrase 'feel angry' is readily interchangeable with 'feel anger' and then takes on the logic of 'feel angora wool'.

Locke's blind man similarly lacks not confrontation with an object, scarlet, but having his visual activities coordinated in a certain way around light of certain wavelengths (although this custom of mentioning only wavelengths of light seriously oversimplifies the complexities of colour perception). It is the presence of a response to such wavelengths within a total transaction which constitutes *having* scarlet qualify an experience. It is hard to imagine someone, on the other hand, who has *had* scarlet make a contribution to the quality of an experience and not know it. (Someone close to this is the person made uneasy by the presence of red, but who does not understand why.) Examples in other sensory modes are easier to find. A room may loose its spaciousness because a hitherto uninterrupted line has been broken. A person may easily *have* the contribution which the line (broken or unbroken) makes to the quality of the experience of a room and not know it.

The temptation to treat the having of an experience as though it were always and exclusively the awareness (the knowing) of an object gives rise to the conceptual pressure to speak of the subjective aspects of experience as though they have their own field of objects and constitute a special domain of (non-natural, non-objective) facts. There is a special domain of this kind for each subject of experience which is (not as a matter of fact, but as a matter of logic) accessible only to that subject and this is what constitutes subjectivity. Dewey was a consistent opponent of all manifestations of this doctrine, but the doctrine seems to have such attractiveness that his arguments made little headway. Even those who professed general agreement with other parts of Dewey's philosophy expressed puzzlement, as did Philip Blair Rice, at Dewey's 'standpoint-less psychology' (Rice, 1943b. p. 654).

Dewey might well have replied that the notion of a standpoint was indispensable to our dealing with other people and with the world, but that the doctrines which he opposed tried to employ this concept where it simply had no application. This reply will be developed in the next section by way of drawing together the theory set out in this chapter and drawing out one of its most important implications. As a preliminary, it will be useful to return briefly to Locke's distinction between primary and secondary qualities, which figured in Section III.a, for a doctrine associated with this distinction reinforces the view of subjectivity which Dewey opposed. This is the doctrine that a vocabulary referring only to 'primary qualities' is fully adequate to describe the natural, objective, world as it really is, and the other qualities enter only into descriptions of the experience of subjects.

Section III.e: Illusory viewpoints

To understand the motivation of Locke's distinction between primary and secondary qualities it is important to recall the role which certain concepts had in the corpuscularian conception of scientific explanation. Things were to be explained as having the colours and odours which they had, and as producing the sounds and tactile sensations which they produced, in terms of the properties of their 'insensible parts'. Likewise the powers of things to affect or be affected by other things[22] were to be explained in this way. The concepts used in providing these explanations, figure, number, motion and rest, texture, solidity, etc., were designated primary qualities. Modern defenders of Locke's distinction will point to our explanations of the differences in colours of light given in terms of differences in frequency of electromagnetic radiation as wholly within the spirit of Locke's distinction, even though it points to the need to modify Locke's list of primary qualities.

One feature of the spirit of Locke's distinction, however, was the core of his empiricism, viz. the claim that our basic explanatory concepts are derived directly from the canonical sources, our five sense organs. This was the point of designating them 'qualities' in the same sense as colour, sounds, smells, etc. Now it has become increasingly clear, in the light of scientific developments since Locke wrote, that such concepts as length, motion, resistance to penetration, etc., which we gain from everyday experience can do no useful explanatory work until they are taken up into a mathematical framework. They must in effect be replaced by concepts which derive their power, precision and comprehensiveness from their contributions to theories which provide complete representations of some range of possible relations, e.g. between continuous quantities as such, between mass, force and rate of aceleration, between frequency, amplitude and mass. Dewey invites us to compare the differences between 'movement as qualitative alteration' and the concept of motion treated in Newton's laws, or stress as involving the exertion of effort and the concept of force per unit area: '. . . in actual treatment,' he declares, '. . . these primary qualities are not qualities but relations' (L5, p. 241).

What is still thought to be alive in Locke's distinction is the suggestion that some of our concepts represent what is actually, objectively in the world ('because they are in the things themselves' (Locke, 1690, II vii 23)) as opposed to how it affects us. Secondary qualities were for Locke simply the subjective effects on us of the primary qualities of things. Locke may have overlooked a subjective, 'secondary quality aspect' (e.g. motion or solidity as we experience it) to the concepts he placed on his list of primary qualities, thereby exposing himself to Berkeley's criticisms, but it remains important to distinguish how the world affects us (how it is for us) from how the world really is. Were there no living beings there would be no colours, no odours, no feelings of exertion, no experience of trees slipping by as one skies downhill. These refer to how the world is for a conscious being, and the difficulties we have relating these 'facts' to the facts represented in objective physical accounts of the world are, according to Thomas Nagel (Nagel, 1979, pp. 165ff.) what makes the mind/body problem intractable.

Dewey, we have seen, readily accepts that mathematical-mechanical concepts are adequate to describe, explain and give us powers of prediction and control over inanimate nature – that part of nature which appears on his first 'plateau'. The reluctance we have to regard the natural world as including more than appears in our conception of this plateau moreover is, according to Dewey, one of the root causes of the mind/body problem: we deny 'quality in general to natural events' (L1, p. 194). And part of Dewey's strategy for dissolving the metaphysical premises which give rise to the mind/body problem rests on the claim that the 'qualities characteristic of sentiency are qualities *of* cosmic events' (L1, p. 204), viz. of interactions between organic and extra-organic things (L1, p. 199). If, however, all cosmic events are in themselves only as they are represented by the mathematical-mechanical concepts which describe inanimate nature, it would seem that even if we carefully avoid thinking of qualities as we think of objects and carefully regard them as felt or directly had, they still cannot be qualities of natural events.

Nagel makes clear the problem which secondary and tertiary qualities represent and why the move of treating them as qualities of cosmic events will not (seem to) be available. The problem is to relate the single points of view with which every subjective phenomenon (such as the secondary and tertiary qualities) is inevitably connected (including everything which Dewey would say is *had* rather than known), and the general viewpoint of an objective physical theory, which will with equal inevitability have to abandon those points of view (Nagel, 1979, p. 167). To make what he sees as the root of the difficulty vivid Nagel invites us to consider the subjective viewpoint of a real (i.e. not imagined) but 'fundamentally alien form of life' (ibid., p. 168), a bat.

'There is', he contends, 'something it is like to *be* a bat', something which involves among other things perceiving the external world primarily by sonar, echolocation, detecting the reflections of one's own high-frequency shrieks. This is a mode of experience which, it would appear, is subjectively unlike anything we can experience or imagine. The very unimaginability (for a human) of the qualities of this subjective experience underscores the difficulty there is relating experience in its subjective manifestations to facts about the physiology of bats objectively considered, facts about which there is no similar difficulty. But there are such facts, their inaccessibility to our imagination notwithstanding; we recognize their existence in so far as we are prepared to regard bats as conscious.

Dewey's claim that, because (as far as we can tell) bats do not possess language or culture, their consciousness is of the 'anoetic'[23] kind, containing no objects, no events with meanings, arises from his way of developing a thesis which Nagel disputes, viz. that experience is a certain kind of objective event. But Nagel could accept Dewey's conclusion as suggesting how difficult it would be for us to have knowledge of bat experience (possess the full bloom of its fused qualities) from the bat's point of view and thereby how difficult it is to make sense of identifying that experience with objective events. 'We cannot genuinely understand the hypothesis that their nature [namely, experiences] is captured in a physical description unless we understand the more fundamental idea that they *have* an objective nature (or that objective processes can have a subjective nature)' (Nagel, 1979, p. 178).

It is not, it should be noted, 'the hypothesis' which is in dispute between Nagel and Dewey, but rather 'the more fundamental idea'. Dewey does not hold that experience is captured in a physical description, if by 'physical description' is meant one given purely in the mathematical-mechanical concepts which now perform the role once assigned by Locke to primary qualities. That Nagel has something like this in mind seems clear from the fact that throughout he addresses his argument to reductionists. A reductionist holds that nothing fundamentally new is added to the natural world by the appearance of life or culture. The thrust of Dewey's 'emergent' theory is that the qualities of sentiency (not to mention the qualities of mental life proper) are *added* to the natural world when it comes to contain animals of a certain complexity in the sense that qualities like red, an odour or sound become causally efficacious. It is only because events (interactions between animals and the world) are qualified by red that certain changes occur in the world.[24]

Resistance to abandoning the metaphysical premise which precludes qualities from the natural (objective) world is linked to a second 'preliminary assumption about existence' (L1, p. 202) at the root of the mind/body problem, 'the dogma of the superior reality of "causes" ' (L1, p. 194). Life and the qualities of sentiency are causally dependent on events which take place on the physical 'plateau', but there is no warrant for holding that causes operating on one level cannot, through coming to be organized in a certain way, release new forms of causation, which were only potentially present on that level, or that when such potentialities are realized they do not count as part of nature. ' "Effects," since they mark the release of potentialities, are more adequate indications of the nature of nature than are just "causes" ' (L1, p. 201). The metaphysical premise which should replace the dogma is more reasonable, 'For it is reasonable to believe that the most adequate definition of the basic traits of natural existence can be had only when its properties are most fully displayed – a condition which is met in the degree of the scope and intimacy of interactions realized' (ibid.).

But while Dewey does not subscribe to the hypothesis which Nagel seeks to undermine, he does subscribe to the claim that we cannot understand the more fundamental idea of what it is for experience to have an objective character or for objective processes to have a subjective nature. The difficulty this more fundamental idea is supposed to face comes down to this: each event which constitutes an experience has (by virtue of being the experience of some creature) a subjective nature, which is the *what it is like* or the *how it is for* the subject of the experience. These are facts which constitute the viewpoint of the subject of experience. It is common to treat such viewpoints as peculiar to each individual and hence logically private, but Nagel insists that members of the same species by virtue of having similarly constituted sensory modes may share a viewpoint without affecting the problem (Nagel, 1979, pp. 171–2). For the problem is that the essence of an objective conception of an event must leave behind all that is peculiar to individual or species-specific viewpoints, must leave out the very features which consititute it as an experience. There is a straightforward logical conflict between what is required to regard an event as being an experience and its having an objective nature (or its being an objective fact and its having a subjective nature).[25]

Nagel's contradiction, between the demands of objectivity and of the subjective viewpoint, might be thought to survive intact within those experiences which Dewey insists are *merely had* rather than known; there would appear to something *it is like* (*the how it is for*) even a creature, whose experience lacks the structure and complexity which enables it to contain objects. But Dewey could well argue that the contradiction is still the product of continuing to treat 'having an experience' as behaving like 'knowing an object'. The idea that what constitutes something as an experience is that it is a 'viewpoint' gives this away. A viewpoint is an object (a place) defined by certain relations to other objects, from where one's experiences may be said to be experiences of those objects. From a viewpoint one can see, for example, the south-west side of the Jungfrau.

Consider, before confronting Nagel's claim directly, in what respect 'viewpoint' is a logically inappropriate concept with which to treat the logical privacy of experience. A viewpoint is (necessarily) something which can be occupied by more than one person, and the objects of which (the same objects) can enter the experience of more than one person. To say that however much George learns about his brother's experiences he will fail to discover what they are like from his brother's viewpoint, is a misleading way of saying that however much George learns, he will fail to *have* his brother's experiences. To say in that case that George fails to know some fact is like saying that however closely George studies and adopts the mannerisms of his brother he will still fail to achieve the feat of acquiring his brother's mannerisms. In the same sense that George cannot have his brother's mannerisms (only X can have X's mannerisms), George cannot have his brother's experiences. As there is no feat which consists of George performing what, logically, only his brother can perform, there is no fact which George can experience which consists in something only his brother can have.

Nagel would appear to avoid this argument, and justify his use of the word 'viewpoint' by considering *types* of experience. 'One person can', he says, 'know or say of another what the quality of the other's experience is' (Nagel, 1979, p. 172). He does not mean (what Dewey would mean by this) seeing that Michael is aroused (his colour, breathing, etc., altered), is hurling abuse and threats of physical violence, and saying that Michael's experience is qualified (pervasively) by anger. Nagel means putting oneself in a conscious state resembling the thing (Michael's state) itself (ibid., p. 176, n. 11). This we can do for our fellow human beings, but cannot do for bats; we can adopt the viewpoint of a fellow human being, but not (it seems) of an alien form of life.

But the 'viewpoint' is no more justified in the cases Nagel is considering than it is in the case of logical privacy. We can know the qualities of another human being's state of mind, and in this sense 'adopt the (individual) viewpoint' of a fellow human being, because we already 'occupy the (type) viewpoint' of a human being. We cannot 'adopt the (type) viewpoint' of a bat because we are not bats. The impossibility of a human having bat experience reduplicates, on the level of species of animals, the impossibility, on the level of individual animals, of one animal having the experience of another. A human cannot have bat experience without being a bat.

Nor is it clear what to make of Nagel's account of what is involved in having the quality of the experience of another person. To know that his brother's experience is qualified by anger, George has to put himself in a conscious state resembling that of his brother. Does this mean George (in order to bring his own experience of anger to bear on understanding the situation) has to become angry himself? If (as only seems reasonable) he does not, there seem to be two possibilities. Either 'George's conscious state resembles that of his brother' means 'George has in his conscious experience an object resembling one revealed in his brother's state' or 'George is able to rehearse certain behavioural patterns and thereby put himself in the dispositions and emotional attitudes characteristic of those conditions of the organic body which constitute the state of consciousness (mind) of his brother'.

The second of these two translations (which follows Dewey, especially at M7, p. 33) does not require George to become angry, merely to approximate in his dispositions and attitudes the unity of organic action to be found in his brother. Clearly George will find his own past experience of being angry (occasions when his responses have been unified in a similar way) a help in calling together the *partial* organic behaviors' which according to Dewey are the 'stuff' of imagination (images being the qualities of such partial behaviours) (L1, p. 221). There is here no difficulty relating conceptually the objective and subjective nature of the angry man's experience. Objectively the experience is a unity of organic responses; subjectively the experience is the unity, the pervasive operative presence of the whole in the parts and of the parts in the whole, which constitute all of a certain individual man's responses, receptivities and efforts as those of an angry man. The qualities of his response are those which make it objectively the response that it is, and subjectively what are *had* by someone who is, as this subject is, angry.

The first of the translations separates the subjective aspects of the experience (of anger) from the subject and stands them over against the subject, creating what looks like a place which could be filled by another subject, but in which the original subject (because we are discussing the subjectivity of that particular subject) is logically stuck. Here arise all the epistemological difficulties of knowing when another subject stands in a similar (since it cannot be the same) place, or even knowing what it would be for a subject to stand in a similar place – difficulties all fed by the illusion that there is something to be *known*. The illusion in turn is fed by the move of treating the experience as a kind of place, a 'viewpoint', and its qualities a field of objects on view. And this move in turn is not possible unless one conceives a subject as distinct from, logically antecedent to, its experiences, instead of as Dewey saw it, even before he knew how to free the idea from all dualistic entanglements,[26] as activities (i.e. experiences) united in a certain way.

While Dewey offers an understanding of what Nagel called 'the fundamental idea' that experiences have an objective nature (or objective processes have a subjective nature), the hold of the logic of the word 'viewpoint' is not the only obstacle to accepting what Dewey offers. One must also break the hold of the correlative assumptions about the self or mind or subject of experience. The assumptions are not unrelated to those lying behind the ancient Pythagorean doctrine of the transmigration of souls between different orders of the animal kingdom. Nagel's argument, of course, does not in any way rest upon the notion that the soul or mind of an individual of one species might actually come to inform the body of an individual of another species. But his diagnosis of the intractability of the mind/body problem does, nevertheless, rest on the challenge to inhabit *imaginatively* the body of an alien form of life such as a bat. This is what the talk of 'viewpoint' amounts to. One is not merely to imagine what the world looks like if one hangs upside-down, and what it is like when objects must be negotiated in rapid flight while being perceived by echolocation, etc.; not what it is like for a *human being* to behave and perceive in this way but 'what it is like for a *bat*' (Nagel, 1979, p. 169).

The Aristotelian response to the Pythagoreans (Aristotle, 414ᵃ 20–25) was that, as the *psyche* of a man is an organized set of capacities and dispositions, it is not *logically* the sort of thing which could be present in a body which lacks the organs to realize those capacities and dispositions or possesses organs for which a human *psyche* did not include the capacities and dispositions. The reply to Nagel, which has just been given on behalf of Dewey, was in this Aristotelian spirit, that as the states of consciousness (mind) of a human being *are* attitudes and dispositions of an organic body of a certain type, they cannot *logically* be those of a bat, and the failure to imagine the logically impossible does not reveal the existence either of humanly unimaginable facts nor of an intractable problem, but only of a misconception on the part of the person making the attempt.

But the impulse to make the attempt is endemic in the conception of mind (*psyche* or consciousness) as independent of and logically antecedent to the body, the interactions it undergoes, and even of the subjective aspects of those interactions. The qualities of experience can be conceived as objects because the subject is conceived as something wholly apart from the realization of those qualities. One will not break the hold of the assumptions which make talk of 'viewpoints' natural in connection with subjectivity, unless one supplants this conception of mind or self. We have looked at Dewey's alternative to this conception largely from the perspective of psycho-physiology in this chapter. It was noted at the end of Section III.c that, according to Dewey, mind is dependent in important ways on linguistic abilities and social relations. The next chapter will consider those dependencies.

IV

Language and Self

The ideas explored in the previous two chapters had their origins and embodiments in psychological material, although the doctrines advanced were sufficiently general to count as belonging to *philosophical* psychology. In this respect Dewey's approach (it was noted at the beginning of Section II.a) sets him apart from most of what regards itself as analytic philosophy. When, on the other hand, Dewey in 1925 urges philosophy to pay more attention to the phenomena of (natural) language (L1, p. 133) his concerns appear more familiar. But even here Dewey's ideas have their origins and embodiments in anthropological and sociological material, which analytic philosophy also keeps at the periphery of its concerns. It is, however, at least possible to compare what Dewey says about the way to understand the phenomena of language and communication with recent developments in analytic philosophy.

In a lecture delivered in 1969, P. F. Strawson reduced the debates in the philosophy of language to what he described as 'a Homeric struggle' (Strawson, 1970, p. 172) between partisans of truth theory and partisans of 'communication intention'. Dewey's approach bears more resemblance to that of the second party and in Sections IV.c and IV.d it will be compared with a recent product from that camp due to Jonathan Bennett. Bernard Harrison (1979, Chapter 12) claimed that Wittgenstein should be assigned to neither camp and the upshot of these two sections will be the same claim made for Dewey. Section IV.e will then explore the possibility of an alliance between Dewey and Wittgenstein.

What stands in the way of an alliance between Dewey and Bennett, on the other hand, is an assumption, which Bennett makes, about selves prior to their entering into relations constituted by linguistic practices. These assumptions are not unconnected with Bennett's professed 'meaning nominalism', which in turn reflects an outlook which is nominalist in the more general sense and individualistic in the sense that claims regarding the dependence of individuals on social institutions make no contribution to Bennett's theory.

Peirce once wrote of 'those daughters of nominalism – sensationalism, phenomenalism, individualism, and materialism' (8.38). Dewey, we will see in the next section, also had a quarrel with the parent, but on the whole his disagreements with this family were addressed to one of the daughters, individualism. These disagreements made a considerable difference to the way Dewey regarded the concept of mind and the nature of linguistic phenomena.

In the previous chapter, for example, it was taken for granted that where Nagel wrote of a 'state of consciousness', Dewey's phrase 'state of mind' (e.g. as used in M7, pp. 31ff.) was sufficiently close in intention for the two men to be regarded as disagreeing about the nature of something. This assumption could not be made about the words 'consciousness' or 'mind' used on their own. Dewey takes 'mind' and 'consciousness' as labelling different aspects of human life, 'consciousness' for him by no means exhausts all the ways in which mind is actualized or manifested. 'The greater part of mind is only implicit in any conscious act or state; the field of mind – of operative meanings [the whole system of meanings as they are embodied in the workings of organic life] – is enormously wider than that of consciousness' (L1, p. 230).

This doctrine is a consequence of Dewey's 'emergent' theory of mind, which was set out in the previous two chapters. In summary: the field of interaction from which sentiency emerges is that of the coordinated multitude of responses which constitute a body as a living organism. These responses in 'higher' organisms (with 'distance receptors' (L1, p. 213)) acquire a temporal structure (anticipation/consummation) to which we allude when we apply the generic term 'habit' to such structured responses. In yet higher organisms, those whose habits are not confined to the instinctive, this temporal structure is formed and reformed as the organism interacts with its environment, so that any given habitual response is the product of the way previous habitual patterns were consummated (i.e. by satisfaction or distress). On the plateau where mind emerges, simple habits are brought into complex structures, so that some habitual responses come to be subordinated to larger, more inclusive patterns. In these more inclusive patterns the included habits function as organs or instruments: a stimulus to a subordinate pattern serves as a *sign*. The total situation which elicits the total pattern acquires a *sense*, and this is what it means to say 'meanings' are embodied in the workings of organic life.

As the qualities had in sentient experience are not a field of distinct elements, each representing the contribution of an individual organic function, but rather are fused, 'vague and massive', so likewise habits which are subordinated to a more comprehensive organization do not each require a stimulus picked out in high relief. Subordination to a more comprehensive pattern may inhibit a 'sub-pattern', but it may also reinforce it by lowering the threshold at which a stimulus will elicit it. And once a subordinate pattern has been elicited, it may by itself, or through its consummation, alter the sense of the situation. 'Polite' or 'civil' people are said to be 'sensitive to the feelings of others': they will glean clues to, say, a recent bereavement from aspects of other people's behaviour, which are not easy to distinguish, and will be led to an appreciation of the sense of the social situation in which they find themselves without adding to the distress of other people. A great many of the features which give sense to a situation need not appear at the focus of an experience, they may shape the experience from the 'fringe'. Mind is 'the larger system of meanings' which 'suffuses, interpenetrates, colours, what is now and here uppermost' (L1, p. 231).[1]

There is, thus, for Dewey an important controlling area of mental life (all mental life) which is *sub*conscious. This is not, as in Freud's *un*conscious, a separate realm of beliefs, purposes and strategies. Dewey's subconscious, far from reduplicating the structure of consciousness at a level not readily accessible to consciousness, should be thought of as the remainder of an organism, of which consciousness is but one important organ. The capacity for conscious awareness is an organ or instrument, which can be applied to the subconscious, but only by refashioning some of the controlling habits which constitute mind, and this does not leave untouched the capacity for conscious awareness itself.

The *sub*conscious, it should be noted, extends further than mind. It incorporates all the 'immense multitude of immediate organic selections, rejections, welcomings, expulsions, appropriations, withdrawals' (L1, p. 227) which we engage in at all times. These responses which contribute to the qualities had in sentiency play a part in controlling even our most intellectualized inferences. 'They give us our *sense* of rightness and wrongness, of what to select and emphasize and follow up, and what to drop, slur over and ignore' (ibid.). But all these responses in human beings have been taken up into and modified by the social relations, the culture which is a necessary condition, according to Dewey, of human participation in the plateau of mind. Humans can contemplate the alternative of giving themselves over completely to the guidance of the subconscious – can contemplate acting without ever 'taking thought' – only if they can be confident that civilization has not left them with 'malcoordinations, fixations and segregations' (L1, p. 228).[2]

But the most remarkable feature of Dewey's concept of mind, which distinguishes it as a 'constant background and foreground' (L1, p. 230) from anything Nagel would appear to mean by 'mind', and which distinguishes its implicit, *sub*conscious aspects from Freud's *un*conscious, is that mind, conscious and subconscious, is not as such a personality, a self; it is not in all its embodiments individualized. Personal individuality is declared at the opening of the sixth chapter of *Experience and Nature* to have its basis and conditions in simpler events; selfhood is an 'eventual function', which means, among other things, something which, although a development out of a certain field of relations, is commonly fallaciously taken for an antecedent condition of that field.[3] It transpires as the chapter unfolds that Dewey does not regard 'self' and 'mind' as synonymous and hence necessarily emerging simultaneously. There is, he claims, a radical difference between an *individual with a mind* and an *individual mind*. The former is in effect an individual instance of a universal differing from another instance with the same 'mind', as one occurrence of the letter 'H' differs from another occurrence. Two letters need not be occurrences of a different letter (type). Two *individuals with minds* need not be different minds, but two *individual minds* differ as *minds*.

> . . . the whole history of science, art and morals proves that the mind that appears *in* individuals is not as such individual mind. The former is in itself a system of belief, recognitions, and ignorances, of acceptances and rejections, of expectancies and appraisals of meanings which have been instituted under the influence of custom and tradition. (L1, p. 170)

There is no doubt that this doctrine is a direct descendant of Hegel's 'objective' mind. When preparing a brief biography of their father, Dewey's daughters asked him to expand on the statement which he had made in his autobiographical sketch (L5, pp. 147ff.) that acquaintance with Hegel had left a 'permanent deposit' in his thought. His quoted response began, 'Hegel's idea of cultural institutions as "objective mind" upon which individuals were dependent in the formation of their mental life . . .' (Schilpp, 1939, p. 17). Although he discarded the further Hegelian idea that an 'absolute mind' is manifested in social institutions, Dewey claimed that this remaining idea was the source of his 'belief that a ready made mind over against a physical world as an object has no empirical support' (ibid., pp. 17–18).

It might seem difficult to find empirical support for the notion of an mind that appears *in* individuals, but is not individual mind. If, however, one allows Dewey to use 'mind' as a label for a system of organic responses of a certain high level of complexity and considers patterns of response in abstraction from the individuals who respond, as well as from the individual responses which they make, it is easy to see what phenomena suggest the phrase 'self *with* a mind'. As one participates in fashion, comes to regard certain things as 'done' or 'just not done', or takes certain beliefs as setting the bounds of sanity (so that to reject them is a sign of madness or sickness) a person does not thereby derive anything which could reasonably be regarded as individuality. These are features of response shared with other people; none of these features reflects 'mind *as* individual'.

It is not a matter of facing and either resisting or capitulating to social pressure. An individual mind is not necessarily one which resists fashion, rejects dogma and flouts prevailing moral standards. Individual minds do sometimes do these things, but in themselves such actions tend to subvert what Dewey means by 'mind'. They tend to break up habits which constitute a system of meanings. The mind that appears *in* individuals can of course survive a fair amount of deviant behaviour without losing its local dominance. Not everyone has to conform to a fashion, do only what is done, believe as every sane man believes. Sometimes, indeed, deviation initiates changes in fashions, morals or beliefs. Often these changes take place in the midst of the continual process of reproducing institutions through education, imitation or proselytization. An innovation is taken up and necessary adjustments made in the whole system of meanings that constitutes mind. Individuals in their individuality, their uncoordinated impulses, their peculiar histories, import new twists and turns in the reproduction of institutions and customs, are a source of change (L1, pp. 164f.).

Mind becomes individual as opposed merely to informing individuals – in other words, we have individual minds as opposed to individuals participating in mind – when an individual introduces deviations as instruments in the 'novel reconstruction of a pre-existing order' (L1, p. 164). Social factors as much as non-human natural phenomena present individuals with problematic situations, the sort of conflict of which the child and the bright object (used as an illustration in Section II.e) is the prototype. There are various unsatisfactory responses to such situations, resulting either in missed opportunities or painful outcomes. They may also be resolved by 'reconstructing' the situation, resolving the conflict by introducing distinctions and selections which realize benefits and reduce distress.

Representing the situation in order to effect such a reconstruction is what Dewey defines as 'inquiry'.[4] When one represents the factors which create a social conflict (or a conflict between an individual and the social environment) one is representing, more or less adequately, the structure of a kind of 'objective mind'. And when one acts to reconstruct these factors by modifying one's own habits of response and working to modify those of other people, the mind that is *in* one individual becomes that person's individual mind. Dewey locates subjectivity (and its 'peculiar intrinsic privacy and incommunicability') in the experience of this remaking of an objective order at the point where there is 'a dissolution of the old objects and a forming of new ones in a medium which, since

81

it is beyond the old object and not yet in a new one, can properly be termed subjective' (L1, p. 171). This notion of subjectivity is held in sharp contrast to that which either in philosophy or in daily life is thought to consist in 'escape to the enjoyment of an inward landscape' (L1, p. 185).

In societies which structure few people in a relatively homogeneous way, all such 'subjective' deviation from norms tends to be treated as a threat (L1, p. 164). Where social relations are 'heterogeneous and expansive' (L1, p. 167), Dewey contends, it is possible for society in general to recognize the important contribution which differences in individual thought can make to the common good. But this attitude toward individuality, which in Western Europe emerged in the seventeenth and eighteenth centuries, was caught up in the political rhetoric which was used by a rising mercantile class and its allies, and resulted in serious distortions in the way we are still taught to see ourselves, our individuality, and our relationships to (democratic) institutions of government.[5] The philosophic manifestations of these distortions have contributed to a view of human beings as standing not only on the margins of – imposed on by, and opposed to – society, but also on the margins of nature.[6] In the remainder of this chapter we will consider how this alleged distorted conception of the relations of individuals to social institutions bears on Dewey's approach to the philosophy of language.

Section IV.b: Individualism and nominalism

The distinction which Dewey sees between 'mind *in* individuals' and 'individual minds', and the way he marks that distinction can thus be given an accessible empirical interpretation. Whether the distinction is important and the way of marking it (which is bound to strike some as objectionable) can be justified, is another matter. If, as Dewey contends, self-hood and along with it personality and subjectivity (in the sense of an 'inner realm of experience') are 'eventual functions', it is clear that the distinction is of crucial importance and the way of describing it quite appropriate. For according to a pattern by now easily recognizable in Dewey's thinking, individual minds emerge by a process of functional differentiation from an organic whole which was only potentially differentiated in this way. And once they have emerged they retain the status of functional parts of a now more complex organic whole. The distinction in question is between the *termini* of this development; and the *terminus a quo* is evidently a system of responses to things as meaningful, a system which is universal and in which individuals do little more than participate (in both the ordinary and the Platonic sense).

There is, however, a philosophic tradition, dating back to a series of movements in the seventeenth and eighteenth centuries, which saw itself as standing in revolt against tradition in science, religion and economic affairs.

> If the given science of nature and given positive institutions expressed arbitrary prejudice, unintelligent custom and chance episodes, where could or should mind be found except in the independent and self-initiated activities of individuals? Wholesale revolt against tradition led to an illusion of equally wholesale isolation of mind as something wholly individual. (L1, p. 174)

Two doctrines deriving from this tradition reveal clearly what it is that Dewey's view calls into question.

The first is the claim that individuals may be credited with native wants, a clear perception of what it is they want and the ability to work out both the means by which their wants may be satisfied, and the limits which circumstances impose on the possibilities of satisfaction. Thus regardless of how social institutions came about historically, the 'social compact' represents an adequate model of social institutions. People's participation in social relations reflects a desire or choice on their part, the free or voluntary adoption of means to maximizing certain individually adopted ends. According to Dewey's position, on the other hand, the horizon of choice and the assessment of means available are socially given. The mind is not 'open to entertain any thought or belief whatever' (L1, p. 169). What individuals can do, if they are able sufficiently to 'free their minds from the standards of the order which obtains' (ibid.), is to transform the institutions in which they live and which determine their horizons of choice. But discerning where the weight of custom and tradition fall, and breaking out from under it, are not easy tasks.

While the first doctrine raises an issue of social and political theory, the second touches epistemology. With the notion of an isolated individual mind goes a doctrine of pure observation, the limit reached when judgment is scraped clear of the encrusted layers of custom and tradition. 'This notion of course is fiction. . . . We bring to the simplest observation a complex apparatus of habits, of accepted meanings' (L1, p. 170). Unless we do so we can only stare blankly. Without habits, meanings and techniques we have nothing with which to see and perceive. 'To *perceive* is to acknowledge unattained possibilities; it is to refer the present to consequences . . .' (L1, p. 143), in other words to follow the meaning of something (L1, p. 147).[7] We cannot resort to pure observation; we can only refine the habits and techniques which enable us to perceive. We cannot free ourselves wholesale from custom and tradition because we are not wholly individual minds capable of locating ourselves in a position of wholesale isolation from which to observe.

Those who are attracted by either or both of these disputed doctrines will find Dewey's distinction and his way of motivating it most unsatisfactory. From their perspective, which Dewey labelled an illusion, the notion of (a) mind operating *in* individuals is a philosophic nightmare, invoking the surreal image of our awakening to discover that what is in our minds is not our own thoughts, but the thoughts of some transcendent super-mind. The nightmarish appearance, however, is a product of the very identification between mind and self which Dewey wants to call into question. It is because the belief that empirical individuals could not 'carry the burden of science and objective institutions' (ibid.) was combined with the assumption that all facts are realized as particulars, that nineteenth-century idealists had recourse to a 'transcendental supraempirical self making human or "finite" selves its medium of manifestation' (ibid.). This is none other than the Absolute Mind which Dewey claimed to have discarded.

One can, of course, repudiate a doctrine and that doctrine nevertheless appear to be a necessary consequence of one's position. To anyone unprepared to think outside the nominalist principle that the only realities are particulars, there will seem to be only two alternatives. Either social organization is reducible to the particular acts of individual human beings[8] or one must entertain the notion of some kind of supra-empirical self. Dewey's thought, we have seen,[9] developed out of a tradition directly opposed to nominalism, and his removal to a location well outside this tradition later in his career did not alter this orientation. But it is not the familiar claim that we must recognize a *one* standing *over* and constituting the basis of the similarity between the *many* members of some class, which Dewey is at pains to preserve. It is 'interaction, operative relationship', which nominalism denies and which Dewey maintains 'is as much a fact about events as are particularity and immediacy' (L1, p. 145).

Even if Dewey did not early on take the trouble, which he took later in the *Logic*, to emphasize the breadth of his concept of language,[10] it is clear that from the start meaning was for him a concept applying well beyond speech and writing: '. . . to be a tool, or to be used as means for consequences, is to have and to endow with meaning' (L1, p. 146). To recognize something as a tool is to recognize its potentiality for some consequence, hence tools have meaning. And it is to recognize the potentiality of something else to be manifested through its use, hence a tool endows other things with meaning. Language has meaning and endows things with meaning because it is essentially an instrument; it is 'the tool of tools, the cherishing mother of all significance' (ibid.). It is the emergence of a temporal structure bestowing on certain activities the role of instrumentality which constitutes the emergence of mind.

Regardless of how this doctrine stands as the basis for a theory of meaning, it reveals clearly how incompatible nominalism is with the general approach of Dewey's mature philosophy. A way of using something is general; its application involves distinguishing and retaining 'the *relationship* between it and its consequence' (L1, p. 147). The consequence, as Dewey's one-time colleague and life-long friend, George Herbert Mead, made clear, is that the particularity of a thing used is quite accidental to its employment. Wishing to drive a nail and failing to find his hammer, a man will reach for anything, brick or stone, which promises to deliver the necessary momentum. 'That sort of response which involves the grasping of a heavy object is a universal' (Mead, 1934, p. 83). The foundation of this universality lies on the 'plateau' beneath that of meaning or mind. An organism does not respond to a stimulus in its individuality or particularity; its responses are always to a class of individual stimuli. That animals have patterns of response is a fact about the world. If an object calls out a response, 'no matter what its particular character may be, one can say that it has a universal character' (ibid.).

For this reason Dewey's mature philosophy was just as antipathetic as his early philosophy to the idea that experience presents us with a stream of particulars which are immediately perceived in their particularity and 'the experience of ordinary life' arises through a process of generalization which consists of 'a comparing, contrasting, classifying process among, between, with or upon the data'.[11] 'It would be difficult to imagine any doctrine more absurd', Dewey claims (L1, p. 147). This is a description of a sophisticated procedure used by reflective people who already possess a system of meanings, but in the acquisition of a system of meanings.

> generalization is carried spontaneously as far as it will plausibly go: usually much further than it will actually go. A newly acquired meaning is forced upon everything that does not obviously resist its application, as a child uses a new word whenever he gets a chance or as he plays with a new toy. (L1, pp. 147–8)

This freedom to impose a meaning, a way of responding to things, is clearly risky in a world where survival depends on producing certain responses and avoiding certain others. This characteristic of human beings (not just of immature human beings yet to be fully initiated into a culture, but also of artists and innovators) is possible because human culture to some extent insulates its members from some of the drastic consequences of their spontaneity. It does not follow, although this too is part of what nominalism holds, that the universals manifested in meaningful responses are wholly arbitrary, adventitious or subjective. Apart from the constraints imposed on the exuberant application of new toys in new circumstances by non-human natural forces, there is also another class of constraints which Dewey urges us not to regard as nonnatural, viz. the responses of other human beings. 'Meanings are objective because they are modes of natural interaction; such an interaction, although primarily between organic beings, as includes things and energies external to living creatures' (L1, p. 149).

It was the way in which nominalism obscures the importance of the interactions between organic beings, more than the issue of whether the uses of words (regarded as instruments) reveal universal characters in things, which formed the basis of Dewey's criticism of nominalism. Nominalism invites us to consider the context in which humans use language in abstraction from all social interaction, to regard a linguistic act or its vehicle purely as a particular existence. It follows that all that could constitute either the process of speaking or writing or its product (the sound or written marks) as language would be its standing in a contingent (logically external) relationship to a further particular, 'a ready made exclusively individual mental state: sensation, image or feeling' (L1, p. 145). Thus arises a theory of language which corresponds to Darwin's theory of emotion:[12] an antecedent internal state finding its 'expression' in an overt movement.

Darwin was drawn to explaining emotional 'expression' as a serviceable outlet for the pressure of an antecedent state, because he appeared to forget the requirements of the explanatory principle which had been introduced by his own theory of natural selection. The movement taken to 'express' emotion must be explained by its role in some pattern of response which 'serves life' (has adaptive value). When this principle is consistently adhered to, what was treated as an antecedent inner state causing the movement becomes, à la James, the subjective aspect of the movement, the immediate presence (had not known) to the animal of the qualities of its own experience. It is not altogether surprising to find Dewey adopting a similar way with the nominalist approach to what it is for an overt movement to constitute a linguistic act.

Section IV.c: Communication intention

The most recent version of this approach is to be found in the programme which Jonathan Bennett developed out of ideas put forward by H. P. Grice, and which Bennett himself named 'meaning nominalism' (Bennett, 1976, pp. 7ff.). Grice (1957) proposed to shed light on the concept of meaning by an analysis of the sense of the word 'mean' which appears in the sentence, 'The Rev. Spooner meant to refer to the reigning monarch, when he used the words "our queer dean".' Grice analysed this concept of 'speaker's meaning' in terms of a complex intention on the part of the speaker to instil a belief in his audience (or to get them to do something), to have this intention recognized and to have the effect brought about through the recognition on the part of the audience of the speaker's intention. This intention on a given occasion constitutes the individual mental state corresponding to a Darwinian emotional state, and which finds its expression in a linguistic utterance corresponding to an emotional expression.

This approach belongs, moreover, to the tradition of Locke for whom the *'primary or immediate signification'* of words was *'nothing but the idea in the mind of him that uses them'* (Locke, 1690, III ii 2). In Gricean terms this can be understood as the claim that if we are to take an event as constituting the use of words, we must take it first of all as a sign of a certain intention (idea) on the part of the person producing the sounds or marks. And the underlying assumption of the tradition from Locke to Bennett is that which Dewey attributes to 'empirical thinkers', viz. that 'language acts as a mechanical go-between to convey observations and ideas which have prior and independent existence. . . . Language thus "expresses" thought as a pipe conducts water' (L1, p. 134).

It was observed by more than one critic[13] that Grice's work leaves us without an account of what *words* mean as opposed to what speakers mean when they use words. The Rev. Spooner's *words* did not after all mean the reigning monarch but rather an incumbent of a certain college office. And it was argued in some quarters that what people can mean by the words they use is so severely tied to what the words mean as to make the analysis of the former dependent on the latter. This was the claim which Bennett proposed to answer by combining Grice's analysis with an account due to David Lewis of how convention could come to be established without explicit agreement. Bennett argued that rudimentary expressions could come to be linked conventionally with certain intentions, becoming in effect frozen signs of speaker's meanings and thereby acquiring a meaning of their own. This made it possible to treat linguistic universals, the rules governing the uses of words (the systems of meanings embodied in linguistic practices), as a growth out of, and ultimately reducible to, particular events in which indivdual mental states give rise to individual outward manifestations.

Bennett's programme is committed to yielding a plausible genetic account, an account of how language might arise among a group of human beings (or similarly equipped animals) which previously had no language. Even if Lewis had provided Bennett with an account of a way convention could become established without presupposing the use of language, the initial scenario requires a prelinguistic 'audience' to recognize in a prelinguistic 'speaker' a complex intention which we can express (indeed, must express in order to identify the intention) using language, but which 'speaker' and 'audience' are both unequipped to express in this way. What could possibly be the basis for the 'audience' attributing such an intention to the 'speaker'? What basis could we, trying to think precisely about this situation, have for attributing either the intention to the 'speaker' or the recognition to the 'audience'?[14]

To give Bennett's prelinguistic anthropoid mammals mental states, intentions and beliefs about the communication intentions of others, which conform to descriptions we are able to give (e.g. 'He is signalling his intention that the others should follow him'), is for Dewey, as it would be for James, to commit 'the psychologist's fallacy'.[15] Moreover it begs what for Dewey is *the* question. For in rejecting the view that language expresses thought the way a pipe conducts water, Dewey is holding out for the claim that language is what makes thought, reflection, foresight and recollection, possible (L1, p. 134).

Many of those who are persuaded that Bennett's programme faces insuperable obstacles would advocate abandoning any attempt to provide a genetic model and would urge instead the attempt to provide a systematic treatment of linguistic (as opposed to speaker's) meaning by means of a semantic theory. Such a theory would be able to generate the truth conditions of all the sentences of the language. It would in other words concentrate on providing an account of the relationship which holds between types of physical events or objects (linguistic acts or their vehicles) and the world, i.e. of the relationship which is supposed to constitute those events or objects as meaningful. This is something which semantic theory hopes to provide without having to take account of these events or objects as human activities (or as the products of human activity) and, many would claim, without needing to explain how humans arrive at a grasp of this relationship.

If Bennett's approach abstracts in a vicious manner from the social relations which Dewey regards as essential for constituting any phenomenon as linguistic, Dewey would regard this semantic approach as abstracting even more viciously.[16] He would insist that a plausible genetic story is needed to complete any account of meaning. What needs to be abandoned is not the attempt to understand the genesis of language, but the assumption that prelinguistic animals possess a thought structure comparable to our own. This is a mistake of the same order as assuming that an economy based on barter would have a place for a system of national reserve banks.[17]

Darwin, we have seen, failed to consider the adaptive value of an emotional expression and wrote for the most part as though a habit of emotional response was 'serviceable' in providing an outlet for relieving the pressure of an inner state. If instead of assuming a linguistic 'expression' *serves to conduct* an inner state to a place of public accessibility, we ask what *adaptive value* overt linguistic behaviour might have, one answer would appear to be that it allows members of a group of animals to coordinate their responses. Individual animals, which act in a coordinated fashion in a group, gain in some environments a selective advantage. Even if it were felt that Bennett's programme should not be subordinated to Darwinian constraints, this conclusion harmonizes with the sort of genetic stories Bennett constructs and also with Lewis's accounts of convention, on which Bennett's programme rests. For conventions arise, according to Lewis, in response to 'coordination problems'.

Now neither intention nor the recognition of intention is necessary to sustain a coordinated pattern of (social) behaviour. All that is necessary is that the members of a group of animals should stimulate one another to appropriate behaviour at the appropriate time. An uncomplicated example of this would be the way, when one bird of a flock feeding on the ground takes to the air, the rest follow. Often the first bird is responding to a threat and the rest of the birds gain a selective advantage by responding to what amounts to an advance warning of such a threat. The flight of the first bird is, we say, a *sign* of the approach of danger, but the other members of the flock are not responding to it as a sign but as a direct stimulus (L1, p. 140). The flight of the first bird might be said to 'express alarm', but as Dewey remarked when discussing the expression of emotion, the word 'expression' names the facts not as they are, but in their second intention' (E4, p. 154). In other words, ' "Expression," or signs, communication of meaning, exists in such cases for the observer, not for the agent' (L1, p. 140).

It is the failure to appreciate this, which gives rise to the psychologist's fallacy and the temptation to commit the fallacy becomes stronger the more a pattern of behaviour resembles human behaviour in its external aspects. One bird in a clump of trees cries out at the approach of a human on the ground; the rest of the flock are observed to become more alert, wary, prepared for flight. It is all too easy to take the first bird as intending to express alarm and the rest of the flock as regarding its cry as, first of all, a sign of that intention and, secondly, as a sign of possible danger. But it would be more plausible to say that the first bird was responding to an immediate stimulus and the rest of the flock to the cry of the first again as a stimulus.

Phenomena such as these provide an essential starting point for any genetic account of linguistic behaviour. Animals which do not already respond to each other's behaviour cannot respond to each other's *intentions* to produce modifications in their behaviour. Bennett's suggestions for the behavioural criteria by which animals might recognize a communication intention make this clear. One mechanism he suggests is 'repeated association' (Bennett, 1976, pp. 148ff.). A certain gesture is found to be constantly correlated with an environmental situation (e.g. presence of some kind of food), but if that gesture is made in the absence of that situation how are the rest to know what response from them is intended unless there is already a pattern by which, say, the group follow one to where the food is? Otherwise the gesture is no more 'Follow me to the food' than it is 'Does anyone know where there is food?' or 'I'm hungry' or 'Didn't we eat well yesterday?' And being possibly any of these, its (audience) meaning is virtually nil.

The other mechanism, *icons* (ibid., pp. 138ff.), appeals to intrinsic similarities between linguistic vehicles (gestures) and environmental situations. Bennett illustrates by imagining one 'tribesman' emitting a hissing noise and making a 'smooth undulating horizontal motion' with his hand. This is to be taken as an intention to warn of the presence of a snake. But as Bernard Harrison (1979, p. 192) observes, there is no more reason to regard this performance as liable to induce the thought of a snake than of the movements of waves and the hiss of the surf, or the sound and movements of a goose, or of a field of corn in a great wind, or of the pools of mud in a volcanic crater.

The problem here confronts any attempt to assign meaning to linguistic vehicles outside the context of an established pattern of social interaction. It also confronts systematic semantics, the current chief rival to any programme, which like Bennett's is based on communication intention. For it was known almost as soon as the basic semantic idea of what it is to interpret a formal language was applied to mathematical theories, that alternative interpretations could not be excluded by formal means. Formal means could not, in other words, determine the *intended* interpretation. To Quine we owe the argument that this same difficulty will arise whenever this account of what it is to interpret a language is applied to natural languages.[18] It follows that the semantic approach to meaning cannot be used to account for the way individuals rely on the recognition of the communication intentions of other individuals to coordinate their activities, although on the whole advocates of this approach deny that a theory of meaning *should* account for this. (Meaning, they believe, is prior to and independent of what they call 'pragmatics'.)

If language is to have a role in serving the ways in which animals coordinate their activities, there must already be patterns of social interaction to which they reliably conform. If these pre-existing patterns of coordination had to depend on the recognition of communication intentions, and if the possession and recognition of these intentions depended on what amounts to a language, there would be no possibility of tracing, even theoretically, a development of linguistic behaviour from a prelinguistic situation. But prelinguistic phenomena can include patterns of coordination based on one animal being stimulated to act by the behaviour of another.

It would appear, moreover, that before considering behavioural criteria for the recognition of communication intentions, one should consider the criteria for simply recognizing an intention to act and whether this could enter the coordination of activity without presupposing the use of language. If the possibility of one animal stimulating another to act can be taken as an unproblematic phenomenon, so it would seem is the phenomenon of one animal being stimulated by the *initial states* of a pattern of behaviour – by the crouch that comes before the leap. This would (in a description of 'second intention') be a response to an expression (the crouch) of an intention (to leap).

Mead saw in this the possibility of a feedback effect occurring, wherein the responses on the part of the second animal to the initial stages of the first animal's act in turn modified that act before its completion. Mead used the word 'gesture' as a technical term for a manifestation of the early stages of a pattern of behaviour and wrote of the feedback effect as giving rise to a 'conversation of gestures' (Mead, 1934, p. 14). This is not, of course, human conversation; it is still response to stimuli rather than to signs, but it is among the phenomena which need to be placed in contrast to human communication in order for us to begin to comprehend the phenomena in which we ourselves participate.

From the perspective of Dewey and Mead the foundations of Bennett's programme were incorrectly laid with the very first step which Grice made when he began his analysis of speaker's meaning. For he first of all set aside the phenomena of 'natural meaning', e.g. 'Those clouds mean rain', or 'Those spots mean measles', and attempted an analysis of 'non-natural meaning' as something quite distinct from natural meaning (apparently because it was based on convention rather than causality) (Grice, 1956, pp. 39–42). The correct perspective according to Dewey and Mead is found by first looking at the responses of animals to what are in effect the natural meanings of events, especially those events which are the responses of other animals, responses which are not (if a genetic account is to begin in the right place) to things as meaningful, but simply to things as stimuli. To segregate immediately natural meanings on the one hand and human communication on the other is to lose sight of the basis by which prelinguistic coordination is established, to reinstitute the division which prevents human communication from being seen as a development within the sphere of natural phenomena and ushers in the notion that it is the activities of fully formed individual minds which are the foundation of human communication.

This is not the same thing as saying that non-natural meaning should be treated as a species of natural meaning nor that one should look first to what it is to take spots as a sign of measles and from there work toward an understanding of what it is to take someone's gestures (vocal or otherwise) as a sign of an intention that a flower should be handed over. For Dewey the order of explanation proceeds in the opposite direction. What has meaning first of all is behaviour, which things and non-behavioural events acquire significance through their capacity to enter meaningful interactions. 'In the first place it is the *motion and sounds* of A which have meaning, or are signs. Similarly the movements

91

of B, while they are immediate to him, are signs to A of B's co-operation or refusal. But secondarily the *thing* pointed out by A to B gains meaning' (L1, p. 142). For the meanings of events to be used, as opposed to those things merely working their effects as stimuli, language (in a broad sense) is necessary. 'Meanings do not come into being without language, and language implies two selves involved in a conjoint or shared undertaking' (L1, p. 226).

Section IV.d: The grasp of relationships

Different parts of this general position would be disputed by the partisans of two of the currently most popular approaches to language within the analytic tradition. Advocates of systematic semantics (truth theorists) would reject the claim that language involves two selves in some shared undertaking. Language, according to this approach, involves only a symbol system (or syntax) capable of being assigned an interpretation (given a semantics). The symbols could be mechanically produced so long as they possess enough logical structure, and the (material) adequacy of any interpretation could be determined by no more than one 'oracle', so long as its answers to questions of the form 'Is p true?' conformed to minimal standards of consistency. But Dewey is proceeding under the assumption that language is a natural phenomenon, that it is reasonable to be governed by principles of natural selection in explaining its emergence, and that one plausible selective advantage which language offers is that it serves the coordination of behaviour. 'Language is always a form of action and in its instrumental [as opposed to artistic/aesthetic] use is always a means of concerted action for an end' (L1, p. 144).

The partisans of communication intention will agree that language implies (at least) two selves in a conjoint undertaking and will agree with Dewey when he declares that 'Primarily meaning is intent . . .' (L1, p. 142), but they will resist the idea that there are no meanings in this sense without language. Dewey's principal quarrel with this party comes down to his rejection of the project, which has its roots in nominalism, of attempting to treat the intentions of individuals as prior to and the foundation of, the rules and regularities (the linguistic universals) which govern their linguistic behaviour. There are already regularities to which prelinguistic animals conform and which allow them to coordinate their behaviour by responding to various activities of other animals in the group, particularly to the initial stages of those activities. What distinguishes responding to something *as meaningful*, as opposed to responding to it as *a stimulus*, is that the response in the former case is *to the relationship* consitituted by the regular connection between the event (object) and its (potential) consequence. The formation and recognition of an intention to communicate is simultaneous with the recognition of the universal.

The way social interaction requires this response to a relationship is illustrated by Dewey's analysis of a situation in which A succeeds in getting B to bring something which A wants, a flower, by pointing to it and uttering sounds. In the situation where the participants only respond to stimuli, B's reaction 'natively . . . is to the movement, not the *pointing*, not to the object pointed out' (L1, p. 140). B must first of all transfer his response from A's movement to the *object* of that movement. This by itself, however, could be no more than a transference of stimulus. B is stimulated by a movement on A's part to respond to a further thing (what we, indulging in second intention, call the 'object' of A's movement), and this he might well do by just looking at it or grabbing it for himself (especially if it is edible).

To respond cooperatively to A's gesture, to respond to A's *intention*, requires that B not execute his native response to the 'object' of A's gesture, but execute a response from A's standpoint.

> The motion of A attracts his gaze to the thing pointed to; then instead of just transferring his response from A's movement to the native reaction he might make to the thing as stimulus, he responds in a way which is a function of A's *relationship*, actual and potential, to the thing. The characteristic thing about B's understanding of A's movement and sounds is that he responds to the thing from the standpoint of A (L1, pp. 140–1).

Similarly if A is to be taken to have *made* a request, he has to be taken to have responded to the object not as a stimulus but from the standpoint of B. And what establishes the possibility of *thus* adopting the standpoint of the other is the recognition of the regularity of the relationship holding between gesture and completed act. The regularity is prior and the activity is consitituted as involving an intention to communicate by virtue of its being recognized as an instance of a regular relationship between gesture of that sort and its outcome. Meanings do not come into being without language because what brings meaning into being brings a gesture up to the level of language.

A criticism of the situation, with which Dewey illustrates his analysis, is that it involves what would seem to be conventional gestures, pointing and uttering articulate sounds, and that this hardly illustrates a situation which could serve as a prelinguistic starting point, one in which the only regularities on which the communicants can rely are natural. Pointing and uttering sounds, however, are not essential to the example. Reaching with an open hand is a natural preliminary to grasping, so is directing one's gaze toward an object.

Another criticism might be that the stress on 'cooperation' is overdone, indeed cooperation is not essential to the recognition of the relationship that constitutes an event or object as meaningful. An illustration of this occurs in anecdotes told by Jane Goodall (1971, pp. 96–7) about the wild chimpanzees which she studied. Her procedure at one time was to tempt the chimps to congregate in a place where they could be observed, by leaving bananas for them to eat. One small chimp, whom Goodall named 'Figan', and who was finding it hard to compete with larger chimps for the food, was observed to notice a banana overlooked by a larger chimp sitting beneath it, and to move off and wait until the larger chimp left before securing it for himself. Goodall attributed to Figan some grasp of the fact that if he looked toward the banana too much, his gaze would betray it to the larger chimp.

Larger chimps do not on the whole share food; even when well fed they will treat the reach of a smaller chimp as a stimulus to snatch a piece of food for themselves. Chimpanzees who have fed will, however, follow another of their number (regardless of that chimp's place in the dominance hierarchy) who gets up abruptly and moves off. On one occasion Figan was observed to do this when the moment was ripe, to be followed by the rest of the group away from the feeding station, and then to double back some minutes later for an unhindered share of bananas.

An important feature of these episodes is that Figan was competing, rather than cooperating, manipulating rather than helping his fellow chimpanzees. This rather undermines the connotation of mutual aid and succour which festoon Dewey's prose whenever he writes of language and its relationship to thought and social interaction.[19] But otherwise these anecdotes serve only to reinforce Dewey's analysis. Figan clearly appeared to be regarding the situation from the standpoint of the other chimpanzees and responding to relationships, both natural and general, between certain actions and their potential consequences. It is, of course, possible that Goodall's reports are laced with second intention, but they nevertheless contain important clues to what it is we regard as grasping the meaning of an act.

We are prone to look upon Figan's performances as not only exhibiting some grasp of the (natural) meaning of an act, but as exhibiting a degree of intelligence, because we see in it a feature which Kant advanced as a criterion of rationality. 'Everything in nature works according to laws. Only a rational being has the capacity of acting according to the conception (*Vorstellung*) of laws' (Kant, 1785, p. 412). Figan was acting according to some grasp of the effects of looking at something another chimp might want, or of the effects of getting up and moving off. And Dewey makes it plain that the grasp (at some level) of a relationship is the foundation of the meaning, e.g. of a tool; 'a stick even though once used as a lever would revert to the status of being just a stick, unless the *relationship* between it and its consequence were distinguished and retained' (L1, p. 147). This ability to act according to the conception of a (law-like) relationship is moreover seen by Dewey to be tied to the capacity for 'contemporaneous response to a thing as entering into the other's behaviour, and this upon both sides' (L1, p. 141), although Figan illustrates how one-sided this entering may be. Thus Dewey claims, 'Possession of the capacity to engage in such activity is intelligence' (ibid).

There remains, however, an important further level of development to which, it would appear, Dewey pays insufficient attention. We have seen what is involved in a gesture coming to have significance and reaching a level where it is not inappropriate to think of its use as linguistic (in a broad sense). But one or several isolated gestures do not constitute a language in the sense of a system of artificial signs. The passage quoted above about the use of a stick as a lever belongs to a context in which Dewey stresses how important 'language or some form of artificial signs' is, if a chance use of something as a tool to secure some effect is to be registered and reapplied in other contexts. The usefulness of things may be hit upon by accident (serendipity factor) but only 'repetition through concerted action accounts for their institutionalization as tools, and this concert of action depends upon the use of memoranda and communication . . . communication is a condition of consciousness' (L1, p. 147).

The difference in level of development presupposed here is the difference between responding to E in the light of a relationship which it has to some consequence, C, and responding to an event S, whose consequence somehow incorporates the relationship between E and C. Only thus does one have (in S) what might be called a 'memorandum' of the relationship. If E is *used*, in the light of its relationship to C, as a sign, then its adoption as an instrument lays over its natural relationship to C a thin veneer of artificiality. If S is produced to modify a response in the light of the relationship between E and C, we have an artifact, artificial through and through. And indeed it may be too hasty to credit animals with intelligence or rationality before they can respond to such a representation, spoken, sung or mimed, of such a relationship. Kant's dictum, after all, literally reads, 'only rational creatures have the capacity to act according to a *representation (Vorstellung)* of laws'.

Although Dewey says little to account for this further linguistic capacity, there are resources, some of them hinted at elsewhere in Dewey's work, for developing such an account. A general mistake to avoid is that of attempting to account for a sophisticated development before one has observed less sophisticated stages leading up to it. In this case the mistake would be to concentrate too soon on the purely arbitrary sign, the sign whose own qualities efface themselves as it ushers into experience the consequences which it serves to signify (e.g. the way the word 'red' is written, what colour it has, does not usually contribute to its functioning as a sign of that colour). This does not, however, mean we must avail ourselves of Bennett's notion of iconicity, nor that the next phenomena to be considered are signs whose qualities may be scrutinized for clues to their significance.

In several places Dewey discusses 'symbols' (e.g. L1, pp. 72–3; 288–90), placing them in contrast to 'signals'. Signal flags 'convey information, ideas and directions', a function not enhanced by having the audience dwell on the qualities of the vehicle of communication. A national flag symbolizes the nation and where potent as a symbol is accorded respect, woven into ritual, and has care over its design and display lavished upon it. It does not function by resembling anything but by acting as a 'condensed substitute' of the nation (L1, p. 70). In a similar way children lavish attention on dolls[20] and mourning relatives, on the graves of the deceased.

The notion of a symbol in the sense of substitute is explored in an essay by E. H. Gombrich, 'Meditations on a Hobby Horse or the Roots of Artistic Form'. The hobby horse is Gombrich's paradigm of a symbolic image. It, he conjectures, began like all artistic forms not as a portrayal but as a substitute (Gombrich, 1951, p. 1). 'The "first" hobby horse . . . was probably no image at all. Just a stick which qualified as a horse because one could ride on it. . . . The *tertium comparationis*, the common factor, was function rather than form' (ibid., p. 4).

Gombrich sees this, wholly in the spirit of Dewey's approach, as a phenomenon continuous with instinctive patterns of response, which will be triggered by objects which are very broadly similar. A cat will chase a ball as if it were a mouse; a baby will suck its thumb as if it were the breast (ibid.). Our, perhaps physiologically based, predisposition to find faces in a wide variety of configured material is a further illustration (ibid., p. 6). All that is required to make an object into a symbolic substitute is, firstly, that there is a possibility of acting toward it in the relevant way (chase it, suck it, scrutinize it for emotional expression, sit astride it) and, secondly, that acting in that way matters (ibid., p. 7). And acting toward things in such ways (using and interpreting) is what for Dewey constitutes meaning.

Iconicity of a kind is involved in this phenomenon. There has to be, as Gombrich observes, enough similarity in a substitute for it to be taken into an established pattern of behaviour, but this could rely very little on similarity in appearance. The behaviour elicited by a symbol, however, must be *similar* to that *regularly associated* with the thing symbolized, and here is where both of the mechanisms to which Bennett appealed combine to yield a reference to absent circumstances (to a relationship which is not wholly present), and for which Bennett otherwise fails to provide a plausible account. But it is not a reference to a *particular* absent situation, and nothing may follow immediately for the way those involved in mimetic symbolic communication will behave toward the things symbolized. Nevertheless it does offer an opportunity to rehearse elements of an episode of cooperative behaviour (e.g. a hunt) and to rearrange those elements so as to produce a more effective performance on the day.

The origin of the use of things as substitutes could well arise from the phenomenon to which Dewey alluded when he insisted that generalization of a way of responding is carried out spontaneously as far as it could plausibly go.[21] This spontaneous generalization is what leads us to speak of children as imaginative, and this may well provide the first medium in which the imagination finds scope for realization. 'Imagination is primarily dramatic, rather than lyric, whether it takes the form of the play enacted on the stage, of the told story or silent soliloquy' (L1, p. 77).[22]

But the basic impulse may not be imagination but desperation. Deprived of an appropriate partner, caged birds are reported to perform courtship routines before all manner of objects. Gombrich, who saw his account of symbols as substitutions as a foundation for a potentially powerful theory of meaning, offered a name for the general theory along the lines of the 'pow-wow' theory (the roots of language lie in imitation) and the 'pooh-pooh' theory (the roots of language lie in emotive interjection).

> We might term it the 'niam-niam' theory postulating the primitive hunter laying awake through hungry winter nights and making the sound of eating, not for communication but as a substitute for eating – being joined, perhaps, by a ritualistic chorus trying to conjure up the phantasm of food. (Gombrich, 1951, p. 5)

If it seems these resources are too thin to provide a foundation for spoken language, it may be because we have so little understanding of the way vocal sounds serve to coordinate the activities of prelinguistic social animals. The grunts and whistles exchanged as dolphins swim excitedly around before the herd goes off to feed do not seem to function like human language, but they still seem to have some role in forming the individuals into a coordinated group. If such vocal sounds provide the focus for the coordinated activity, they could easily shift to being substitutes for activity.

Here perhaps lie resources for circumventing a major difficulty which Harrison presses against Bennett's programme. How do the vehicles of acts of communication come to have propositional structure? This is, in other words, the problem of 'passing from "whole utterances" to structured ones' (Harrison, 1979, p. 190). We have seen how a gesture can come to function as a sign of an act to be completed on the part of another animal able to place itself in the role of the animal making the gesture. We have seen how an object (including a sound) can come to function as a substitute for an object involved in an action and how a vocal gesture which performs a role (as a stimulus) in coordinating a social activity could play a role in dramatic substitutions for the actual activity. We have, thus, sounds which can substitute for both action (predicate) and object (common noun), so our hungry hunters could lie awake rehearsing not only the hoped for consummation of their hunt, but also the activities which prepare the way to that consummation.

Section IV.e: The tool of tools

There is clearly ample material here to develop a third philosophic approach to the phenomena of language, an approach which would be allied to neither of the two camps already mentioned, semantic theories (theories of truth) or theories based on communication intention. It would be tempting to see Dewey's approach (strengthened as it would be by the substantial contributions of his friend, George Herbert Mead) as finding an ally in the Wittgenstein of the *Investigations*, who also appears not to fit comfortably with either of the two groups of partisans (Harrison, 1979, Chapter 12).

Dewey's insistence that 'objects do not identify themselves apart from discourse'[23] places him firmly against the Augustinian picture of language which is set up at the beginning of the *Investigations* as Wittgenstein's principal stalking horse. The common form of life, on which Wittgenstein came to rest a great deal, has a role very similar to that of Dewey's 'mind *in* individuals', and where Wittgenstein wrote of 'agreement in use', Dewey wrote of 'agreement in action'. 'To fail to understand is to fail to come into agreement in action; to misunderstand is to set up action at cross purposes' (L1, p. 141).

> the convention or common consent, which sets [speech] apart as a
> means of recording and communicating meaning is that of
> agreement in *action*; of shared modes of responsive behaviour and
> participation in their consequences. . . . Agreement in the
> proposition arrived at is significant only through this function in
> promoting agreement in action. (LTE, pp. 46–7)

Both men rejected the notion that purely private experience could be what gives our words meaning; rather the reverse is the case, a publicly shared language is a condition of being able to refer to our inner states. This is what Wittgenstein's private language argument establishes, if it establishes anything. This is what is entailed by Dewey's belief that our experiences are the interaction of our bodies with our environments, and that we live (have) our experiences before we can know them; 'what made [organic psycho-physical action] identifiable objects, events with a perceptible character, was their concretion in discourse. . . . If we had not talked with others and they with us, we should never talk to and with ourselves' (L1, p. 135).

On the basis of having recommended that we not ask for the meaning but for the use, Wittgenstein is credited with the doctrine that meaning is use. If it were worth arguing over precedence for this doctrine, Dewey would have a better claim. '. . . the sound h-a-t gains meaning in precisely the same way that the thing "hat" gains it, by being used in a given way' (M9, p. 19); '. . . it is the characteristic use to which the thing is put, because of its specific qualities, which supplies the meaning with which it is identified' (M9, p. 34).

There are, of course, many points of difference, but one which above all is likely to reflect adversely on Dewey is that where Wittgenstein offers the private language argument(s) to show the incoherency of the position which he (in common with Dewey) rejects, Dewey appears only to dogmatize. An examination of one of the consequences of Dewey's overall position will illustrate this apparent difference. Dewey, we have seen, claims that meaning requires language and language involves a community of action; he also claims that to be a tool is to have and to endow with meaning. It follows that a prelinguistic animal cannot use tools. Since, moreover, signs are tools, because they are *used* by a creature who grasps their significance to adjust its responses to the (potential) consequences which they mark, prelinguistic animals cannot, for example, treat clouds as a sign of rain. In so far as we seem to be able to imagine non-social animals, let alone prelinguistic animals, using tools and signs, there seems to be a conclusion here which (to put it no more strongly) cries out for further support.

We have surveyed enough of Dewey's argument to see why the involvement of the perspective of a second creature in a response would be regarded as a sufficient condition for raising the behaviour of the first creature from the level of a response to events (e.g. gestures) *as stimuli* to the level of response to events *as signs*. But we look in vain for an argument that this is also a necessary condition. For example,

B's understanding of the meaning of what A says, instead of being a mere reaction to sound, is an anticipation of a consequence, while it is also an immediate activity of eyes, legs, and hands in getting and giving the flower to A. The flower is the thing which it immediately is, and it also is means of a conclusion. All of this is directly involved in the existence of intelligible speech. No such simultaneous presence of finality and agency is possible in things as *purely* physical – in abstraction, that is, of potential presence in a situation of communication. (L1, p. 143)

The final sentence states the claim that a situation of communication is a necessary condition for the simultaneous presence of finality and agency, the very thing which constitutes anything as an instrument, a tool. All Dewey's considerations support the penultimate sentence, that it is a sufficient condition. Nothing appears to support the ultimate conclusion, nor to mediate the *sequitur*.

It could be that Dewey means no more than to claim that there is a severe psychological limitation on the possibilities of retaining and developing the use of a tool which has been hit upon accidentally if that use cannot be integrated into a culture. This would appear to be the drift of the passage about the stick used as a lever.[24] Read on its own this passage appears to allow the possibility of the use of tools (including the use of events as signs of potential consequences) to arise on occasion outside the context of social interactions. Language and concerted action would only be necessary to perpetuate these uses.

But this would amount to a climb-down from Dewey's claim about the dependence of meaning upon social interaction and his clear rejection of the belief that 'the correspondence of things and meanings is prior to discourse and social intercourse' (L1, p. 136). It would open the door to the individual mind which does not arise within the context of a group of individuals *with* mind(s), to the individual who perceives the utility of having some means to keep track of experience and invents a language for that purpose. It is this image of the individual mind as constituted prior to language and social interaction which, Dewey would argue, we are projecting onto the prelinguistic or non-social animals, whom we imagine to hit upon the *use* (properly speaking) of a sign or tool. But what is wrong with this image? What incoherency is buried beneath this apparently innocent and plausible anthropomorphism?

Dewey clearly appears to need something which, like Wittgenstein's private language argument, purports to show that our assumptions about what a prelinguistic or non-social animal could do are incoherent, and moreover needs a conclusion far stronger than anything which could be established on the basis of Wittgenstein's general strategy. For one might plausibly argue, even if the argument is disputed, that one cannot establish rules for the use of a conventional sign simply by deciding for oneself how the word is to be used, because on subsequent occasions all one has, on which to base the judgment that its use conforms to the rule, is that it appears to conform. 'One would like to say: whatever is going to seem right to me is right. And that only means that here we can't talk about "right" ' (Wittgenstein, 1953, p. 92e). But the relationship between a tool or a natural sign and its potential consequences is not conventionally established. Whether one has grasped a real simultaneous presence of finality and agency, whether one has in other words assessed correctly that responding *thus* will ensure *that*, will before long be made manifest.

It is not, however, reasonable to expect Dewey to proceed along the path chosen by Wittgenstein, nor to criticize his conclusions because they appear to find no support in the style of argument pioneered by Wittgenstein and brought into prominence only after Dewey's death. Nowhere does Dewey draw our attention to what constitutes an act as following (correctly or incorrectly) a rule. His preoccupation is with a distinction, which may be another form of that involved in the question which Wittgenstein posed, or which may be a prior distinction: what constitutes a response as anything other than a 'mere reaction to sound' (or to any other stimulus)? What constitutes a response as conscious?

On the basis of this distinction one might launch an internal critique of one's opponents, show that they have made crucial use of a distinction in developing their position and at the same time undermined the very distinction on which they have placed important weight. What prospects this strategy has can be judged by the success of Wittgenstein's argument, which has by no means been accorded universal acquiescence. Dewey in his younger days displayed a penchant for constructing internal critiques, but though as he matured he rarely declined to enter into debate, he came to place less weight on such 'formal exercises'.[25] One does not supplant a firmly held view by challenging its coherence. Its more dogmatic adherents will feign deafness, its less dogmatic adherents will rise to defeat the challenge or to redeploy their position in such as way as to make it appear less vulnerable.

Dewey tended in his later years to put more effort into articulating his alternatives to the views which he rejected. The accusation of absurdity, which (we have seen) he did not hesitate to throw at his opponents, was not backed up by deductions of contradictions in their position but by the development of an alternative perspective from which their doctrines appeared insufficiently comprehensive and in their unacknowledged partiality absurdly pretentious. But if Dewey declined to advance *reductio ad absurdum* arguments, the conclusions of which are contradictions in his opponents' positions, the lack of an argument for the clearly implied claim that language (communication) is a *necessary* (as well as a sufficient) condition for the recognition of meaning, stands as an obstacle to those who wish to see all that is encompassed in his perspective. Some sympathetic speculation is needed to indicate how the picture might be completed.

It is necessary for this to return to one of the main conclusions of the analysis of the reflex arc concept.[26] An objective stimulus was there said to be transformed into sensation as possible (as conscious) stimulus – and motion as conscious response was said to emerge – in situations where the stimulus became the intersection of conflicting responses. Dewey continued to regard this as a valid insight into the nature of consciousness, but it is evidently an incomplete account. For we are conscious for extended periods, while the hesitation of the once burned child in Dewey's example lasts only as long as it takes to resolve the tension created in its patterns of response. It then returns to the immediacy of response, that constitutes consciousness only in the anoetic sense,[27] i.e. to moving as stimulated by whatever internal or external events dominate activity.

Social responses also create this crucial tension. That is clear from what Dewey extracts from the schematic episode in which A gets B to hand over a flower. B is not simply to respond to A's gestures by having his dominant stimulus shift to focusing on the flower and then carrying through his own native response. (If A and B were chimpanzees and the object a banana, rather than a flower, B would seize the banana for his own consumption.) However, this episode too would yield only a momentary flicker of consciousness, not a steady searchlight, the image to which Dewey's opponents help themselves, knowing it will be taken as an appropriate metaphor, without troubling to relate it to other natural phenomena.[28] To keep the searchlight steady for any length of time requires an environment able to produce *constant divided response*. That is either an environment of constant crisis of the sort faced by the child with 'hands-on' experience of candles, or an environment in which one is constantly adjusting one's responses to the perspectives of others.

If A's gesture prompts B to hand over a flower through B's entering into A's perspective and holding it in tension against his own, the gesture serves as an act of communication, an element of language comes into being. If B checks his action (cp. L1, p. 214) to hide something from A, that absent gesture is the language of an undelivered message. These gestures, both present and absent, constitute elements of language in the sense that they are intended acts (or non-acts) of communication governed by a grasp at some level of a rule or regularity. If the environment becomes saturated with demands upon, and stimuli to respond to, others, so saturated that even when alone the objects which enter into acts of communication – food eaten, things handled, routines performed – are responded to with the felt presence of others, language in Dewey's broad sense comes to constitute the most salient feature of that environment and consciousness will be nurtured for as long as the organism maintains this form of responsiveness; 'communication is a condition of consciousness' (L1, p. 147).

Now an animal may manipulate things in its environment to its selective advantage. Animals like beavers have instinctive routines for felling and using trees to create favourable environments; animals like raccoons haved flexible routines which enable them to manipulate human contrivances, especially if there is a food reward at stake. There may well be, especially in the latter cases, flickers of consciousness, evanescent meanings, which are grasped momentarily but then slip away and are never used to transform an environment. Communication of the complex sort that is made possible by human speech creates an environment in which the object is not merely manipulated to a successful consummation, but used in a way informed by the perspectives of others. Its use can be communicated; the pattern of behaviour that releases its potentialities can be established as an institution. It can become what human tools are, permanent and flexible instruments: 'Language is the tool of tools' (L1, pp. 134, 146).

What Dewey means by language, therefore, is any system of responses which incorporate the perspectives of others. The hens who scattered as the farmer threw grain in their direction were said to have 'ego-centric' responses (L1, p. 140). Ego-centric, perhaps, but not with a *self* as centre. A self can constitute a feature of an environment only by contrast to another self, and there are no other selves, no other perspectives in the hens' environment, only stimuli to feed and stimuli to flee. There is virtually nothing which holds a response in check against the completion of a response on behalf of another creature with another perspective. The hen's responses cannot be the operations of a self until its environment is constituted by the perspectives of others, through the medium of a system of responses to things as constituted by such responses. It can react to its environment in such a way as to alter it, but it cannot *use* (properly speaking) any part of its environment until it can respond as a self to other selves: 'the operations of the self [are] the tool of tools' (L1, p. 189).

V

Truth and Inquiry

Section V.a: The instrumentalist conception of truth

It was observed in the first chapter that Dewey entered philosophy as an adherent of a movement, post-Kantianism, which opposed the idea that the truth of a thought lies in its correspondence to something wholly outside experience. The aim of intellectual activity and what it is that constitutes such activity as 'objective' lies in features which are to be found *in* experience. This is an outlook which Dewey retained even after he gave up other features of post-Kantian idealism, such as the principle that everything that exists, exists for consciousness. Even after James's *Principles of Psychology* helped Dewey to a conception of experience as a biological phenomenon, only part of which qualifies as conscious, he retained the idea that the truth of our thoughts should be 'an experienced relation among the things of experience' (M3, p. 126).

We are now, after three chapters in which Dewey's account of the origin and nature of conscious experience has been set out, in a position to take up Dewey's distinctive doctrines regarding truth and our knowledge of the natural world. The philosophical psychology which lies at the centre of Dewey's thought will bear directly on what Dewey sees as the nature of inquiry. For, as it was remarked at the end of Section IV.a, the once burned infant confronting another bright object is a prototype for Dewey not only of conscious experience, but of what it is that brings about knowledge and hence of what takes place when inquiry is conducted. Inquiry will be taken up in Section V.b. The present section will explain how the weight of the analysis of 'truth' (later 'warranted assertibility') comes to rest on inquiry and will consider some of the implications which follow from the way inquiry is made to carry this burden. Later sections will consider how Dewey resists certain metaphysical impulses which are commonly stimulated by discussions of truth and knowledge.

We can begin with a drill which Dewey recommended for keeping such impulses in check.

> It would be a great gain for logic and epistemology if we were always to translate the noun 'truth' back into the adjective 'true,' and this back into the adverb 'truly'; at least, if we were to do so until we have familiarized ourselves thoroughly with the fact that 'truth' is an abstract noun, summarizing a quality presented by specific affairs in their own specific contents. (M3, p. 118)

What Dewey is recommending here can be usefully expressed in terms which he used on another occasion when addressing 'The Problem of Truth': concentrate your attention on 'truth', the noun common and distributive, rather than on 'truth', the noun singular and absolute (M6, p. 14). The former 'denotes *truths*, that is specific verifications, combinations of meanings and outcomes reflectively viewed . . .' (M3, p. 126). And we are urged to rest our understanding of the noun singular and absolute on these. 'Truth is a collection of truths' (L1, p. 307).

But the cognates of 'true' have connotations which undermined Dewey's efforts to concentrate in this way on specific verifications. 'A truth' carries the flavour of participating in something final, certain, which transcends specific verifications. Dewey wanted all 'truths', even if reliably tested, to be treated as tentative, hypothetical,[1] fallible and in no way transcending specific verifications. Eventually he surrendered the word and adopted 'warranted assertibility'[2] to perform the duties of 'truth', noun common and distributive.

Even with the clarification which results from this change of terminology, the recommendation is not unproblematic. There is first of all the question, 'Can we expect there to be a quality present in all specific verifications, which 'truth,' noun singular and absolute, can summarize?' Are our verifications not simply too diverse in character to be summed up and labelled by a single abstract noun? What Dewey had in mind was that if we look at what leads up to our verifications, if we examine them within a sufficiently wide temporal context, we will find a common pattern; and because 'consummations' acquire specific qualities as a result of their anticipatory phases,[3] this common pattern will bestow a specific quality on our verifications. If we want to avoid the talk of qualities, we can simply say that what 'truth', noun singular and absolute, does is to point to a common structure in what gives rise to a verification, viz. a problematic situation, and the way the verification brings that situation to a (temporary) close. This is why 'inquiry', the process of dealing reflectively with a problematic situation, is central to Dewey's analysis.

But there is a second problem, which is that if our idea of truth, noun singular and absolute, simply sums up the character of verifications so far experienced we will have no basis for the tentative, 'fallibilistic' outlook, which Dewey insists upon. What will sustain the thought that a great deal of what we carry away from our verifications is likely to be inaccurate, one-sided and from certain standpoints false (*not* true)? This thought cannot be sustained by what we find in our verifications.

In his *Logic* (LTE) Dewey drew on Peirce's definition of 'truth'. He first of all cited 5.407 ('How to Make Our Idea Clear', 1878):

> The best definition of *truth* from the logical standpoint which is known to me is that of Peirce: 'The opinion which is fated to be ultimately agreed to by all who investigate is what we mean by truth and the object represented by this opinion is the real.' (LTE, p. 345n)[4]

He continued, citing 5.565 (the entry on 'truth' in Baldwin's *Dictionary* of 1901):

> A more complete (and more suggestive) statement is the following: 'Truth is that concordance of an abstract statement with the ideal limit towards which endless investigation would tend to bring scientific belief, which concordance the abstract statement may possess by virtue of the confession of its inaccuracy and one-sidedness and this confession is an essential ingredient of truth.' (Ibid.)

In Peirce's account we *have* a foundation for our 'confession of inaccuracy and one-sidedness'. There is plenty of scope for this, if our verifications come as the upshot of our investigations (i.e. our inquiries) and if inquiry is, as Dewey stressed, a *'continuing* process' (LTE, p. 8), in which what is settled at one stage is exposed to further inquiry at later stages, at which times it may be reconfirmed or overthrown, deepened or revised.

Now the index of the *Logic* gives a measure of how important this limit-of-inquiry notion was for Dewey. There is but one entry for all the cognates of 'true', viz. 'Truth, defined', and the only entry is to the footnote just quoted, which is tucked away in an obscure corner of a fairly long-winded book. The index also contains a cross-reference, 'See *Assertibility, Warranted'*. The noun singular and absolute remained at the periphery of Dewey's concerns, and it is not difficult to understand why in the light of what has already been said. If truth, noun singular and absolute, is defined in terms of the outcomes of an indefinitely extended series of activities, i.e. inquiries, the burden of our understanding of that noun will have to rest on what inquiry is and what its individual instances yield (viz. 'warranted assertibility').

Many people feel, however, that an important question can be put to any statement we regard as verified or 'warrantedly assertible', viz. 'But is it *true?*' If this question is asked without any specific doubt in mind,

Dewey (like Peirce) would suggest this was an idle question. If it was thought to be important that it *have* a meaning, Dewey would suggest that it was asking, 'Is this a statement we will continue to regard as warranted so long as inquiry is pursued with the utmost vigour under the most favourable circumstances?' This way of understanding the question at least avoids appeal to anything which transcends possible experience, but giving this question a meaning is by no means the central task of logic, and it is a waste of time to ask the question except in the context of some specific doubt.

To some this indifference to a question which has been central to analytic philosophy, particularly over the past two decades, and the insistence that it cannot be asked on its own, is tantamount not to Dewey's challenging prevailing views, but to his recommending a change of subject. Dewey does not share the concerns of, and hence does not appear to have anything to say to, those who are working in philosophical logic. But a sign that Dewey is not just off somewhere else, looking into a different subject altogether, is the way Dewey's account of intellectual advance or 'inquiry' differs radically from that offered by someone whose concerns are much closer to those of contemporary philosophical logicians. We will begin to explore this difference over 'inquiry' in the next section of this chapter. For the remainder of this section we will explore the source and implications of Dewey's refusal to consider the truth of statements on their own.

If Dewey treated Peirce's limit-of-inquiry notion as peripheral to his concerns, it was because his approach did not rest on there being a unique limit to human inquiry, although Dewey did not offer any reason to think there was no unique limit. This will emerge in Section V.c. It was, however, important to him that inquiries be regarded as connected to one another, that they form a 'continuum' (LTE, p. iii). He understood this to mean that any positive achievement made in the course of inquiry at one stage is subject to revision or reversal at a later stage. This represents Dewey's adherence to what Peirce called 'fallibilism'. It warns us not to view the results of any inquiry in isolation from the context provided by subsequent inquiries, which will draw upon its results, just as it has (very probably) proceeded by drawing (critically) on results of previous inquiries.

But the doctrine implies not only that there are other inquiries which feed and are fed by any individual inquiry, but that each inquiry is conducted *in its own context* and its results are determined relative to that context so that such results cannot be moved freely from one context to another without the need for critical scrutiny. But surely what is *true* in one place at one time is true for all places and all times? Is that not part of the goal of inquiry in general? Perhaps, Dewey would reply, but a fallibilist adopts a cautious attitude about how often our inquiries succeed in this respect.

In Dewey's case the caution that constitutes his fallibilism is a consequence of his conviction that the contexts determining all particular inquiries are created by problems which are *in form* practical problems. The basic idea is that intelligent thought is a natural (biological) response of certain (viz. human) organisms to a (possibly only threatened) breakdown in the coordination of some activity: '. . . thinking starts . . . from an effort to get out of some trouble, actual or menacing' (M10, p. 333). The route to realizing some goal or end is blocked and means have to be found to remove or overcome the obstacle.

In the course of *thinking* how to overcome the obstacle, human beings represent to themselves what are in the first instance possible courses of action. Inquiry, the reflective form of intelligent response, proceeds by dividing the situation into 'what is there (whether as obstacle or as resource)' (M10, p. 334) and projections of something which can be brought to bear on the problem. 'Knowing [that is to say acquiring knowledge] always has a *particular* purpose and its solution must be a function of its condition in connection with *additional* ones which are brought to bear' (M10, p. 327). The former, the conditions taken as 'there', are all in some measure the products of previous efforts to deal with trouble. The latter, the 'additional' conditions or 'projections', are instruments to be tested by whether the trouble is removed or ameliorated, the breakdown averted or repaired.

The components of these representations used in the course of applying reflective thought to overcoming problems thus include what we think of as straightforward 'statements of fact', and inadequacies in them may be the root of what is creating or perpetuating the problem. So they may in turn call for separate subordinate inquiry. But if one forgets the wider context in which these subordinate inquiries arise, and to which their results answer, one becomes prone to what for Dewey would be a serious error and which, although Dewey did not give it a name, we can for convenience refer to as 'the autonomy of factual discourse'. Belief in the autonomy of factual discourse is a specific form of the error of 'neglect of context';[5] it is the neglect of the problem which gave rise to the question which the statement of fact answers. In Section V.d we will see this (what for Dewey is an) error at the bottom of a belief that it is possible and necessary to conduct a certain form of what is described as 'pure enquiry'.

In the first two decades of this century it was not unknown for philosophers (e.g. F. C. S. Schiller) to claim that ultimately all judgments were practical, and for others to distinguish theoretical or factual judgments from practical judgments only as a preliminary to reducing the former to the latter.[6] Dewey evidently had considerable affinity with these philosophers, but he did not deny that theoretical or factual judgments had their own distinctive characteristics, nor is it fair to say he attempted to *reduce* them to practical judgments. His position was rather that of holding such judgments to be specific organs of larger organic wholes, wholes which consisted of those contexts which required practical judgments to be made. (To say a kidney is an organ of a complete organism is neither to claim it can subsist on its own as a complete organism, nor is it a preliminary to reducing it to a complete organism.)

What this means in practice is that any statement setting out the facts pertaining either to the course to be pursued, or the means to pursue it, must be advanced under the general condition that it is both relevant and adequate in dealing with the matter in hand. Thus all statements of fact made in the context of coming to a settled judgment about what is to be done are hypothetical, i.e. made on the condition that they have not left out something important nor included something irrelevant. The adequacy or otherwise of a statement of fact, in other words, cannot be considered in isolation from the context determined by the situation which has called for a practical judgment. Statements of fact cannot without proper care and attention be moved from one context to another, 'A purely geological statement may be quite accurate in its own universe of discourse and yet quite incomplete and hence inaccurate in another universe of discourse' (M8, p. 20n).

The claim which Dewey is making here is important and needs to be stressed. A statement of fact cannot be judged to be true or false on its own, but only in relation to the role which the statement has in a wider context. All factual statements, moreover, have to be assessed in terms of their role in a context which is provided by a practical project.[7] Factual statements have in effect the status of functional parts in a machine being designed for a purpose. In terms of this image the denial of the autonomy of factual discourse is the denial that factual statements are universally interchangeable parts; a factual statement established as adequate in one domain cannot be used in another without at least being marked as possibly needing reconsideration.

Belief in the autonomy of factual discourse is bound up with the belief that what constitutes the truth (or otherwise) value of a factual statement consists in a relation it bears to some part of 'the world', and which can in principle be grasped in isolation from all else. This is commonly taken to be the burden of the classical correspondence conception of truth. Dewey's view of the functional nature of factual statements suggested to him that although there was a sense in which truth did involve a correspondence with the world, concentrating on statements in isolation from the context in which they are used meant the correspondence had been misunderstood. His approach had produced a better 'explanation of the traditional theory of truth as correspondence or agreement of

109

existence and mind or thought. It showed that the correspondence or agreement was like that between an invention and the conditions which the invention is intended to meet' (M10, p. 334). 'The agreement, correspondence, is between purpose, plan, and its own execution, fulfillment; between a map of a course constructed for the sake of guiding behavior and the results attained in acting upon the indications of the map' (M4, p. 84).

The central thesis is, thus, that the virtue commonly called 'truth', the hoped-for outcome of particular inquiries, belongs to the genus 'things which fulfil a function'. This is why Dewey chose the label 'instrumentalism' for his own brand of pragmatism. 'Own brands' (cp. Schiller's 'humanism' and Peirce's 'pragmaticism')[8] served to mark varying distances from what James was calling 'pragmatism'. Dewey, for example, did not welcome the way James attributed to him the claim that 'truth is what gives satisfaction' (M4, p. 109),[9] and made it clear that consequences unrelated to the content of the instrument (such as general feelings of being at peace with the universe) were quite worthless ways to test what he regarded as intellectual instruments.

> If ideas terminate in good consequences, but yet the goodness of the consequences was no part of the intention of an idea, does the goodness have any verifying force? . . . If an idea leads to consequences which are good in the *one* respect only of fulfilling the intent of the idea (as when one drinks a liquid to test the idea that it is a poison), does the badness of the consequences in every other respect detract from the verifying force or consequences? (Ibid.)

Section V.b: 'Inquiry' vs. 'Enquiry'

'Instrumentalism', however, is an unfortunate word in many respects. Nowadays it is a word used almost exclusively for a positivist approach to the status of scientific theories. Like the positivists, Dewey insisted that theories were to be *used* to make predictions and stood or fell on the strength of their ability to do this. But there are still two quite different things called 'instrumentalism' and it is important to bear the difference in mind. For a positivist there is always a contrast between things known in some favoured sense (e.g. 'immediately known') and things *used* in the course of making inferences in order to anticipate what can be known in the favoured sense. For Dewey, as we shall see, we know something precisely to the extent that we can use it successfully to make inferences; 'instrumental' does not mark a contrast to what is *really* known.

To Dewey's contemporaries, 'instrumentalism' suggested that all was to be subordinated to 'utilities of a bread-and-butter type' (M10, p. 366). Dewey protested that no restrictions were to be placed on the consequences which served to test an idea or proposition; the consequences could be, 'aesthetic, or moral, or political, or religious in quality – anything you please' (ibid.). The notion of practical project is not to be interpreted narrowly as a project necessarily directed toward narrow gratifications or marketable products, but widely to include the most disinterested projects of theoretical and experimental scientists.

Such protests did not entirely purge the odour of crass utilitarianism. One reason it clung was that Dewey's doctrine undermines a widely held conception of the supposedly noble project of pure inquiry, the pursuit of truth for its own sake. This is not to say that pure, in the sense of autonomous, inquiry had no place in Dewey's scheme. Dewey did not deny that people could work at problems or puzzles with no immediate bearing on human welfare, enjoyment or prosperity (other than what may arise from the activity of inquiry itself). Scientists are free to develop their own problematics and to pursue solutions to problems thus generated like exponents of any autonomous intellectual activity from chess 'problems' to cryptic crossword puzzles.[10] (Whether science should be allowed to conduct itself in this manner is another question altogether.)

But the conception of pure inquiry to which Dewey stands opposed remains powerfully attractive to those who hold to the autonomy of factual discourse and the associated correspondence conception of truth. Recently, in the course of expounding the philosophy of Descartes, Bernard Williams (1978)[11] advanced arguments to the effect that the aspirations embodied in our ordinary 'enquiries'[12] presuppose an achievement which can only be delivered by a 'project of pure enquiry'. Consideration of this claim will in the next section highlight important features of Dewey's position. Equally instructive is the contrast between the way the two men regard the aim and structure of more mundane forms of investigation, and in this section we will explore the contrast. The difference will turn out to rest on points where Dewey's philosophical psychology informs his conception of the 'problematic situation' which elicits inquiry. Williams's conception, on the other hand, rests in no way on the general features of a problematic situation and he consequently displays a commitment to the automony of factual discourse.

Williams's commitment to the autonomy of factual discourse leads him to the following characterization of 'the most primitive situation of wanting the truth. [The enquirer] has no elaborate or reflective demands – it is not, for instance, that he wants to acquire or found a science. . . . He merely wants the truth on certain questions' (Williams, 1978, p. 37). Let us call this 'a project of primitive enquiry' to distinguish it from what Williams calls 'the project of pure enquiry'. A difference between the projects is that a primitive enquiry is usually embarked upon for some motive additional to the desire simply to know, while in pure enquiry, enquirers suspend 'all interests other than [the] interest in knowledge' (ibid., p. 47) and devote themselves to getting the 'truth ratio [for their beliefs] up to the absolute maximum' (ibid., p. 49).

The goal of a primitive enquirer, on the other hand, is to reach a state which consists in his having a true belief about the answer to a question of the form 'Whether *p*?' for some proposition *p*, a state which has been appropriately produced in such a way that beliefs produced in that way are generally true (ibid., p. 45).[13] The way this account applies can be illustrated by a child, who may be said to know whether the postman has been, if he believes truly that the postman has been and his belief has been produced by seeing mail, which the postman has put through the letterbox that morning. (Saying that he has seen mail which the postman put through the letterbox that morning, satisfies the condition that his belief be 'appropriately produced'. He has not seen letters wrongly delivered to another house the day before and put through the letterbox by a neighbour sometime after the postman had been that morning.)

For Dewey, given his opposition to raising questions of fact in isolation from particular problems, the form of question which will direct our inquiries will be not 'Whether p?' but something along the lines of 'Does hypothesis *p* help with difficulty *d*?' But Williams has, as far as Dewey is concerned, begun in the right place, with a human being who is not going to be satisfied with just having belief states somehow befall him. His beliefs will be worth calling knowledge because they depend upon his 'adopt[ing] purposive means to get into' (ibid., p. 39) the desired belief states. But if a primitive enquiry is embarked on with an ulterior aim, is it not more apposite to describe the goal of inquiry in such a way as to reflect its subordination to the ulterior aim? Surely a primitive enquirer will in the first instance seek to have a belief appropriately produced in such a way that beliefs produced in that way are in the circumstances *sufficiently reliable* (cp. Williams's 'generally true'). In general in primitive enquiry, as Williams acknowledges, the effort invested in securing reliable ways of having beliefs produced 'turns importantly on what is at stake: we check the petrol tank more thoroughly before a drive across the Sahara than before a drive across town' (ibid., p. 46).

But by far the most crucial difference between the approaches of the two men is the different accounts of the 'state' of mind which is transformed by the investigation. For Williams the state is a 'belief' and he says little about beliefs other than that they contribute to our representations of the world. 'Belief' is not a technical term which Dewey favoured;[14] in the *Logic* (see LTE, chapter I) he justified avoiding a number of such traditional terms because they were too prone to be read in terms of purely personal (logically private) mental or psychical states. (Williams, indeed, takes our everyday psychological vocabulary in precisely this way (ibid., 295ff.)). What Dewey wanted was a vocabulary that would not be read as committed to the dualistic interpretation of the relation of experience to nature.

For Dewey the basic elements of experience, and what ultimately constitutes 'states' of mind, are input-output *cycles* or habits. These elements combine ('interpenetrate', see M14, pp. 29–31) in a fashion which John Stuart Mill would recognize as 'chemical' (Mill, 1843, Book VI, Chapters vii and ix) as opposed to 'physical', i.e. the results of combining them are not the sum of their individual effects. As we saw in Section II.e, if two habits conflict one need not extinguish the other. A child's disposition to reach for something bright may, after several occasions of giving rise to a satisfying outcome, have a painful result. A new habit of withdrawing from such a stimulus may be formed from that one occasion, but it need not supplant the old habit, if a discrimination, that is if a new selectivity determining which environmental stimulus elicits which response, can be formed.

While the discrimination is being formed, an organism will hesitate over a stimulus, caught in a tension between two responses, open to the other influences in its environment which might form the basis of a new discriminatory response. It is here that Dewey located the most primitive (and transient) kind of consciousness in an account providing consciousness with a functional role (as the reforming of an organism's patterns of response, (cp. L1, p. 233)), a role that was tied to the context of a problematic situation. The problem has the form 'How to proceed given S?' and the organism's response is mediated by opening itself to further signs of the alternative possibilities between which it is caught in a tension.[15] What it actually lets determine its response, say S*, in this situation in which S is no longer adequate to determine a response, has the function which is, where cognition is fully operative, performed by a judgment. If S* proves to be the basis of a discrimination that yields satisfactory outcomes it will form the basis of an altered complex of habits and constitute a new solution.

This same pattern holds for more cognitive uses of sense perception, e.g. a physician diagnosing a disease. The doctor's knowledge is constituted by a habit of inference from perceptual input (symptom) to diagnosis. His *intelligence* is engaged when the available data do not fully determine the situation and he must call for, or (in the case of medical research) devise, tests which will lead to a determinate diagnosis – and ultimately (because for Dewey all such judgments are practical) to a course of treatment. 'The labor of intelligence is thus transferred from inference to the determination of data, the data being determined, however, in the interests of inference and as part of an inference' (M8, p. 55).

113

Dewey, however, sharply distinguished what he was saying about perceptual knowledge from the claim that to recognize something involves an unconscious inference *from* sensory data. This he set to one side as a possibly true but irrelevant psychological thesis. The relevant claim pertains not to what leads to the perception of a table, but to what *follows from it*, 'to say that to see a table is to get an indication of something to write on is in no way to say that the perception of a table is an inference from sensory data' (M8, p. 53).

Where belief fits into this scheme of epistemological psychology, and in what sense a belief can be said to contribute to our representations of the world, are matters needing careful treatment. Peirce set out (in a manuscript dated 10 March 1873), with a clarity and precision which Dewey seldom managed, the *sort* of account Dewey's framework requires. 'We have seen that an inference is the process by which one belief determines another. But a belief is itself a habit of the mind by virtue of which one idea gives rise to another' (7.354).

> . . . it further appears that in reference to a belief not only can we not have it in an instant, but it can not be present to the mind in any period of time. It does not consist in anything which is present to the mind, but in an habitual connection among the things which are successively present. (7.355)

Dewey, for whom knowledge was simply the best grade of belief[16] which we could achieve (in given circumstances), agreed with this account to the extent that he denied repeatedly and emphatically that knowledge was ever 'merely immediate' (L1, p. 243, and LTE, Chapter VIII). Knowledge and hence belief consisted in the connections our minds can trace between things: 'The more connections and interactions we ascertain the more we *know* the object in question' (L4, p. 213).

Dewey, however, used the word 'inference' more generously than did Peirce, allowing that 'anticipation and prevision' were simple forms of inference (M8, p. 95), so that in effect a belief is a habit of inference.[17] Dewey, moreover, used the word 'idea' not as a term for what is present, but what is present as signifying something else (usually not present). This is what constitutes a representation; it is not a belief state (habit or disposition), but a stage in the actualization of such a dispositional state. A habit, where it is considered as a response to something, *qua* sign or representation, is a mode of interpretation. By treating beliefs as habits and in effect always approaching representations from the standpoint of their modes of interpretation, Dewey avoided the common error of forgetting that no sign or representation provides its own interpretation.

Dewey also linked belief more firmly to action than did Peirce. In LTE he set out the objective sense of 'belief', which he favoured but feared he could not disentangle from the subjective sense, as 'the settled condition of objective subject-matter, together with readiness to act in a given way when, if, and as, that subject-matter is present in existence' (LTE, p. 7). If we apply the framework of habits of response to this definition, then the way to interpret 'settled condition of objective subject-matter' is that the perceived features of a situation do not in the light of the aim or goal (which in part defines that situation) elicit conflicting responses (either inferences or overt action). The habits that the environmental features elicit are as much objective features of the situation as the features themselves. 'Habits enter into the *constitution* of the situation; they are in and of it, not, so far as it is concerned, something outside of it' (M6, p. 120).

Thus the environmental features plus the response patterns constitute the subject matter; they are to be viewed as the unfolding of events in the natural world, and where these events are settled and will unfold in a determinate fashion there is belief. Where they are not settled, there is doubt and the situation needs to be transformed by developing and coordinating responses to those features of the situation that will remove the conflict and restore unity to the developing event. Thus instead of describing the upshot of a successful inquiry as a (true) answer to a question of the form 'Whether p?' Dewey's account points to an objective change in the problematic situation, instituting or restoring it into a single coherent whole.[18]

We are now in a position to understand Dewey's definition of 'inquiry'; what he regarded as 'the most highly generalized conception of inquiry which can be justifiably formulated, viz. '*Inquiry is the controlled or directed transformation of an indeterminate situation into one that is so determinate in its constituent distinctions and relations as to convert the elements of the original situation into a unified whole*' (LTE, p. 104). Dewey offers judicial proceedings as a model where the features of inquiry which he wants to stress are difficult to overlook. There is first of all an indeterminacy about what is to be done because there is a dispute about the significance of certain facts. (Even where there is a dispute ostensibly about what the facts themselves are, this turns on questions about how to interpret certain other facts, viz. evidence or purported evidence.) Secondly, 'The *significance* of factual material is fixed by the rules of the existing conceptual structure which interprets them. And yet, the quality of the problematic situation determines which rules of the total system are selected' (LTE, p. 121). Finally, when the case is settled, the 'unified whole' consists in an unambiguous disposition of the liberty or property of the persons concerned. This is represented in a proposition having a directive effect on future conduct.

When a proposition acquires this directive status, either at the termination of the inquiry or at any intermediate stage (e.g. that certain evidence is admissible, that the defendant is fit to stand trial or has a case to answer), Dewey calls such a proposition a 'judgment'. All judgments are 'asserted',[19] and when an assertion is made on the basis of a controlled use of data, i.e. when the precise significance of the data is determined and further data are called forth as needed, so that the proposition is seen to do the work which it purports to do, the assertion is 'warranted'.

What Dewey calls 'inquiry' and what Williams calls (primitive) 'enquiry' are thus conceived in very different ways. The extent of this difference will emerge more fully in the next section when we consider Williams's claims regarding the need for a project of pure enquiry. But one consequence of the way Dewey ties 'inquiry' to a problematic situation can be noted here: the two concepts are not coextensive. Williams's concept, we have seen, applies to a case where a child has been sent to find out whether the postman has been. Inquiry for Dewey is concerned with 'problems', and 'A problem is not a task to be performed which a person puts upon himself or that is placed upon him by others – like a so-called arithmetical "problem" in school work' (LTE, p. 108).

An arithmetical 'task' can easily be brought into the form which Williams gives to primitive enquiry, e.g. 'Whether the quotient of these two numbers is $23\frac{7}{8}$?' A primitive enquirer might seek a true belief concerning the answer to this question which is appropriately produced in such a way that beliefs produced in that way are generally true, but this would not, according to Dewey, be an inquiry.

Section V.c: Enquiring after the absolute

Inquiry, for Dewey, is *thinking*, but even thinking can be conducted more and less reflectively. Logic, as Dewey conceived the subject, is the attempt to improve through reflection the way people go about the business of inquiry. Formal representation of patterns of inference might contribute to this project but, either because Dewey had a low opinion of how useful mathematical devices were, or because he was not particularly gifted when it came to their development or use, his contributions to 'logic' have made next to no impact on what now passes under that name.

Nevertheless the project Dewey proposed is by no means silly. The methodology he outlines is not unlike that urged recently in some quarters for the philosophy of science. Philosophy from this perspective can only reflect on the history of science, locate what appears to have constituted progress and offer hypotheses about what might give rise to similar advances – all in order to try to feed back into scientific practice a heightened awareness of itself. Dewey's approach to 'logic', it could be argued, is simply a more general application of the same methodology, and as it would be undertaken solely in the interest of improving the general techniques of inquiry, it could be characterized as a 'project of pure inquiry'.

Whatever the upshot of Dewey's project, it does not appear he would have welcomed or endorsed what Bernard Williams claims would become apparent to enquirers who undertook to reflect on their (primitive) enquiries. For according to Williams they would see the need for a 'project of pure enquiry' in the sense of an effort to arrive at a set of beliefs with a 'truth ratio up to the absolute maximum' (Williams, 1978, p. 49), a project for which they would need 'an exceptionlessly truth producing method of acquiring beliefs' (ibid., p. 69). The reason for this lies in a

> very basic thought, that if knowledge is what it claims to be, then it is knowledge of a reality which exists independently of that knowledge, and indeed (except for the special case where the reality known happens itself to be some psychological item) independently of any thought or experience. Knowledge is of what is there *anyway*. (Ibid., p. 64)

Williams refers to this conception of that 'reality which is there "anyway" ' as 'the absolute conception [of reality]' (ibid., p. 65). Such a conception of reality is precisely what Dewey does not want people to think acceptable, let alone inevitable, so it is worth considering carefully the way Williams motivates the need for an 'absolute conception'.

We are invited to imagine two individuals or groups of people, A and B, who have different and *prima facie* conflicting beliefs, experience or ways of conceptualizing the world. Taken together, these beliefs, experience and ways of conceptualizing the world are what Williams calls their respective 'representations' of the world or of part of the world. If both A and B can claim to have representations which constitute knowledge, it seems that it must be possible to treat A and B as having adopted different perspectives on one and the same world or reality. So we need a conception (representation) of the world which includes the representations of A and B as limited perspectives. A and/or B can, of course, achieve this reconciliation by disengaging themselves from their original representations and moving to a more inclusive representation. And it seems there is no end to the possibility of needing to do this; for yet more individuals may come along with further differing representations needing to be reconciled with whatever representations we have thus far accommodated in our most comprehensive framework.

So far this characterizes a wide if by no means comprehensive class of what Dewey would regard as genuine problems or situations calling for inquiry. Philosophy of science in recent decades has become preoccupied with the possibility of clash between different theoretical perspectives. But the general form of scientific problems was not, for Dewey, one of reconciling such conflicts. Nicholas Jardine, who like Dewey rejects the idea of 'theoretical context-free canons of rationality', presents the outcomes of actual inquiries as a series of consensuses and writes as though the philosophic problem of scientific inquiry were to describe how it is possible to generate consensus under constraints strong enough to avoid 'mob-rule' (Jardine, 1986, pp. 34–6). How to reach a consensus on an issue or a way of reconciling differences by relating them as 'perspectives' would be for Dewey only some of the problems calling for inquiry; problems also arise for individuals or for groups which are not simply about how to reach agreement. Problems arise with the *things* in our experience; their resolution is, like 'truth', 'an experienced relation among the things of experience' (M3, p. 126).

Nevertheless it is a straightforward matter to apply Dewey's definition of 'inquiry' to the problem of reconciling differing perspectives: '*Inquiry is the controlled or directed transformation* [by constructing an inclusive representation] *of an indeterminate situation* [how and when we should accept the guidance of the respective representations of A and B] *into one that is so determinate in its constituent distinctions and relations* [e.g. A's representation may be followed only up to here, where B's perspective offers better guidance] *as to convert the elements of the original situation* [A's and B's conflicting representations] *into a unified whole* [within which the representations of A and B are partial views or perspectives].'

One possible (but as it turns out incorrect) way of interpreting Williams would be to say that the limit of the process of reconciling all possible different representations is the conception 'of what there is *anyway*', 'the absolute conception of reality'. But there is under this interpretation no obvious reason why, as we build more and more comprehensive representational frameworks, we should necessarily move toward what is independent of *any* thought or experience. Surely a more comprehensive framework is a *way* of relating experiences, not something which dispenses with them altogether. When Dewey considered (M3, pp. 158–9) the way different people experience a horse – depending on whether one is a horse trader, a jockey, a timid family man 'who wants a "safe driver" ' (the article was published in 1905), a zoologist or a palaeontologist – he stressed that the experiences of each were equally real. There was, he insisted, no need for 'a contrast . . . between *a* Reality, and the various approximations to, or phenomenal representations of Reality, but [simply a need for a contrast] between different reals of experience' (M3, p. 159).

One should, moreover, approach with caution the claim that this conception is presupposed by the very fact that we undertake enquiries. In order to undertake to reconcile the perspectives of A and B we do not have to assume it can be done, we simply need no strong reason to think it cannot be done. Dewey was himself cautious about the assumption that there had to be a solution to every problem we tackled, and reluctant to totalize over all the problems we might seek to resolve.

> That problematic situations are resolv*able* (though the means of attaining solution may not be practically available at a given time) is certainly a working postulate of inquiry, and it is true that such resolution renders intelligible what was previously unintelligible.
> But the extension of these principles beyond the bounds of plurality of problematic situations has no warrant. (LTE, p. 532)

Achieving a reconciling representation will unify a previously ununi-fied subject matter; that is achieved by all successful inquiry. 'But it is always a unification of the subject-matter which constitutes an individual problematic situation, it is not unification at large' (LTE, p. 531).[20]

The idea of the absolute conception as the limit of a process of reconciling differing representations is clearly akin to Peirce's limit-of-inquiry conception of truth. Williams, however, feels that to settle for giving this sense to the absolute conception is insufficient. If the final state is 'regarded as entirely empty, specified only as "whatever it is that these representations represent" ', or, in Peircean terms, 'whatever will remain without substantial modification among the results of continuing inquiry', then it will not do 'the work that was expected of it' (Williams, 1978, p. 65). What, apparently, is expected of it is that it mediate between competing conceptions or representations. But as soon as we reach for a conception of 'how things are anyway' with enough content to perform this function we face 'a basic dilemma'. How can we tell that this conception is not just one more particular representation of the world subject to being superseded by something more comprehensive? Whatever conception we choose, it seems that 'we have no independent point of leverage for raising this into the absolute representation of reality' (ibid.).

For Dewey this dilemma arises from a familiar fallacious pattern of thought. There is no reason to think we cannot or should not aspire to a framework which will include all representations as perspectives and which will (we hope) anticipate any potentially conflicting ways of representing things. But we must not ever assume we have reached this happy state, or that without it knowledge is impossible. We should not suppose 'Knowledge . . . to consist in attainment of a final all comprehensive Unity, equivalent to the Universe as an unconditioned whole – a demand which accounts for . . . absolute idealism' (LTE, p. 531). This is to commit the 'fallacy of an all comprehensive unification' (LTE, p. 532), which is evidently one more instance of '*the* philosophic fallacy',[21] in this case the conversion of the goal of a comprehensive representation ('eventual function') into a condition ('antecedent existence') of having any representation that could count as knowledge.

Section V.d: Context and the conditioning of inquiry

It is not entirely clear on closer examination how pure enquiry is supposed to help achieve an absolute conception. Consider two examples of the sort of problem which is supposed to motivate the need for an absolute conception, the first a literal instance of the metaphor which governs the topic. Reports which reached Aristotle (297^b30–298^a5) that men had visited places where unfamiliar stars appeared in the sky, and familiar ones failed to appear, required the conception of a curved surface to relate such places to places in Europe. An example, which does not involve 'location', 'perspective' and 'viewpoint' quite so literally, concerns the assumption that the mass of bodies is distributed throughout most of the space they occupy. This was challenged by the results of bombarding them with very small particles. Observing the scatter of such particles introduced a quite different 'perspective' on the distribution of the mass of such bodies.

The problem faced by people who are seeking (or, without realizing it, need) to reconcile conflicting descriptions of phenomena by arriving at a hitherto unthought-of way of relating perspectives, is not the problem of finding an answer to something of the form 'Whether p?' And an exceptionlessly truth-producing method of selecting answers to questions of that form will offer no benefits. The problem is to find a way of posing the right question. The situation is more like that in law or mathematics where there is need to generalize a concept so as to incorporate different definitions or procedures under a single notion. In this circumstance it is seriously misleading to suggest the enterprise is concerned simply with the truth of propositions. The reason it is misleading will emerge if we turn to the question of how the results of primitive enquiry may be affected by being delivered from a perspective which is limited in some way, which is not the absolute conception of reality.

A new device for relating phenomena, which represents them as different perspectives, does not affect every belief which had been incorporated in more limited representations. Beliefs about how to get from A to B within Europe, or about what was to be seen in the night sky over Europe, were not shown to be wrong when people were forced to accept that Europe was located on a sphere rather than a plane. Beliefs about what will happen when two medium sized bodies come into contact were not shown to be false by the discovery that there is a great deal more 'empty space' in them than we hitherto had imagined. Before these new 'perspectives' were introduced *some* wrong answers had been accepted as true, but no reason was discovered for thinking this was the case with *many* other answers hitherto believed to be true, and it is hard to imagine what would show that primitive enquiry into all questions had failed in its objective.

There is a difficulty, of course, in untangling the unaffected beliefs from the affected beliefs, when the representation which they constitute is altered to incorporate new perspectives. The way to get from London to Moscow is pretty much the same whether we represent their relation on a 'flat Earth' or on a 'spherical Earth'. But the belief that the geometrically shortest distance between them lies overland (rather than through the Earth's crust) has to go when the former gives way to the latter. And it is possible that accidental features of the 'flat Earth' representation could have produced a false belief about where the shortest air or overland route lay. But the key worry here is that it is only from the more inclusive representation that we can assess which beliefs can still stand.

From this we might conclude that, as long as more inclusive representations are possible, we can never be *certain* of any of our beliefs. This, however, is not the source of what Williams sees as the need for an absolute conception, for he does not suggest certainty is a necessary condition of (primitive) knowledge; in fact the discussion of primitive enquiry was designed in part to establish that this is not a necessary condition (see Williams, 1978, p. 45). There is little mention in Williams's discussion, moreover, of the case where it is concluded that one of the conflicting representations just had it (or much of it) wrong.[22] This is, however, a possible (perhaps even inevitable) result of effecting a reconciliation. One representation may be treated as a limited perspective within the other and hence as mistaken in some respect, if only in the generality originally assumed for that representation. (If both representations are incorporated in a wider framework, then both undergo correction in this sense.) Aspects of a corrected representation may, moreover, be dismissed as, say dreams or myths.

This, however, involves an epistemological evaluation ('*merely* a dream') which may make it difficult, if not impossible, to settle which perspective is the most inclusive. ('No, not *merely* a dream; dreams are significant indications of how experience as a whole is to be understood.') The presence of such evaluative elements in a representation is one reason why it cannot simply be *assumed* that every pair of differing representations can be incorporated into a single framework. Williams, significantly, does not include patterns of evaluation[23] in his list of the components (viz. beliefs, experiences, ways of conceptualizing) of a representation and the assumption that his 'very basic thought' will be accepted without protest rests in a crucial way on a general omission, which includes this as a special case.

The difficulty of untangling beliefs which are affected by a new

121

perspective, and beliefs which are not, has this important feature. Perspectives, both narrow and inclusive, 'condition' enquiry. What this means is that moving to a representation which is wide enough to locate two conflicting claims to knowledge in such a way as to resolve a conflict which appears between them, involves altering what is to constitute a sensible question, *and* (more importantly from Williams's point of view) what counts toward a satisfactory answer. Details, which are accessible to a narrower perspective but are regarded as not worth noticing or looking out for, become crucially important. Some things which hitherto were thought to be very important are seen to be insignificant. Standards of precision shift, usually toward the more rigorous, but not always. These are not shifts just in what is to be regarded as a reliable way to arrive at *the truth* of *p*, they are shifts in *what is to count as having arrived at* the truth of *p*.

This is why it is seriously misleading to characterize an enquiry into how to reconcile representations as asking after the truth of propositions. And if this is the case, then pure enquiry is not relevant to attaining an absolute standpoint. Not only does it now appear highly unlikely that maximizing the truth ratio among ordinary beliefs (products of primitive enquiries) will result in achieving the absolute standpoint (for a pure enquirer has no way of telling in advance how his initial limited perspective has conditioned his primitive enquiries and their results), it also appears that 'an exceptionlessly truth producing method of acquiring beliefs' cannot be sought on its own, for attaining an improved perspective may well be prior to knowing what (in a particular field of endeavour) is to count as truth and hence what is to count as a truth-producing method of acquiring belief (not to mention what is to count as achieving an increased truth ratio).

The irrelevance of pure enquiry to the function which the absolute conception of reality is expected to perform is hidden from Williams because of the way he characterized primitive enquiry. For although something like the notion of an enquiry being conditioned must operate when motivating the notion of a limited perspective, there is nothing in the way Williams characterizes primitive enquiry which corresponds to this notion. Consider: in primitive enquiry 'truth' labels the goal of the activity, but this goal is not typically pursued for its own sake. (That rather is what constitutes pure enquiry). But if the goal of believing 'the truth' about some matter serves, as Dewey insisted, as a means to some further end, might we not have to say something about that further end in order adequately to characterize the goal of a primitive enquiry?

This natural question is never raised by Williams. He assumes that for primitive enquirers truth is something which *could be* (although typically is not) sought for its own sake, independently of what further goals it might serve. Whatever purposes which primitive enquirers have in

122

seeking to know 'Whether *p*?', are assumed not to have any bearing on the object of their enquiries, or on what is to count as an answer. Indeed some particular purpose in wanting to know 'Whether *p*?' *may* not condition the result of an enquiry so as to render it limited on some other occasion. But *it is not* safe to proceed as though a general complex of purposes and interests will not impose limitations on the methods and the results of enquiries, limitations which will only emerge when those results confront a different complex of purposes and interests.

This is only one aspect of a very large assumption, for nothing whatever is acknowledged by Williams to condition primitive enquiry. The enquirer wants the truth about *p* as though from *just* the description 'Andrew wants to know where Moscow is in relation to London' we could tell whether he is making a map or considering trade prospects; as though from just the description 'Brenda wants to know how much space the matter of this body occupies' we could tell whether she is engaged in atomic physics or packing for a holiday.

This way of treating enquiry is tantamount to the assumption that truth is to be determined independently of any conditions imposed by the context which determined the need for investigation. But a condition is what restricts an enquirer to what, in the context of a more inclusive representation, is a narrow perspective. Thus the notion that pure enquirers can achieve the absolute conception by purging the results of their primitive enquiries of beliefs which are not true, and raising their truth ratio to the absolute maximum, is a consequence of imagining that as primitive enquirers they can proceed unencumbered by the conditions of context which are supposed only to be shed once the absolute conception is attained. But the assumption that primitive enquirers aspire to do something which can only be done from the standpoint of the absolute conception is what leads to Williams's 'basic dilemma'. It is assumed that primitive enquirers need the standpoint of an absolute conception because the account given of what they are doing on a particular enquiry omits any mention of the factors which condition their enquiry.

If the account of primitive enquiry is placed back in the context of the goals, interests, standards of relevance and general habits of mind which condition every actual enquiry, then it is obvious that ordinary enquiry does not (and does not need to) appeal to a determinate absolute conception. Although the argument which Williams used to reach the need for an absolute conception involved what Dewey, in *Experience and Nature*, identified as '*the* philosophic fallacy' (turning an eventual function into an antecedent condition) the root of the impulse lies in what Dewey identified[24] as the more general mistake of neglect of context.

Section V.e: Actors and spectators

Williams's enquirer 'adopts purposive means to get into' a desired belief state. Dewey's inquirer acts to transform the problematic situation in which he finds himself. Does not Dewey's inquirer take unjustified liberties? Is it not incumbent on people who confront a situation about which they have a question or problem – particularly one about a matter of fact – to keep their activities carefully in check so that they do not inadvertently answer the question with what they want, hope or expect to hear, and report as independent 'fact' something which is partly their own doing? Does Dewey's analysis do justice to the principle that objective inquiry must be conducted in a detached manner?

Dewey for his part was prone to stress the extent to which modern *experimental* science recognizes the need to control artificially the conditions in which observation takes place, but he was as alive as anyone to the constant vigilance which experimenters must exercise to ensure that what they report are not 'artifacts of preparation' or products of wishful thinking. He repeatedly affirmed that coming to know results in changes in the situation and in the initial experience[25] which elicited inquiry, but this was not a claim that coming to know should be allowed materially to affect either the (warranted) answer to specific questions posed in an inquiry or the test of (hypothetical) answers by subsequent experience. It was the claim rather that the formation of the question, the suggestion of an answer, the working out of the implications of that answer and the subsequent treatment of experiences as confirming or disconfirming that answer, all take place in a wider context of practical concerns. That wider context does not remain unaltered by such a procedure, even as efforts are made to isolate and control phenomena so as to yield a 'warranted' answer, i.e. one not influenced by the inquirer's hopes, expectations or activities.

Nevertheless the suggestion that coming to know necessarily involves any change in the things which provoked the inquiry seems to many people counter-intuitive. One has to bear in mind how comprehensively Dewey viewed the context of an inquiry. The inquirer's habits, recall, 'enter into the *constitution* of the situation . . .' (M6, p. 120). Either these habits will have to undergo a restructuring, or the circumstances which elicit them will need to be restructured, if the problematic situation is to be transformed. If the situation comprehends as much as this, there is no way to avoid the conclusion that coming to know changes things.

In reply it will be maintained that this trivializes the thesis or is simply irrelevant. That knowers change when they come to know is not in dispute. But the relations are such, Dewey would insist, that the change in the knower cannot be treated in isolation from the resulting change in the total situation, nor from the difference this change in the situation makes to the knower's environment. The total situation is made up of – its real features include – the potential interactions between knower and known. And these also alter when a creature comes to know:

> the difference which the natural event of knowing makes to the natural event of direct organic stimulation . . . is no change of a reality into an unreality, of an object into something subjective; it is no secret, illicit or epistemological transformation; it is a genuine acquisition of new and distinctive features through entering into relations with things with which it was not formerly connected – namely possible and future things. (M10, p. 35)

The thesis applies at the level of sentience. If a predator spies prey, that prey acquires an immediate liability, which it did not previously possess, to become a meal. If the eye of a small primate which is able to fling pebbles, falls on a pebble, that object acquires a potentiality for movement through the air, and for impact on nearby objects, which it did not possess prior to this. This potentiality may be dismissed as trivial, but a pebble, whose new potential is realized as it is thrown, has its history materially affected and nature along with it is altered in a way it would not have been had the pebble not been noticed. Dewey's doctrine, however, is prone to be exaggerated by his opponents. Dewey is not advancing the preposterous claim that when we come to know something about stars light years away, a change has to take place somewhere, say in the nuclear reactions which feed the star. Nature has changed in its relations if the star comes to affect the behaviour of a creature on a distant planet in a different way.

Dewey stressed this consequence of his position to keep before people's attention the context in which humans come to know: 'the purpose of knowing is to effect some alteration . . .' (M6, p. 140). The doctrine nevertheless conjures up images of humans reaching out to 'apprehend' facts and finding that in 'grasping' them the facts change or shift, so that what is attained is never what was intended. Far better, it is felt, that we should follow the lead of images which draw on the visual mode of perception. We can peer and not interfere with what arouses our curiosity. Dewey more than once derided 'spectator' notions of knowledge or consciousness (M10, p. 41; L1, pp. 235, 259), although this theme is not as prominent in his writing as some critics would lead one to believe. The reason Dewey did not identify this model of awareness as 'the philosophic fallacy'[26] is not hard to see. To press too hard on the claim that cognition is not 'spectatorship' is to allow that one's opponents have a correct understanding of what is involved in being a spectator.

'Spectatorship' does, nevertheless, provide an image which usefully encapsulates an assumption about human knowledge, which Dewey consistently opposed. We are invited to think of human experience as unfolding before each individual in his or her private cinema,[27] where any involvement in the (ongoing) scripting of the plot or design of the set is wholly irrelevant to that experience. The spectator has only one concern, 'How much of this is true? How much can I count as knowledge and how much is a trick played on me by the producer or by my own tendency to be misled by what I experience?' This is a truncated image of our cognitive relationship to nature. It represents the causal flow on which rests the validity of our thoughts about reality as a one-way traffic flowing inward; all outward causal flow is irrelevant to the truth or validity of a thought.

Dewey in effect would have us return to a way of looking at human knowledge which was common in early Greek thought, i.e. in the thought from which Plato and Aristotle developed their doctrines. The Greeks saw human intellectual efforts as directed not primarily at attaining assurance of some fact, but at reducing the extent to which human beings are left at the mercy of events that just happen, of fortune or *tuche*. What reduced human vulnerability to such events is intelligent foresight and control, which when organized into a teachable body of precise and universally applicable explanations constitutes *techne* or *episteme*. These two words rather than words for cognitive states like awareness (*eidenai*) or acquaintance (*gignoskein*) are the focal points of the epistemologies of Plato and Aristotle. *Episteme* derives from a verb meaning to be able; *techne* applies most frequently to practical and productive activities which are carried out under the guidance of principles which require intelligence and reflective understanding to formulate and grasp.[28]

Dewey does not seem to have fully appreciated the extent to which his own outlook is reflected in early Greek thought. He makes much more of the origins of the spectator conception in Plato and Aristotle than of the presence in Greek thought (including that of Plato and Aristotle) of an orientation similar to his own, which looks at intelligence as functioning to preserve or bring about a better state of affairs. In Section VIII.b we will see Dewey approve the way the Greeks conceived of experience (*empeiria*) and miss the extent to which 'art' (*techne*) is akin to his own conception of intelligence. All of Dewey's doctrines regarding science, value, aesthetic experience and social life are shaped by this conception of intelligence as constituting a variety of 'arts' (classical sense, i.e. *artes, technai*) to equip humans to meet a variety of problems. What is distinctive about his doctrine, we will see in Chapters VII to IX, arises from the way he applies this conception of art in the light of a claim about practical reason (which is also found in, but not as thoroughly applied by, Aristotle).

Regardless of whether it is Plato and Aristotle, or those who interpreted their philosophies after them, who should be held responsible for the spectator concept of knowing, its error (as Dewey sees it) is that it removes the activity of mind from the context of a practical project; it is continuous with the belief in the autonomy of factual discourse.[29] 'Inquiry into the facts' is a constituent of a wider complex process. One has to take 'constituent' seriously here; it implies that coming to know is *not* the same as accomplishing some particular project, getting satisfaction. What is known functions as an instrument and moreover one not fashioned for a once-off purpose, but to be used on future occasions (contribute to the 'continuum of inquiry'), and hence it answers to constraints imposed by the environment which are additional to those imposed by any immediate practical concern.

What takes place when humans acquire factual knowledge cannot, therefore, be considered in isolation from alterations which (necessarily) take place in the potential properties of, and potential interactions between, things involved in the situation. As soon as humans learn that clay alters its properties when heated to a very high temperature, lumps of clay acquire potentialities to perform certain roles which they previously did not have. It might be argued that clay must possess these potentialities regardless of what humans know, but there is a clear sense in which those potentialities move closer to actuality when humans come to know what 'firing' does to clay. To insist that this does not make a *real* difference is to treat human knowledge and action as somehow apart from, or outside of, nature.

Bernard Williams, we have seen, claims we need a conception of the world as it is, independently of any thought or experience. Williams thus not only seeks to leave out of nature altogether essentially active knowers (whose knowing is tied to their capacities to act) and knowing agents (whose capacities to act are tied essentially to their knowledge). He also pushes 'observers', which he conceives in isolation from their capacities to act, out to the margins of nature. It was argued above that the claim that our scientific endeavours are progressively yielding 'a conception of the world as it is, independently of the peculiarities of any observers', can be supported, if taken in the sense that this conception enables us systematically to relate the peculiarities of viewpoints. But Williams goes on to draw a much stronger conclusion. 'That, surely, must be identical with a conception which, if we are not idealists, we need: a conception of the world as it is independently of all observers' (Williams, 1978, p. 241). What idealism is here and why it should be avoided are not spelled out. We are told on the previous page, 'Berkeley was an idealist, something that there is reason not to be', and no more.

Now although Dewey began his career as (a non-Berkelian) idealist, who thought of the world as coextensive with the objects of conscious experience, he came to view conscious experience as just one kind of natural event.[30] There are in Dewey's framework ample resources for describing a world as it was before there was experience of any kind, sentient or conscious. This would be the world on the first of Dewey's 'plateaus'.[31] Dewey makes some claims about the truth or falsity of statements made about the remote past, which look like he is denying the reality of such periods. But this is a consequence of his claims only under an account of meaning, which he repudiates, and which he has replaced by the doctrines based on the approach set out in Chapter IV above. These claims and counterclaims will be examined in the first two sections of the next chapter. At the bottom of the repudiated conception of meaning from which it appears that Dewey denies the reality of the past, we will find the old (Cartesian) correspondence conception of truth.

Berkeley certainly rejected as incoherent a conception of the world as existing *at any time* without being the content of the thought of some mind. Dewey would not, however, regard the dogmatic defence of the conception, which Berkeley rejected, as sufficient to resist idealism. Berkeley is a paradigm case of someone who operates with the spectator conception of conscious experience, and it is this which Dewey believed led to idealism. Any dogmatic defence of material reality, any 'presentative realism', we will see him argue in Section VI.c below, already gives away too much to idealism.

Williams for his part is not pressing merely for a conception of reality as it was *at some point* without any thought or experience in it, but as it *is* independently of any thought or experience. What Dewey counts as experience, i.e. certain interactions between organisms and their environment, does not count as experience for Williams, for his idea of experience is based on '*how it is for* A' (A being a subject of experience), which, like Nagel's conception, is explained in terms of taking up A's point of view imaginatively (Williams, 1978, p. 295).[32] It is true that arguments are adduced in Chapter 10 of Williams (1978) that this conception of experience is highly problematic and extremely difficult to relate to the absolute conception. Dewey would concur with this negative conclusion. But Williams uses it to cast doubt upon the possibility of psychological and social sciences. Without an alternative concept of experience such as Dewey offers, distinctively human phenomena are squeezed out of reality and, more to the (practical) point, the status of human inquiry into human phenomena is left in doubt (ibid., p. 302).

Dewey looked to the application of scientific (especially experimental) methods of inquiry to give us greater control over our social environment and the dispositions and capacities which constitute us as individual selves. The locating of human phenomena on the margins of nature, which one finds in philosophies which treat human experience on the spectator model, works against Dewey's belief that we can apply such methods and hope for anything like the success we have had in natural science. One way in particular in which the spectator model works against the hope for this success is that human wants and desires, and ultimately values, tend to be located, along with the 'subjective aspects of experience' (secondary and tertiary qualities),[33] on the margins of nature, not part of nature, not subject to criticism in the light of what is learned about nature. In the latter part of Chapter VII, we will see how, by treating our habits of desire, along with our habits of perception, as subject to intelligent correction, Dewey mounted an account of value which did not, as do so many contemporary accounts, assign it the role of tyrannical step-child of a faculty of intelligence, a faculty whose only true-born offspring is natural science.

The obstacle which the spectator conception places in the way of Dewey's philosophy does not lie simply in the way it tends to locate human experience on the margins of nature. It lies in treating human experience as something which can be isolated from the proper context(s) which must be grasped to know or understand it, which indeed must be grasped in order to understand anything at all. A conception of nature, the whole of which consisted simply of an aggregate of such isolable phenomena, would be just as effective a block to Dewey's philosophy. This is indeed the sort of view advanced by the 'new realists', who claimed they were treating human minds and human knowledge as part of natural reality, as standing in real albeit external relations to the rest of nature. The qualification 'external' meant precisely that the terms of the relation could be grasped in isolation from one another. In Section VI.d we will see Dewey opposing this monistic way of treating human phenomena as a part of nature as strongly as he opposed the dualism of 'presentative realism'. What is crucial for Dewey's philosophy is the view, which he articulated against 'nominalism', that there is real 'interaction and operative relationship', and the view, which he articulated against 'individualism', that human minds are not constituted as individual things prior to their entering into natural (including especially social) relationships.[34]

VI

Dewey and the Realists

Section VI.a: Meaning and means of verification

In the previous chapter we saw how, when the cognates of 'true' still had an important place in Dewey's vocabulary, he sought to explicate the concept of truth by an account of the general features of the context in which verification takes place. Among the reasons Dewey eventually relegated the cognates of 'true' to a relatively unimportant role in his vocabulary was the difficulty he encountered in persuading people not to think of truth as a property or as a 'value' which statements or judgments possess prior to their becoming known through being verified. It was not that he denied that it made sense to treat statements of judgments as possessing such an antecedent property or value. It was rather that building a philosophic account on this notion readily led to (what Dewey saw as) distortions in the way we regard our thought and our relationship to our natural environment.

Of course it is natural to treat a statement of the fact that when sulphuric acid comes into contact with copper, copper sulphate is formed, as something that would be a truth regardless of whether anyone had verified or knew it.

> If anyone wishes to so use the word truth, I have of course no objection provided the definition is consistently stuck to. But then we have to use a different word than truth to apply both to verification and to the alleged antecedent property of judgment *qua* judgment. . . . in my vocabulary a *known* truth is alone called a truth, it being simpler to call the prior judgment a *claim* to truth or a hypothesis or a meaning. (M13, p. 22)

It is clear from this passage (1922), where Dewey is still trying to reform the habits of thought associated with the cognates of 'true', that he did not actually regard talk of an 'antecedent property as unintelligible'.

Later, as we saw in Section V.a, he appealed to Peirce's limit-of-inquiry notion to give a sense of 'truth' that rendered it independent of particular verifications. But he still rested the weight of his discussion not on something which would be found in the 'continuum of inquiry' if properly conducted and sufficiently prolonged, but on what was involved in conducting and concluding particular inquiries. Failure to do this leads to misdescribing our intellectual goals and achievements. We treat the former as requiring some kind of absolute standpoint and the latter as not answerable to our continuing efforts.

We saw in the previous chapter some of the consequences of Dewey's approach as we contrasted his conception of 'inquiry' with Bernard Williams's notion of 'enquiry'. There are further consequences, which were felt by many people in Dewey's day – most notably Arthur Lovejoy – as well as by many today, to reveal a fundamental incoherency in what he recommends. These consequences bear upon the conduct of intellectual endeavours, such as history, which are continually raising questions which it may never be possible to answer. To understand what is at issue, it will be useful to consider this context where it *seems* Dewey's policy is most difficult to follow and *seems* to lead to unacceptable paradox, viz. the context of the statements which we make about the remote past.

In 'A Short Catechism Concerning Truth', published in 1910 (M6, pp. 3ff.), Dewey portrays a critical pupil calling into question the pragmatic notion of correspondence which is recommended by his teacher, who in this dialogue represents Dewey. This notion of correspondence, we have seen,[1] is a species of the genus 'things which fulfil a function', and the pupil correctly infers that the correspondence of a statement *about* the past in virtue of which it is 'true' (later Dewey will use 'warranted') is to something existing after the statement has been made, something which 'does not exist till after ideas have worked' (M6, p. 6). Common sense, however, treats the correspondence as one between the statement and something existing before the statement is made. But how, comes the teacher's reply, can we *know* whether this correspondence obtains if one term, the past, is gone for ever? Surely the correspondence constituting knowledge consists in this:

> The past event has left effects, consequences, that are present and
> that will continue in the future. Our belief about it, if genuine,
> must also modify action in *some* way and so have objective effects.
> If these two sets of effects interlock harmoniously, then the
> judgment is true. If perchance the past event had no discoverable
> consequences or our thought of it can work out to no assignable
> difference anywhere, then there is no possiblity of genuine judgment.
> (M6, p.7).

This, the pupil continues to object, means there cannot be any truth about the past, for pragmatism makes all objects of judgment future. The teacher replies by distinguishing between 'content' and 'reference of content' (a distinction which Dewey later marked by 'subject matter' and 'object', e.g. M13, p. 44). The content (subject matter) does involve the past, but 'the characteristic aim of judgment is none the less to give this content a future reference and function' (ibid.).

The pupil's response at this point is to accuse the teacher of making an absurd identification of truth and verification. But the teacher insists that the 'organic connection' between what constitutes truth and what constitutes knowledge must not be overlooked. And if it is admitted that statements *are verified* in the way the pragmatist suggests, then we can ask first of all how the further and separate claim about what truth consists in can be verified (what difference to the course of events does *it* make?) and, secondly, what it *means* to say an idea (proposition) has truth in advance of its verification, its being 'made true'? If verification shows a proposition to be true (warranted) because it can be made to work in a certain way, can it have any property antecedent to this other than 'the ability to work – an ability revealed by its actual working' (M6, p. 8)?

The pupil does not press the teacher further on this point, but there are clearly cases where a proposition about the past will lack 'the ability to work'. In order 'to work' a proposition has to connect to present or future effects or consequences of the past events which form the subject matter of the proposition. If these effects do not survive in any accessible form, the proposition will not be verifiable. It seems nevertheless that such propositions can be, indeed should be, thought to have the ' "antecedent" truth property'. In an article written in reply to an attack on his views by Arthur Lovejoy (1920, especially pp. 466–74), Dewey cheerfully grasped the nettle of paradox.

> Take the case of questions about the past which are intrinsically unanswerable, at least by any means now at our command. What did Brutus eat for his morning meal the day he assassinated Cæsar? There are those who call a statement on such a matter a judgment or proposition in a logical sense. It seems to me that at most it is but an esthetic fancy such as may figure in the pages of a historic novelist who wishes to add realistic detail to his romance. . . . Only when the past event which is judged *is a going concern having effects still directly observable are judgement and knowledge possible.* (M13, pp. 42–3)

Lovejoy had acknowledged the difficulty in attaining *knowledge* where there were no surviving consequences of the events in question, but was insisting that,

However singular may appear the fact that a judgement about the past should find its *locus* of verification in the future, the singularity of the fact does not entitle one to argue backward and declare that the judgment could not have meant what it expressly presents itself as meaning – and *what the verification actually presents itself as proving*. (Lovejoy, 1920, p. 471)

Lovejoy pressed hard this distinction between means of verification and what, as he put it (ibid.), 'the original judgment knew itself to mean' ('A judgement is its own master in deciding what it means . . .' – ibid.). Dewey's remarks about Brutus's breakfast, however, were intended to undermine this sharp distinction by reinforcing the insistence, put in the mouth of the teacher, that what truth consists in (what is meant) and means of validation must be intrinsically connected. The lesson he wanted to draw was that the object of a judgment about the past should be seen not as the past event by itself but as 'a past-event-having-a-connection-continuing-into-the-present-and-future' (M13, p. 43).

It needs to be stressed that Dewey was not trying to terminate prematurely any historical inquiry. (He was not, as Peirce would have put it, 'blocking the road to inquiry'.) The claim was about what constitutes a *real* historical inquiry and fanciful examples like the question of Brutus's breakfast merely represent the possibility of a question we cannot possibly answer for want of surviving evidence. Such examples embody no claim that what we have here *is* such an example, nor even that there are such examples. The claim is about how to respond to the challenge of an opponent who raises such a possibility.[2] It would have helped Dewey's case measurably to have argued that our grasp of the meaning of a question like 'What did Brutus have for breakfast the morning he assassinated Cæsar?' consists in our ability to recognize what *would* count as present or future evidence in favour of some answer, even where no such evidence may exist. This tactic seems not to have occurred to Dewey and he rests his case instead on developing a series of illustrative examples.

In the first, a case of pure reminiscence, there is only aesthetic interest: in the second, the past is considered with a view to providing the basis for giving advice about what to do. In both cases the subject matter may be embellished: in the former, for the sake of enjoyment; in the latter, to render it 'more pertinent to the case in hand'. In this second case there emerges a clear distinction between subject matter (past event) and object meant (the present or future situation on which its significance is brought to bear). The second case may, moreover, in the light of the fear that embellishments are destroying the value of the subject matter, lead to a third form of question, one directly (and properly thought of as) *about* the past, viz. 'Just what was it that happened, anyway?' It is clearly possible that such a question remains in a context of concern about the present or future, in which case the distinction, on which Dewey insists, between subject matter and object remains essential to the inquiry.

Dewey acknowledges that it would be unsafe to generalize from the evident possibility of this third sort of question arising within a practically oriented inquiry, to the claim that all such judgments remain tied to such a practically oriented context, but he is eager to embrace this generalization nevertheless. For he claims the subject matter/object distinction is essential to inquiry and he advances the hypothesis that it applies to all cases of judgment about the past, insisting that there is nothing 'forced or paradoxical' in this view. Further illustrations are used to support this. Did I remember to write a letter which I intended to write? The question arises because it affects how things now stand with my correspondent. I find out by seeing if present evidence can interlock harmoniously with the hypothesis that I did write and send the letter. I look for a carbon-copy, or see if, having failed to mail it, I perchance left the letter somewhere in my study, or I write to the person asking if . . . etc.

As this case may be thought to be too much involved with personal affairs, Dewey considers the meaning of puddles on the street. Did it rain last night or is this the effect of the watering cart? I can find out because other effects of each of these possible events will differ. The object of the inquiry is tied up with the bearing the actual event will have on the crops, the price of grain, which pair of shoes to wear, etc.; and precisely which question is asked by the words 'Did it rain last night?' is bound up with which of those is the 'object' of the inquiry.

Lovejoy answered this case by conceding that inquiry into a proposition about the past must proceed on the basis that its object, its *complete* "object" ', is 'a past event having effects, direct or indirect, surviving in the present'. Continuity with the present 'is undeniably a *part* of the meaning of the expression "known past event". But the part is not the whole; . . . the matter at issue has to do solely with that part of the total object of a judgement about the past which *is* past' (Lovejoy, 1922, p. 351) Lovejoy then compared Dewey's concentration on part of the meaning of the expression (viz. continuity with the present) with an astronomer who, recognizing that the red of the spectrum is red-in-connection-with-yellow, decides to study only the yellow, 'disregarding any problems which may have to do solely with red' (ibid.).

Lovejoy's argument here seems a curious defence of the propriety of considering only that about the past which is past. For he first concedes that propositions about the past belong in a wider context; he then treats this wider context as *part* of what he wants to concentrate upon, and then finally compares his opponent to someone who wants to substitute for the thing in question (red in connection with yellow, past in connection with future) some other part of the context (yellow, the present or future). But this in no way reflects Dewey's position, which is simply that it is a mistake to proceed as though the wider context could be ignored.

Lovejoy, moreover, refused to surrender the word 'object' to Dewey. The *complete* "object" ' might be the-past-event-having-a-connection-continuing-into-the-present-and-future, but for 'object' Lovejoy would countenance nothing other than the past event taken on its own. He accused Dewey of equivocating on 'object' and 'objective' (of an inquiry). Dewey had anticipated this allegation, but had not helped matters by applying 'object' not only in contrast to 'subject matter' but also for the 'final object', which 'represents some objective taking settled and definite form' (M13, p. 45, n. 3). This, he explained subsequently, 'includes in an integrated whole both "subject matter" [letter to N.N.] and "object" [bearing on some present or future relationship with N.N.] as they appear in distinction during inquiry' (M15, p. 38).

Although ordinary usage could be called on to support the way Lovejoy insists upon using the word 'object' (as well as the word 'truth'), there are philosophical claims behind Dewey's departures from ordinary usage, which deserve to be considered on their own merits. Would we think more clearly and adequately if we conformed to Dewey's suggested usage? What Dewey is recommending is two-fold:[3]

> (1) We should not pretend that a proposition about the past has any cognitive status in isolation from the connection which past events (subject matter) have to present and future affairs (object). Because truth and falsity are tied to cognitive status, these notions do not apply to propositions about the past considered in isolation from those about the present and future.
>
> (2) We should not pretend that we can divide a problem(atic proposition) about the past into object and subject matter without referring to a context of inquiry, which is determined by the goal (objective) of giving settled and definite form to some objective.

It is worth exploring both of these recommendations at some length. The first will be taken up in the next section and the second at the beginning of the next chapter.

Section VI.b: What truly represents the past

Dewey's position is undeniably a species of verificationism, and verificationism is a doctrine widely thought to have been discredited. In one form the discrediting consists simply in observing that applying verificationism to statements about the past would entail that some are neither true nor false, but we ordinarily regard statements about the past as subject to bivalence.[4] Against someone like Dewey, who is not sworn to 'save all the phenomena' of ordinary beliefs and practices, this argument simply begs the question. Other arguments were directed at the verificationism specific to logical positivism; how well these arguments apply to a philosopher who does not share crucial assumptions with the positivists is far from clear.

One of the crucial differences separating Dewey's verificationism from that of the positivists appeared to him at the time of his debate with Lovejoy to be the crux of the dispute. Dewey saw that Lovejoy assumed that there could be knowledge of 'isolated, self sufficient events or affairs', but 'My theory denies the validity of this conception. It asserts that mere presence in experience is quite a different matter from knowledge or judgement, which always involves a *connection*, and, where time enters in, a connection of present with past and future' (M13, p. 47). Logical positivism (including the logical empiricism advanced by Russell) is based on this notion, which Dewey holds to be without validity. The sense datum statement is precisely what Dewey says cannot constitute a judgment or a piece of knowledge.[5]

The question of whether 'an isolated self-complete thing' can be an 'object of knowledge' raises an issue which touches more that just statements about the past. As Dewey notes, we have here a question about the nature of representation (M13, p. 15). To make a judgment about the past or about the future (or about some remote place at the present time), something which is 'present' (i.e. not absent) must stand for something which is not present. On this much there is common ground with Lovejoy, for he bases his epistemology on a notion of something 'presented-as-absent'. But Dewey applies this notion with much greater generality than Lovejoy and at the same time places a restriction on its application, which serves to define its status as cognitive. Dewey insists, on the one hand, that things (*res*) – not only mental or linguistic things, but things in the natural world – can represent.[6] Present smoke – not just the idea or linguistic act/entity – may represent absent fire. Such a representation is, on the other hand, for Dewey, an intention and like any intention has fulfilment conditions: 'in order to fulfill the meaning of what is given-as-present, the given-as-absent must become present, and this involves an operation which tries to bring the inferred fire into experience in the same immediate way in which the smoke is present' (M13, p. 53).

Lovejoy resisted the idea that a given-as-absent needs any such operation as this. Day-dreams present what is absent, and we can do nothing to realize them; our thoughts may be reminiscences and nothing more. Quite so, replied Dewey, but such events do not have cognitive status; they embody no knowledge.

For, as the remarks about representation indicate, wherever inference or reflection comes in (and I should not call anything knowledge in a logical or intellectual sense unless it does come in), there is, clearly, mediation of an object by some other entity which points to or signifies or represents or gives witness to or evidence of. Nevertheless, thought or inference becomes knowledge in the complete sense of the word only when the indication or signifying is borne out, verifed in something directly present, or immediately *experienced* – not immediately known. (M13, pp. 51–2).

Lovejoy insisted, moreover, that the present-as-absent could only be embodied in a psychical medium. Physical things cannot 'present the absent'; only mental things can do that. Fire may cause smoke, but the smoke does not present or represent the fire. If the smoke leads a sentient, cognitive creature to look for, or expect, fire, the presentation of the smoke does not do this by itself, but only through the mediation of an idea of fire resembling in some way real fire, and occasioned by the smoke (M15, pp. 363–7).

Lovejoy thus dismissed Dewey's claim that the smoke (*res*, not idea) is capable of exercising a function which deserved to be called 'mental' (M13, p. 57) and with it the associated metaphysical thesis that this is all there is to the 'mental realm'. For Dewey was prepared to claim that the mental is simply the natural world in its capacity as representative (of other parts of the natural world). A cloud, a barometer reading, a word, may, according to Dewey, be 'treated *for certain purposes* just as an actual rain storm would be treated' (ibid.). We may in that case term it a mental entity. We have here an application of the idea that for a thing to possess a meaning all it needs is to perform as a (symbolic) substitute.[7] Mind for Dewey, which includes everything to which it is appropriate to apply the word 'mental', is a system of meanings (L1, p. 231), i.e. a system of natural modes of interaction (L1, p. 149), of ways of using and intepreting things, where interpreting 'is always the imputation of potentiality for some consequence' (L1, p. 147).

The dispute between Dewey and Lovejoy thus comes down to how the concepts of knowledge/cognition and representation are to be construed. Dewey rejects, while Lovejoy accepts, the cognitive status of an isolated presence before a conscious mind. The former would not, the latter would, claim to *know*, for example, what is present in his reveries. Representation for Lovejoy consists in a two-term relation between something ('sign') and whatever it represents ('object'). The intention embodied in the use of anything as a sign involves nothing more than the object. For Dewey there must be at least one additional term wherein lies the fulfilment of the intention embodied in the use of the sign. This third term, which Dewey labels 'object' (and speaks of the sign as 'referring to'), belongs among what Peirce labelled the 'interpretants'of a sign or 'representamen'.[8] (Dewey's use of 'object' readily breeds confusion, so Pierce's 'interpretant' will be used here in its place.) It is its reliability when used to make (one or more of) its interpretant(s) present, that constitutes the validity of a sign for Dewey. And if the sign is propositional in form, it is in virtue of this reliability that the sign is accorded 'warranted assertibility' ('truth').

To illustrate the difference between the two approaches to representation consider the thought experiment known as 'Russell's five-minute hypothesis' (Russell, 1921, pp. 159ff.). This hypothesis generalizes a defence of creationism against the evidence of the fossil record, a record which points to geological and biological evolution over vast periods of time. The defence proceeds by arguing that the world was created by God with a false fossil record to tempt the intellectually arrogant to deny the truth of the biblical account. Russell suggested that God could equally have created the world exactly as it is now, five minutes ago, complete with (false) fossil records, (false) historical records and (false) memories in all its inhabitants. According to Russell, Lovejoy and more recent philosophers such as Malcolm (1963, pp. 187–202), all our purported memories of anything which happened (say) yesterday are, under this hypothesis, equally false.

According to Dewey there is an important sense in which the memories God has given us (under the hypothesis) can be divided into those which are true (valid or warrantedly assertible) and those which are not. My memory of having mailed a letter yesterday is true in this sense, if in three days' time I receive the reply I requested, and false if I go home this evening and discover my letter on my desk. The representative character of a memory is not, according to Dewey and Peirce, exhausted by its link to a past event; it is an essential and ineliminable part of its representative character that it *have* interpretants and that some of them have a future reference.

But *truth*, their opponents would allege, is tied strictly and solely to that other essential part of representation, the reference to the (in the case of memory, past) event, which Dewey labels 'subject matter' (and which Peirce labels 'object'). That is all that need enter into God's perspective on the representation of the event, which is in our supposed past; and it is God's perspective on the matter which constitutes truth, *ex hypothesi*, under the five-minute hypothesis. 'God' here represents the view from the absolute standpoint. For a pragmatist no proper sense can be given to this standpoint, which divorces it from the possible experience of finite beings such as ourselves. What constitutes 'truth' in this abstract sense for a pragmatist is what is to be found among our beliefs 'at the limit of inquiry'.

There are thus two possible relationships between God's perspective

138

on the five minutes of real history and our own perspective, only one of which will be accepted by a pragmatist. That one is the possibility we will someday come (via the interpretation of signs present in our experience) to realize that the world began some time in what we have hitherto taken to be a time nearly 2,000 years after the birth of Christ. In this case this fact known so far only to God is something which lies somewhere on the indefinitely extended 'continuum of inquiry'. It points, in ways we do not yet know how to interpret, to future experiences which will compel us to acknowledge its validity.

If we allow that interpretants are not parts of the meanings of signs, then we can entertain the possibility that on this particular matter it is not possible for human beings to attain God's perspective. It is just *true* that the world was created five minutes ago, but created in such a way that there is no way of discovering this. But if this possibility is all that is sustained by arguing that the interpretant is eliminable from the concept of representation, then a pragmatist would dismiss this as worthless, for the possibility is completely idle. But is there anything which is preserved by confining representation to a two-term relation other than this particular way in which reality is supposed to transcend all possible experience?

Russell's five-minute hypothesis is but one of a family of sceptical problems which arise from trying to measure human knowledge against what might be called a 'Cartesian absolute'. The doubt about the nature of the past can be turned into a doubt about whether there is a past at all. (If our epistemic hold on the past prior to any distance from the present, however small – five years, five minutes, five nanoseconds – is uncertain, the present is all we can claim to know.) And the belief that the future constantly reveals its reality may then be only an illusion fostered by the false memory of having anticipated the present moment. Descartes founded this form of scepticism by calling into doubt the world external to his experience. The natural upshot of Cartesian scepticism is what Santayana (1923, p. 15) called 'solipsism of the present moment'; the past is, after all, simply the temporal dimension of the 'external world'. And the *sine qua non* of Cartesian scepticism is a Cartesian absolute; one cannot decry the lack of knowledge unless one can give some indication of what it is one lacks.

What one lacks is assurance that one's judgment or experience represents its object as it really is. This is an assurance which one can fail to have even though every interpretant of that judgment or experience, which indicates the character of future experience, is borne out in that experience.[9] What would it be to have this assurance? It would, presumably, be to know that the object is (was) as the 'original judgment knew itself to mean'. But what the original judgment (experience) knew itself to mean cannot be accounted for by its interpretants. Its interpretants, Lovejoy, Russell *et al.* have insisted, are irrelevant to its meaning in the required sense. So one must know (have grasped) the meaning of one's judgment (experience) in isolation from everything apart from the object it purports to represent. And to have the assurance which is lacking one would have to know the object in the same isolated fashion, isolated except possibly for connection back to the judgment (or experience) which knew itself to mean this very object.

The attempt to measure the human epistemic achievement against a Cartesian absolute thus depends on stressing the *object* of representation at the expense of its interpretant. And it also depends on treating knowledge of that object on the model of the knowledge which there is supposed to be of our (inner) experience. This experience is supposed to consist of a domain of objects which are knowable in isolation from one another. But according to Dewey, although we may *have* such experience we do not thereby *know* it, and it is a mistake to treat its qualities as objects.[10] If we treat the having of such qualities as the paradigm of knowing, then the objects to which such qualities point when they function as signs are all too often obviously not accessible to being experienced in that way and become unknowable. The past is dead and cannot be resurrected; any attempt to 'know it' (in the sense of have experience of it) will deal only with a surrogate after the event.

We saw in Sections I.c and I.d how Dewey dealt with Russell's treatment of the classic Cartesian paradigm of this sort of problem, that of the status of our knowledge of the external world. Russell characterized the problem as whether we can infer anything other than our own 'hard data' from the existence of those data. The assumption built into this problem is that we have knowledge of 'hard data', of self-contained contents of experience. For Dewey there is knowledge (cognition) only where experience prompts 'anticipation and prevision', only where experience is interpreted, only where inference takes place. 'Inference brings, in short, truth and falsity into the world, just as definitely as . . . the existence of banking brings with it consequences of business extension and of bankruptcy not previously existent' (M8, pp. 70–1). The question whether we are justified in making any inference is the non-question of whether we are justified in having experience. The only general question relating inference and justification is, 'Which particular inferences are we (as things stand) justified in making?'

It should be clear how Dewey's denial that there can be knowledge of 'isolated self-sufficent events or affairs' is involved in undermining the whole Cartesian problematic. If Dewey's claim about what gives an experience the staus of cognition (viz. the links it has to other experiences) is sustained, there is nothing which can be called knowledge (cognition) which is the sort of thing sought for by Descartes and his intellectual descendants. There is nothing, moreover, which can be called knowledge which will serve as the paradigm of what is sought; there is no knowledge of bare, isolated givens in experience.

Section VI.c: Perception and the old realism

We have seen that central to Dewey's disputes with Russell and with Lovejoy was the claim that an 'isolated self-complete thing' cannot be an object of knowledge. One implication of this claim is that sense data are not, as such, objects of knowledge; another is that perception does not, as such, have cognitive status (M6, p. 105). An experience is not in the first instance a cognitive event, it is simply a natural event, an organism interacting with its environment. Cognitive status accrues to an experience through its performing a certain function, viz. that of being taken or used as a sign of further natural events.[11]

The force of the phrase 'as such', which occurred twice in the previous paragraph, should be carefully noted. Sense data as signs (rather than 'as such') have cognitive status. Perceptions 'are the sole ultimate data, the sole media, of inference to all natural objects and processes. While we do not in any intelligible or verifiable sense, know *them*, we know all things that we do know *with* or *by* them' (M6, p. 109). In ordinary life we use many perceptions so frequently that 'What they stand for is telescoped, as it were, into what they are. . . . Thus, *for practical purposes*, many perceptual events are cases of knowledge; that is, they have been *used* as such so often that the habit of so using them is established or automatic' (M6, p. 110).[12] And, of course, natural science begins and ends with perceptions, not because they are what is ultimately known, but because of their nature as evidence, as signs of natural things, events and relations (M6. pp. 109–10).

What Dewey is proposing arises from the account of the relationship of sentience and cognition set out in Chapter III, but it undeniably involves terminological legislation. It is common in philosophy to treat perception as having at its core a paradigm case of knowing something – the quality of the experience is known, if nothing else. But Dewey is claiming that a serious error is embodied in this common philosophic practice. The paradigm case of knowledge is not to be found at the heart of perception, when it has been stripped of its leaves of inference. The paradigm is to be found in the leaves (M6, p. 109); at the heart is just something that happens to an organism.

What Dewey is attempting to set on its head is so familiar that his attempts might be thought to amount to a break with common sense, but a break with common sense, it may be argued, is already involved in the claim that perception is ('as such') a case of knowledge. 'The plain man', Dewey contends, 'does not regard noises heard, lights seen, . . . as things *known* (M6, p. 108). They are merely things, which the plain man may welcome or reject, act on or just appreciate. He may also inquire into their significance. In that case he may come to stand to them in the relation of knower to known, but not until he has so inquired. Dewey does not, however, propose to overturn well-established doctrines by appeal to the court of common sense. The main reason which he advances for denying cognitive status to perceptions ('as such') is that giving them cognitive status is the first step on the road to idealism, or, as he puts it, 'lets the nose of the idealist camel into the tent', and before long the camel 'devours the tent' (M6, p. 106).

If one looks at a star in the night sky, what appears in the visual field may be described as a speck of brightness. If this speck of brightness is regarded as known merely through its presence in the perceptual experience of the the perceiver, then because the external cause of this perception, the star, cannot stand in precisely this relation, the cognitive status of the star becomes problematic. It is not known in the same way or the same sense, and we are forced either to accept that what we thought was the real object of knowledge, the star, is not known - hence scepticism – or that the real object of knowledge is not the star, but an idea (the star being part of the content of the idea) – hence idealism. If, however, we stop modelling the relation of cognition on immediate perception and deny that the immediate experience is as such cognitive, then whatever justification we have for the thought, 'This speck of brightness comes from a massive thermonuclear reaction many light years away', is what constitutes that thought as knowledge, and moreover knowledge of *causes of perceptual experience had on cloudless nights*. The spirit of Dewey's terminological legislation, in other words, is realistic; it blocks the depredations of Berkelians.

Dewey himself was clearly not an idealist. He insisted on the right of his own version of pragmatism to be regarded as a 'realism' (M3, pp. 153–7); he was happy to acknowledge that things exist prior to and independently of being known (M6, p. 13); and he acknowledged that 'objects vary in relation to one another independently of their relation to the "knower" ' (M6, p. 127).[13] But he found himself opposed to most of what presents itself as 'realism'. In this section we will see Dewey opposing '[re]presentative realism' and in the next a native American version of the logical realism found in Frege. In the following chapter Dewey's divergence from the realism represented by Peirce will be explored further. It is, however, unhelpful to label Dewey simply as an 'anti-realist'. It invites the assumption that somehow Dewey was opposed to reality rather than being opposed to a variety of (mis)conceptions about our relation to reality, which happen to label themselves 'realism'.

Dewey entertained no illusions, even when he first advanced his doctrine, that would-be realists would be prepared to accept it. He recognized that what is commonly thought of as realism, is based *as much* on the assumption that 'sensations–perceptions are cases of knowledge' (M6, p. 121) as is idealism. Realists, for example, *have* a perfectly adequate defence against familiar idealist arguments based on perceptual illusions. Mirages, half-submerged sticks apparently bent, even the double image which results from dislocating one eyeball with a finger are not delusive experiences. All have physical explanations, all are photographically reproducible (M6, p. 103). Dewey uses this reply when responding on his own behalf to these well-worn opening moves (M10, pp. 29ff.):[14] but, he argues, the realist undermines the use of this reply by clinging to the assumption that the bare appearance is itself ('as such') a known object (M6, pp. 104ff.). What the realist should avoid saying is that the appearance is known, and insist instead that only what is learned after inquiry is known, e.g. that desert conditions produce misleading effects, that the line between air and water does something peculiar to the way the stick looks.

A further consequence of avoiding (subjective) idealism by repudiating the assumption that perception is ('as such') a case of knowledge is that all other presentations have just as good a claim to be treated as cases of knowledge.

> In its epistemological use, the term 'knowledge' has a blanket value which is absolutely unknown in common life. It covers any and every 'presentation' of any and every thing to a knower, to an 'awarer,' if I may coin a word for the sake of avoiding some of the pitfalls of the term 'consciousness.' And, I repeat, this indiscriminate use of the term 'knowledge,' so foreign to science and daily life, is absolutely unavoidable if perception be regarded as, in itself, a mode of knowledge. (M6, p. 112)

Dewey called the sort of realist who lets the camel have the tent a 'presentative realist', and the sort who adopts his own discriminating use of the term 'knowledge' a 'naïve realist'. The indiscriminate use of 'knowledge' is based on a belief which he labels 'the ubiquity of the knowledge relation' (M6, pp. 111ff.). His complaint here is one we encountered above in Section II.d under the label 'intellectualism' (cp. M6, p. 86, and L1, pp. 28ff.). It is this which creates the pseudo-problems of 'the alleged discipline of epistemology' (M6, p. 111).

When characterizing his position as a form of 'empiricism' Dewey used the qualifier 'immediate' to mark the claim that 'things are what they are [immediately] experienced as', where this does not entail 'what they are *known* to be' (M3, pp. 158ff.). If a situation is experienced as depressing, it is depressing. If after inquiry new features emerge which transform the situation, put a new complexion on it, it may be experienced as, *and* known to be, a hopeful situation, this does not however mean that previously it was not *really*, *objectively*, depressing, merely experienced as such.[15] The 'intellectualist' assumption that things are only what they are *known* to be was, Dewey contended, 'the root paralogism of all idealisms, whether subjective or objective, psychological or epistomological' (M3. p. 159).

The (immediate) empiricism, the foxy brand of naïve realism, which Dewey advocated, treats some experiences, notably perception, as non-cognitive: at least *au fond* perception is a stimulus followed by a response. A *cognitive* version of this kind of event would be, as we saw in Chapter III, one that involved extra layers of control over the response, transforming it, perhaps checking the response or integrating it with other susceptibilities and responses. Rather than focusing just on the presentation of the stimulus, this requires considering what happens to a natural course of events when cognition transforms it. Presentative realists, in other words, are like dieticians who confine their attention to the presentation of food, and pay no attention to its ingestion and digestion.

There are two interrelated assumptions made by presentative realists which Dewey challenges. One is what he sees as an inadequate model of a cognitive event, viz. one such that all that is involved in cognition is a mental 'content' of some kind present to a conscious mind. This is assumed to take place wherever a being is conscious, or 'knows', and this leads in turn to the second assumption, 'ubiquity', which is that all the relations into which a mind enters are uniform instances of this same relation. Realists are exposed to idealist taunts, Dewey argues, not simply because they use a model of cognition, which plays into the hands of the idealists, but also because they follow idealists in assuming the model is to be applied everywhere (ubiquitously) (cf. L1, p. 30).

If the relation of eater to eaten were everywhere the same and were the *only* relationship an organism could bear to its environment, one could propound, just like a realist, the 'foodist' doctrine that the eating relation can be ignored, for in the way that 'All propositions which have any intelligible meaning are [said by realists to be] about objects just as they are, and in the relations they bear to one another [, so foods] pass in and out of the relation to eater with no change in their own traits' (M6, p. 116). To which 'eaterists', like idealists, could reply that, as no object exists except in relation to eating, everything is constituted a thing by its relation to eating. Nothing can be said about an object without taking into account its relation to eaters. But, the foodists would reply, a thing can only be eaten if it is in and of itself food. To which the eaterists would riposte, nothing can be said about something in and of itself apart from the ubiquitous relationship in which all things must *ex hypothesi* stand. And so the debate would drag on.

Standing to one side, Dewey contended there was 'no intelligible point at issue' (M6, p. 113) either in this burlesque[16] or in the debate taken seriously by philosophers. If all experience is a cognitive relation, how can it form the subject matter of an intellectual discipline? With what can the relation be informatively contrasted? There is something to say about the eating/being-eaten relationship only because organisms and food stand in other relations (M6, pp. 116, 120). Likewise there is something to be said about the knowledge relation only because knowers stand in a multitude of *other* relations to things known. 'This means, of course, that things, the things that later come to be known, are primarily not objects of awareness, but causes of weal and woe, things to get and things to avoid, means and obstacles, tools and results' (M6, p.120). The gettings and avoidings involve perceptual responses. The means, obstacles, tools and results are monitored perceptually, the weal and woe registered perceptually, before they are dealt with cognitively. A perception is not a presentation to a self, but an event, the unfolding of a habitual response, containing a self (M6, pp. 119–20).[17] This is the sophisticated naïvety which is needed to avoid the toils of idealism.

Nevertheless, as Dewey anticipated, self-proclaimed realists steadfastly refused to drop the assumption that perception is ('as such') a paradigm case of knowing. Dewey's claim to be a realist, moreover, looked suspicious in the light, on the one hand, of the claim, examined in Section V.e above, that cognition was in some way involved in the transformation of its object, and in the light, on the other hand, of his appeal to a paradigm of knowledge based on the relations by which things become the signs of other things. Had not the hero of Dewey's youth, T. H. Green, insisted that 'Nature is the system of related appearances'?[18] Is this not the high road to idealism of the objective sort?

Not at all, for to reach the high road, one needs at least one further assumption made by Green, which, as we saw in Section II.a, Dewey surrendered, and that is that relations are not given in appearances. For if experience is not confined to appearances and perception not treated as something presented to a knowing mind, if experience is something an organism undergoes and perception but one aspect of the unfolding of a (developing) habitual response; then relatedness between appearances is as embodied in the organic events which constitute experience as is sensitivity. The objective idealists argued that relations must be imposed by us through the synthetic activity of our finite minds and this to them was cognition, the truth or falsity of which is measured by the most rational of all the possible relational systems as this is embodied in infinite, absolute mind.

The pragmatist starts with the acknowledgment that a knower is first of all an organism which has already experienced in a multitude of ways the connections of the episodes of experience with one another. This has to be the case for it to have coped successfully with its environment. When cognition supervenes there are already a myriad of unproblematic connections embodied in organic responses, and the function of cognition is simply to facilitate the resolution of such problems as the environment inevitably presents. Doing so gives rise to the development of more elaborate, adaptable and reliable connections. Truth and falsehood are not measured against a structure embodied in absolute mind but in terms of more of the same successes and failures in dealing with the causes of weal and woe.

Section VI.d: The new realism

It was pointed out by one of Dewey's most persistent critics, Evander Bradley McGilvary, that if Dewey's arguments had been intended to undermine all self-proclaimed realisms in order to leave pragmatism as the one viable alternative to idealism, he had failed. For at least one important sect of realists did not make the assumption on which Dewey's attack turned. True, there had been, and still were, realists for whom the thing known in perception stood in relation to a mind, or knower or consciousness. McGilvary (1912, p. 455) cited Russell and Moore as those who still held this thesis. But there were also realists who held that 'consciousness is a relation *between* things and not . . . a relation of things to mind.' Among these realists were three of Dewey's colleagues at Columbia, two of whom had joined with four academics from other universities in publishing 'The Program and First Platform of Six Realists'.[19]

Dewey replied to McGilvary that he had not intended his criticism of realism to apply to those who did not share the presentational doctrine, which he had challenged, but that the doctrine was nevertheless based on an identification of mind with the self and on a conception of knowledge as a relation between object and self, both of which were 'the most characteristic and permeating traits of modern philosophy' (M7, p. 82). Dewey was content to hint that realists who tried to dispense with this assumption still had a lot of work to do to produce a viable account of the self or subject and its place in knowledge. Had he more space, he might have rehearsed arguments to show that the six leopards had not fully shed their presentative spots. The spots were not prominent in the 'Program and First Platform' – indeed 'Cartesian dualism and the representative theory' were explicitly repudiated (M6, p. 477). Nevertheless the spots reappeared when Dewey engaged a spokesman for the Six, Edward Gleason Spaulding, in an extended dispute in the *Journal of Philosophy*, which terminated in an interesting joint document in which the new realist and the instrumentalist set down their points of agreement and disagreement.

A crucial plank in the platform on which the Six proposed to stand was a doctrine of 'external relations'. Absolute idealists, notably F. H. Bradley (1897, pp. 574–82), had built ambitious claims on the principle that all relations are 'internal'. A relation is internal if it affects or contributes to the nature of the things related. If 'husband' were taken to constitute the nature of an individual man, then 'married to' would be an internal relation, for it is only by virtue of standing in this relation that a man can be said to be a husband. If all relations are internal, one must know all the relations in which a thing stands, and all the things to which it is related, in order to know that thing.

The realists thus rested much of their case on relations, aRb, such that 'aR in no degree constitutes b nor does Rb constitute a, nor does R constitute either a or b' (M6, p. 474). Above all, this logical property of 'externality' was taken to be characteristic of the relationship obtaining between a knower and the thing known. For anything to be known it does have to stand in a relation to a mind or consciousness, but the knowing is eliminable in the sense that 'the entity is known as it would be if the knowing were not taking place' (M6, p. 480). Known things are not products of the knowing relation (M6, p. 478); they can come to be known or cease to be known without undergoing any modification (M6, p. 481). No self-consistent or satisfactory logic, the Six Realists claimed, countenanced the organic (or 'internal') view of relations, so that idealists had to appeal to a logic inconsistent with their idealist doctrines.

Dewey held no brief for the doctrine that *all* relations are internal (M6, p. 138, n. 2), but he had some sympathy for the idea that particulars could not be known other than through the relations in which they stood; 'particulars can be identified *as* particulars only in a relational complex' (M8, p. 90). Throughout his career he favoured the view that natural objects (notably living things, but also chemical reactions – M6, p. 140) and natural events (in particular those constituting experience) can only be understood through grasping the organic interrelatedness of their constituents. When he says, 'a living organism and its life processes involve a world or nature temporally and spatially "external" to itself but "internal" to its functions' (L1, p. 212) he means 'external' and 'internal' in this logical sense.

Organic interrelatedness is indeed a prime example of what the new realists opposed. A kidney is what it is only through having a function in an organism. Maintaining a thorough-going 'externalist' approach to relations requires some kind of reductionist approach to chemical and biological systems, one which explains the behaviour of the whole system in terms of constituents which are in no way dependent for their nature on the relations into which they enter – which are not, in other words, like kidneys. Clearly the doctrine of external relations would appear to Dewey as nothing short of institutionalizing what in Section I.e we saw described as the error of 'neglect of context', and enshrining the denial of 'operative relationship', which in Section IV.b we saw to be his chief complaint against nominalism.

Dewey, on the other hand, as we saw in Chapter III, was committed to an emergentist position. Reducing even a chemical system to externally related constituents inevitably leaves something out. There are real features of such complex systems which cannot be accounted for in terms that would be adequate if the same constituents were organized in a less complex way. And he went beyond this familiar position in stressing that to understand a living system, particularly the events that constitute its experience, one has to grasp organic relations which extend beyond what are ordinarily thought of as the boundaries of the organism. Respiration, digestion, perception and social interaction all introduce into the world relations which, when they obtain, affect the natures of the things involved. And Dewey, as we saw in Section V.e, did not shrink from applying the same doctrine to the relation of knower to thing known. In the following three chapters we will see the importance of internal relations in Dewey's account of practical reasoning and the general nature of our ends.

It is clear that Dewey had a stake in internal relations and clear why it was on that point in particular that he should want to challenge 'The Program and First Platform' of the Six. His challenge took the form of alleging a fundamental ambiguity in the doctrine of external relations. Does it make a claim about the terms of a proposition or about the '*existences*' denoted by the terms? If the latter, then Dewey thought it 'demonstrably false' in the light of chemical and biological phenomena.[20] If the former – if it applies to terms – then Dewey wanted to know 'what is the warrant for transferring it [the doctrine] over to the quite different matter of the relation of the proposition (in its content and intent) to *existences*' (M6, p. 140)? In any case the doctrine in its application to terms seemed 'obviously false'. Achieving knowledge often involves altering the meanings of terms; the process is one 'where meanings are continuously modified by the new relations into which they enter' (M6, p. 139).

In response to the claim that the meanings of terms change as knowledge grows, Spaulding on behalf of the Six distinguished between judgments and propositions. The constituents of a judgment ('call these concepts' (Spaulding, 1911a, p. 487)) may be inadequate and need to be altered in the course of inquiry. This procedure, Spaulding insisted (ibid.), was always to reject the judgment as false *in toto*, or to analyse it into two more propositions whose 'contents' were not modified by being related and supplemented. In response to the claim which Dewey made about biological and chemical phenomena, Spaulding appealed to the way mathematical analysis treats time and physical magnitudes generally, viz. as continua of points, each externally related to one

148

another. (Dewey had, after all, admitted that spatial relations were 'external'.) This Spaulding insisted was 'always the ideal for the chemist and biologist' (Spaulding, 1911a, p. 489).

Spaulding's appeal to mathematical analysis only seemed to Dewey to beg the question. One does not have to deny the validity of mathematics, or the value of its applications to natural phenomena, to question whether mathematical concepts can represent all the relations, or all the logical aspects of the relations, which hold between natural phenomena. Dewey said:

> To repeat: External relations *may* hold of the terms of a proposition, without being a description of the relation of the proposition as an *existence* to other *existences*. I did not claim that it does not hold in this existential case; I claimed that to conclude that it holds . . . on *the basis of an analysis of the relation of the terms of a proposition to each other as terms*, is to beg the precise question at issue; it is to assume that one can decide from the *im*-plication of a proposition a question of fact having to do with its *ap*-plication. (M6, p. 144).

Spaulding in reply to Dewey's rejoinder denied that he and his colleagues were inferring something about existences from the logical properties of the terms of propositions. Spaulding maintained that the doctrine in its application to existences rested on empirical investigation. Because the new realist framework applied several categories ('term' was used as a variable ranging over 'terms of propositions, or propositions as wholes, or points or instants, etc.' (M6, p. 502)), the sort of empirical investigation had to vary accordingly. Thus to give an empirical foundation to the doctrine of external relations, one had to recognize not only sense observation and experiment but also 'ideal observation'.

By ideal observation, according to Spaulding, one recognized that the doctrine of external relations applied 'to that cognitive situation in which there is achieved knowledge of theories, of propositions, of numbers, etc. (Spaulding, 1911b, p. 504) and that it also applied to relations between intensity-points, space-points, instants, etc. (M2, p. 505). By observation and experiment (Spaulding does not specify whether it is 'sense' or 'ideal' in these cases), one finds that the theory applies 'to that cognitive situation in which there is genuine knowledge of mental existences' and that it applies to the relations between the terms of a proposition, to the relation between the proposition and that to which it refers, and to the relations of propositions to one another (ibid.). By sense observation we discover that the doctrine applies 'to that cognitive situation in which there is genuine knowledge of physical existents' (Spaulding, 1911b, p. 504).

But in this last case there seems to be – and Spaulding himself admits this – a crucial dependence on the discovery by ideal observation that the doctrine applies to theories, propositions, numbers, etc. There is, without the mediation of theories and propositions, no completely convincing answer to the idealist and phenomenalist claim *'that the so-called physical object known is in some degree constituted by or modified by the knowing'* (ibid.). And Spaulding ends his second response to Dewey on a much less confident note than had characterized the manifesto and his first *apologia*. He concludes by calling for efforts to be made to design a crucial experiment to decide this issue between the realists and the intellectual descendants of Kant (Spaulding 1911b, pp. 508–10).

Dewey did not continue the dispute in print apart from publishing jointly with Spaulding a statement of points of agreement and disagreement, which the two thrashed out in private discussion. Where they agreed to disagree was over the status of 'subsistent entities', in particular propositions. Spaulding gave them a status and validity independent of human cognitive activities, whether it be doubt, inquiry or awareness. Dewey insisted their status and validity depended on their connections to prior and subsequent inquiries. To him it was meaningless to speak of logical entities (propositions) being prior to existents, just as it made no sense to ask whether numbers were logically prior to or posterior to counting (M6, p. 150).

> As a matter of discovery, I think I find that the existence of logical entities and of a process of inferential inquiry are one and the same thing. The process of inferential inquiry has its own characteristic or distinguishing marks, just like any other natural occurrence. Its peculiar marks are precisely those traits and relations that are called logical. This does not mean that they are constituted in the process of *their* being known. On the contrary, inferences, or existences having logical traits, must exist before they can be inquired into. When inquired into, the resulting proposition bears the same kind of relation to the existence it is about – or refers to – as any proposition sustains to the existence it is about. (M6, p. 152)

The disagreement, Dewey concluded, was one of fact. Spaulding and he did not reach the same conclusions in their philosophical inquiries into the nature of logical properties and relations. When Dewey inquired into, for example, 'The Logical Character of Ideas' (M4, pp. 91ff.) he came to the conclusion that an idea (a term which included propositions) only arose in 'situations which are doubtful' and 'judgment in suspense'. When words having a propositional form were used 'merely to enunciate to others facts already in existence' (PM, p. 278), Dewey was reluctant to accord them the status of propositions. These enunciations were the product of previous successful inquiries and were potentially useful instruments to be used in guiding or influencing the behaviour of other people, but propositions had the primary function of projecting resolutions to problems.

> . . . 'study and inquiry' show that the subsistent *is* the existent to which it refers, modified; that this particular sort of modification is just what is denoted by [']proposition[']. . . . The subsistent does not, then, modify the existent, for being logical in status . . . it has no existential efficiency . . . indirectly a proposition is a medium of a practical, non-cognitive alteration of the thing referred to. . . . (M6, pp. 148–9)

Logic, for Dewey, was the study of this activity of dealing with doubtful situations by means of methodically conducted inferential inquiry. Abstractions, which we make from this activity in order to reform it and conduct it more reflectively, lead us to identify propositions and principles of inference, but these are not, as the new realists claimed, prior to 'all scientific and metaphysical systems' (M6, p. 474). Rather, they are tied to human cognitive activities in much the way intuitionists claim that mathematical entities and principles are tied to human cognition – not something we discover, but features of our own activities which nevertheless objectively constrain us.

Dewey's discussions of logical issues typically lack precision, but his position does follow roughly the lines taken in intuitionist philosophy of mathematics.[21] In a debate which took place in 1929–30 between Dewey and Ernest Nagel, Dewey argued that one could not rest an argument for existence on the law of the excluded middle (or on any other purely formal principle) (L5, p. 197), and he objected to a (what he took to be illicit) move very similar to that which he had identified in 'The First Program and Platform' of the Six two decades earlier: 'to assume that the actual event has the same properties as has the subject-matter by means of which we reason about it, is to make precisely the same conversion of the logical into the existential, the formal into the material, which is at issue' (L5, p. 200).

Section VI.e: The new idealism?

McGilvary, who sympathized with the Six Realists, contended, we have seen, that Dewey's objection to presentative realism did not touch the new realism. If one denies that knowledge consists in a presentation of something to a mind or consciousness and insists that it consists in an external relation (on a par with any other relation in nature), have not Dewey's criticisms been avoided? Dewey's attack on presentative realism did not, however, depend on the presentation being *internally* related to the mind receiving it, but on the inability of any simple relationship to constitute knowledge.[22] Any isolated relationship between knower and known (or knower, proposition and known) which is abstracted from the temporal and causal connections, in which both are inevitably caught up, is inadequate. The Six may have repudiated the Cartesian mind, but in practically the same breath they insisted that 'physical nature . . . is, under certain circumstances, directly present in consciousness' (Spaulding *et al.*, 1911, p.477). But does even this logically refined ('externalist') whiff of presentationism amount to the ominous nose of the idealist camel?

It is important to note how, in order to maintain the central thesis of the new realist logic, viz. the doctrine of external relations, Spaulding's argument comes to rely on an ideal mental faculty and an ontology of ideal objects, in particular propositions. Propositions embody the requisite logical principle, viz. the externality of relations. If actual judgments and actual experiences do not manifest the principle, there must be these (ideal) things related in some way to our actual thought processes which do display the required logical properties. Spaulding is not able to argue that sense observation and experience support an externalist view of the relations embodied in chemical and biological phenomena. He has to insist that the application of externalist approved mathematical techniques are 'always an ideal for the chemist and biologist'. He has to affirm his faith throughout that analysis will in the end reveal the correctness of the doctrine of external relations.

In a brief (page and a half) discussion note which Dewey published in 1909 (M4, pp. 76–7), he advanced the thesis that an 'intellectualist' view of truth led either to 'anarchistic' subjective idealism or to absolute idealism. 'Intellectualism' at this stage was used by Dewey to denote the doctrine that truth is a property either of ideas or of things *antecedent* to any process of verification. Anarchistic subjective idealism follows from taking the former course but leaving out Berkeley's God. For if truth is a property of ideas, but ideas are not taken as Berkeley took them, as signs of God's intentions with regard to the future occurrence of ideas, then:

> If these properties of truth and falsity are ultimate, self-contained, and unique properties; if an idea is as likely to have one kind of property as the other; and if there is nothing in an idea which reveals upon bare inspection which of the two kinds of property is possessed, surely the intellectualist is committed to a belief in the thoroughly atomistic nature of truths. (M4, p. 76)

Truths, moreover, would have to be regarded as coming into existence when certain ideas are first entertained. (The position that ideas have existence antecedent to being thought is subsumed under the other alternative.)

On the other hand, if truth were a property of things, events or objects, then physical reality as much as thought must have logical properties; 'the universe must be conceived as a truth-system, i.e. a system of relations of reason, or as "objective thought" ' (M4, p. 77). Dewey then quoted a passage from Bossuet, which he had found in Janet's *Final Causes*:

'If I now ask where and in what subject these truths subsist, eternal and immutable as they are, I am obliged to own a being wherein truth eternally subsists and is always understood; and this being must be the truth itself, and must be all truth; and from it is derived the truth in all that is'. (Ibid.)

This had been the principal argument for the existence of God used by absolute idealists.[23] The natural world had to have the character of thought, for the opposite of thought, matter, is characterized by the externality of the relations in which each of its instances otherwise stand. The cognitive characteristics of full intelligibility, to which we aspire, are well beyond our present grasp and represent only the ideal limit of our cognitive aspirations. But thought cannot exist without mind. An actually intelligible universe is unthinkable without an actual Absolute Mind to think it.

Remove now the condition that there is an Absolute Mind (God) and with it the demand for intelligibility (in the sense of a recognizable unity to the system of nature) as the goal of human cognition, and one has the sort of logical realism of the Six: propositions which subsist without there necessarily being a mind to think them, and which represent as the ideal of human cognitive activity the 'thoroughly atomistic nature of truth'. If phenomenalism is Berkeley without God and is still idealism ('subjective idealism'), why, if neo-realism is absolute idealism without God, is it not also an idealism?

The new realists have so far been allocated a relatively obscure corner in the history of twentieth-century philosophy. Their brand of logical realism, however, did not die in the cradle but flourished on a diet of Frege and remains alive today, a curious half-breed which maintains a discreet silence about the idealist blood that flows through its veins.

VII

Objectivity, Value and Motivation

Section VII.a: The aims and means of inquiry

Dewey's rejection of what in Section V.b was called 'the autonomy of factual discourse' was the negative side of the claim that inquiry into matters of fact always takes place in the context of a practical enterprise, an attempt to bring about some change or preserve some state of affairs. One would expect from this that claims about the nature of practical reasoning should have an important bearing on what Dewey regards as the nature of factual inquiry. We will see in the first two sections of this chapter how a disagreement over a central principle of practical reasoning lies at the root of an important divergence between the doctines of Peirce and Dewey. In the remaining sections of this chapter we will consider how Dewey's view of this principle gives rise to his distinctive doctrines regarding the nature of value and the correct understanding of the philosophical psychology that lies behind objective inquiry into values.

The doctrine, which (as we saw in Section V.e) Dewey favoured, that knowing makes a difference to the thing known was greeted with distaste not only by various realists, but also, as it turns out, by at least one important pragmatist. In a manuscript of about 1906 Peirce wrote (in response to ripples created as much by James and Schiller as by Dewey), 'It appears that there are certain mummified pedants who have never waked to the truth that the act of knowing a real object alters it. They are curious specimens of humanity, and as I am one of them, it may be amusing to see how I think' (Peirce, 5.555). How Peirce thought on this matter is indeed, irony aside, very instructive.

Peirce traced the origin of the claim to 'a new analysis' which equated 'the true' with 'that in cognition which is Satisfactory'. To evaluate this analysis, he observed, we need some agreement on what we mean by 'the True' so that we can see whether this is a plausible analysis. Peirce supposed that what we mean by 'the True' is 'that at which inquiry aims'. And before proceeding to ask whether inquiry aims at 'that in cognition which is Satisfactory', we need to consider what the latter means. If it means 'excites a certain feeling of satisfaction', this is nothing but hedonism. 'For when hedonists talk of "pleasure," they do not mean what is so-called in ordinary speech, but what excites a feeling of satisfaction' (5.559).

The end or goal of inquiry is not for Dewey a feeling of any kind, but an objective change in the situation which elicited the inquiry, viz. its unification into a single coherent whole. The characterization of a situation as 'doubtful' or 'problematic' is not a subjective characterization even if it takes an organism (traditionally referred to as a 'subject') to constitute in part such a situation. Russell read Dewey's view of the task of inquiry in terms of 'satisfaction of personal desires, of success in activities performed in order to satisfy personal desire', and Dewey replied:

> Mr. Russell proceeds first by converting a doubtful *situation* into a personal doubt. . . . Then by changing doubt into private discomfort, truth is identified [upon my view] with removal of this discomfort . . . [but] 'Satisfaction' is satisfaction of the conditions prescribed by the problem. (PM, p. 348)[1]

We have seen in Sections I.c and V.b that Dewey characterized the general change brought about in things by successful inquiry as unification into a single coherent whole. This was not, however, meant to be a single goal pursued throughout all inquiries: Dewey rejected the absolute idealist goal of a 'final all comprehensive Unity'.[2] Each problematic situation requires its own kind of unification, and there is little apart from this characterization which can usefully be said (in general) about what successful inquiry achieves. But are we not left, then, with saying that 'the Satisfactory' means simply 'success' or 'congruence to the aim of action'? This, Pierce thought, was no viable alternative to hedonism.

> . . . the aim must be determined before it can be determined, either in thought or in fact, to be satisfactory. An action that had no other aim than to be congruous to its aim would have no aim at all, and would not be a deliberate action. (5.560)

Dewey seems particularly vulnerable to Peirce's objection here for at times he writes as though we conducted an inquiry in order to find out what would constitute a satisfactory outcome to the inquiry. In replying to Lovejoy's accusation that he had equivocated between 'object of the inquiry' and 'objective of the inquiry', Dewey wrote:

> The argument does not depend upon any ambiguity between objective and object. As long as inquiry is going on the object is

an objective because it is still in question. The final object represents some objective taking settled and definite form. (M13, p. 45, n. 3)[3]

In dismissing the idea, that the aim of an activity could be nothing more than to be congruous to its aim, Peirce was implicitly appealing to a commonly accepted principle, that to deliberate and thereafter act deliberately, one must have a determinate idea of one's objective, of what it is one wants to achieve. Deliberation then takes the form of discovering means to realize that objective. Does Dewey flout this principle and thereby lapse into incoherency when describing inquiry as deliberate action? If, in fact, Dewey's position is incoherent, it is not inadvertently so, for he made persistent explicit efforts to overturn the principle that deliberation and deliberate action require a fully determinate aim.

One such attempt occurs in the course of a series of two articles under the title, 'The Logic of Judgments of Practice' (M8, pp. 14ff.), published nine years after Peirce penned his manuscript appealing to this principle. Practical judgments are about what is to be done (*agenda*) and are made in a situation which is incomplete. Now any judgment made about an ongoing process is about a situation which is incomplete. ('We're on our way to Coventry', i.e. we are not there yet.) But what is peculiar about judgments of practice is that the judgment to be made is itself a factor determining how the situation will complete itself. This presence of the judgment in the situation it is about marked for Dewey an important formal difference between practical judgments and other kinds of judgment, and marked the source of the doctrine that coming to know changes things; for coming to know is always the result of trying to make some practically oriented determination.

In addition to this reflexive kind of incompleteness, a practical judgment has to determine both what is to be done, X, and the means available to carry through with X. If the end is fully determinate, then practical reasoning may be set the task of hitting on some means to realize that end, and its success will be measured by the success of the means it selects. It would seem, indeed, that practical reason has no other office. It would seem that we deliberate, as Aristotle said, 'not about ends but about what contributes to ends' (1112^{b}12).

What Dewey proposed we should recognise instead of the principle of determinate ends (or aims) was 'the thoroughly reciprocal character of means and ends' (M8, p. 37). The principle of determinate ends acknowledges only one side of this reciprocal character while totally obscuring the other. The reciprocity arises, according to Dewey, because our ends are not always determinate, and it is only in working out the means to some vaguely specified end that we come to discover at what, exactly, our activity is aimed. To want X and not to know what would realize X, is not yet to know (fully) what X is: 'only by the judgement of means . . . is the end determinately made out in judgement' (ibid.). And in what (in its context) is a far from transparent *sequitur*, Dewey cites Aristotle's remark about deliberating only about means, never about ends, in support of his own position (M8, p. 37).

Section VII.b: Means to the determination of ends

Recent interpretations of Aristotle[4] suggest that Dewey's appeal to Aristotle's dictum is by no means fanciful, and they offer a useful route to understanding Dewey's claim about the reciprocity of means and ends. The crucial point is that Aristotle's word translated 'means' is homonymous, covering what appear to us to be two quite different notions. We expect that where 'means' are sought, someone is looking for an instrument to achieve some specified objective. If the only available source of coffee is a vending machine requiring 2 × 20p, then two 20p pieces are the means to a cup of coffee. It is common[5] to refer to this as the 'instrumental' sense of means'.

It appears, however, that where there is only a vague specification of an aim and what is sought is a more precise description or a specification of a concrete instance, this too would count as a 'means' for Aristotle. If someone wishes to express sympathy, show solidarity or serve some cause, the next step may be to seek some more precise specification or a suggestion for a concrete action of some sort. Unlike two 20p pieces, which will never in the full sense *be* what they are a means to – a cup of coffee – sending flowers, taking a collection, canvassing door to door, may well *be* an expression of sympathy, a show of solidarity or the serving of some cause. These latter sorts of means are commonly referred to as 'constituents' (or 'constitutive means'). What constitutes an X is (in the logical sense) internally related to X. An instrumental means to X is typically thought to stand in an external relation to X.

An excellent example of deliberating about constitutive means in an effort to spell out an end or aim more precisely, is Aristotle's exploration of *eudaimonia* in the first book of the *Nicomachean Ethics*. *Eudaimonia*, Aristotle observes, is what (Greek-speaking) people agree in using as a label for the aspirations which they have for their entire lives. This, he acknowledges, amounts to a platitude (1097[b]23).[6] Aristotle recognizes three traditional ways to fill out the concept of *eudaimonia* and thus to render the claim less platitudinous, viz. *eudaimonia* is a life of pleasure, a life of honour or a life of wisdom (1095[b]15–20).[7] Aristotle's own way of approaching the problem of specifying more precisely what *eudaimonia* is, proceeds via the notion of the function (*ergon*) of man (1097[b]25ff.).

What united both the instrumental and constitutive notions of means in Aristotle's mind may have been this: if we set down a description of an end, X, and then write down something, Y, which would serve to bring about X, and then something, Z, which would serve to bring about Y, and continue until we reach something we can straightaway act upon or undertake, we will have written down a series of mediating or middle terms, or means to X. And whether we have started with a precise end and are seeking instruments to realize it, or are starting with an imprecise end and are seeking something more precise to constitute – and thereby realise – it, our procedure will, from the standpoint of writing a series of descriptive terms, look formally the same. Because each such intermediate term serves in its turn as something to be aimed at, Dewey calls the terms 'ends-in-view':

> . . . the last end in view is always that which operates as the direct or immediate means of setting our own powers in operation. The end-in-view upon which judgment of action settles down is simply the adequate or complete means to the doing of something.
>
> We do deliberate, however, about aims, about ends-in-view. . . . (M8, p. 38)

To see what Dewey means by the reciprocal character of ends and means, it is necessary only to add to these observations a caution about the artificiality of the distinction between instrumental and constitutive means. Means are never wholly external to the end which they are used to realize. The discovery of the only available means, M, to some aim, X, however precisely X has hitherto been specified, adds to the specification of X. It becomes 'X at the cost of using M', and *may* be abandoned simply because the cost is too dear, or because what using M will entail is unacceptable. 'Wanting a cup of coffee' is not fully determinate, and when it is discovered that in present circumstances this amounts to 'wanting a cup of coffee costing 40p', one may realize one does not want *that*, and decide not to have a cup of coffee.

Ideally, Dewey thought, one should always be able to integrate whatever means one used in pursuit of some end into that end: so that 'instrumental' in the sense Dewey most favoured meant something like 'an organic constituent'. On this basis he criticized modern culture for encouraging the alienation of means from ends and mounted an account of the role which art *should* be able to play in human life. This doctrine will be explored in Chapter IX, especially Sections IX.c and IX.d, and it is here that we will find the source of Dewey's reluctance to surrender the doctrine of the reciprocal character of means and ends. We can, however, explore further the consequences of this reluctance before examining its source.

Peirce might have resisted the idea that our aim may (indeed must) become more definite as our inquiries proceed, but does his own philosophy not contain just such a move? In the 1906 manuscript, Peirce admitted that his article published in November 1877 ('The Fixation of Belief', 5.358–87) had laid the foundations of pragmatism on a kind of feeling of satisfaction , viz. the 'feeling firm belief' (5.567). Nevertheless, Peirce insisted, out of this intellectual hedonism, through stages in which firm belief is fixed in turn by wilful belief (or 'self-mendacity'), the authority of organized society, and the fermentation of ideas, men finally reach 'the idea of truth as overwhelmingly forced upon the mind in experience as the effect of an independent reality' (5.564).[8] But does this account of reaching the idea of truth – the account by which Peirce in 1906 measured his distance from hedonism – not have the very form which Dewey gives to the development of determinate ends? In passing through these stages humans discover something about the means available to them for fixing belief, which expands the goal of firm belief into that of truth.

Where Dewey would take issue with Peirce is over the artificiality of representing the four crucial methods as separate stages each left behind as the next one is reached. In fact the four methods – of tenacity, authority, fashion (the '*a priori*' method) and science – remain intermingled. If there is anything in the order Peirce imposes on his methods, it might lie in the suggestion that each succeeding method must absorb and transform the previous method. Authority cannot prevail unless there is enough wilful belief or self-mendacity to sustain that authority. Fashion yields its own authority, even if its organization is less obvious than that of, say, an ecclesiastical hierarchy. Science is not embodied in books but in the living thought of a community of human beings, who advance their disciplines by the 'ferment of ideas' (Peirce's more charitable phrase for the *a priori* method). This process has its fashions as well as generating an authority structure, which must be sustained by the tenacity, wilful belief or self-mendacity (although the kinder word is 'commitment') on the part of individual scientists.

Truth is a problem which ordinary men understand, Dewey observed in 1911 (at the start of a series of lectures on 'The Problem of Truth') because the absract noun – 'truth', noun singular and absolute – refers people to those beliefs which 'are of peculiar importance for the guidance of life' (M6, p. 13) 'a general view of things upon which one should regulate one's affairs' (M6, p. 14). What falls within the extension of the term is 'beliefs that are current, that are authoritative in a given community or organization' (M6, p. 12), and these include 'dominant political, moral and religious beliefs' (M6, p. 13). Individual truths – 'truth', noun common and distributive – likewise point to a social virtue, truthfulness, to a social function, the maintenance of common action and common understanding, and to social custom for the criteria of correct representation (M6, pp. 14–19). Whatever self-mendacity may produce as belief *de facto*, it is assessed in terms of the legitimate *de jure*

159

view authorized and demanded by social custom and common interests (M6, p. 25). The tension that occurs between individual belief or inclination and the authorized view is what gives rise to a notion, albeit imperfect, of objectivity.

To insist that this is an incomplete or imperfect notion of objectivity, and that the authority of custom and tradition can be challenged, without turning in the direction of anarchy, one may appeal *à la* Plato or Descartes to a transcendent truth, or appeal like a modest man of science to beliefs which are accepted tentatively in virtue of having been tested *by their consequences*, using what are taken (again tentatively) to be the best available methods. Pragmatism conceived itself as articulating this second version of a more complete and adequate notion of objectivity.

Nevertheless, Dewey observed in the third lecture of the series on 'The Problem of Truth', pragmatism has to face up to a question about the notion of consequences. The imperfect grade of objectivity refers to consequences, to the guidance of life, the regulation of affairs, to socially desired ('desirable') outcomes. When we move to the second, more complete grade of objectivity, must we put aside interest in social benefit, just as individual whim has to be set aside to reach the first grade? If we do not exclude working toward (and working out what is) social prosperity, 'What becomes of the traits of impartiality, of exclusion of preference for a special conclusion, of the impersonal outlook of science and its intellectual objectivity?' (M6, p. 56). But to rule out all elements of general or social value from what counts as the deciding consequences leaves us with only '*knowledge*-consequences . . . intellectual results as the sole mark of truth' (M6, p. 57) This issue, Dewey suggested, was 'the only serious question, as to principle, a wisely pragmatic philosophy need fear' (M6, p. 54).

> Were I an opponent of that philosophy, I do not think I should waste my energy butting my head against an impregnable stone wall: the identification of truth, both descriptively and analytically, with working towards the concrete production of specific consequences. I should press the charge of oscillating between two kinds of consequences: the intellectually objective and the socially controlling. (M6, p. 57)

Peirce made it clear on numerous cocasions (e.g. 8.132–43) that he valued *pure* science, science not entangled in any socially useful projects, not measured by any social benefits, not measured, indeed, by anything other than *intellectual* results. Dewey, equally clearly, favoured socially responsible science and rejected any hard and fast separation of the intellectually objective and the socially controlling (e.g. L1, pp. 128–31). The framework he spells out for practical reason evidently allows scientific results to inform social objectives and for social objectives to shape what is to be sought in particular scientific inquiries. The framework to which Peirce appeals is both traditional and traditionalist. It appeals to a tradition which assumes that aims must be determinate; it leaves us with nothing but established custom as the source of the aim toward which our thought and action are directed. Dewey, for his part, regarded 'the idea that progress consists in increasing our capacity to achieve some antecedently fixed goal as an hypnotic after-image', and he repeatedly urged that the experimental method be applied to social problems, to provide us with more liberating means and more liberated ends-in-view. His hope was to harness science as a socially progressive force, and this may well be the profoundest respect in which his pragmatism differs from that of Peirce.

Section VII.c: The constitution of values

Of the two pragmatisms, Peirce's is closer to the received views of our age. It may be questioned whether his approach really can yield the notion of truth as 'overwhelmingly forced upon the mind in experience as the effect of an independent reality'. But there is little doubt that, for those who (whatever their approach) take objective truth seriously, this phrase expresses their idea of it. In resisting the separation of the 'intellectually objective' and the 'socially-controlling' Dewey seems to betray objectivity. The notion of truth certainly plays a role in that of social dependability, as well as that of authority, but to leave these intertwined and not to seek to extricate truth from such entanglements is to risk corrupting the one enterprise, natural science, where we can hope to attain a view of something which is not biased by our feelings, desires or aspirations. If we let our values mix with our science, we shall only obscure the former and destroy the latter.

It is clear from Chapter V above that Dewey would view the desire for an account of nature which leaves behind all thought or experience as wholly misguided. And the more specific idea that we can undertake (natural) scientific inquiry without at crucial points along the way having to settle important questions of value was, to Dewey, equally misguided. Recall that inquiry is practical activity, the aim of which is to restore unity to some ongoing activity.[9] Inquiry may be concerned with something concrete (the building of some contrivance) or abstract (the development of a mathematical technique) or a combination of the two (the application of a scientific theory to the development of a body of experimental results). If, furthermore, the discovery of even the most 'instrumental' (i.e. logically external) of means will serve to fill out what that end is or could be, the end, the restoring of unity to a situation which has become fragmented, will not be something which can be specified fully in advance of discovering the means to effect the transformation.

In every case there will be some expectation of what it will be like to resolve the problem. We will be hoping for something like a new heat-resistant glaze, a generalization of the notion of Cartesian product, the postulation of a hitherto unobserved planet, or elementary particle, or catalytic agent. The expected solution may only be bought at the cost of additional money, lack of elegance, complicated computations or *ad hoc* hypotheses. In some cases we may not reckon the cost excessive; in others the cost may make us hesitate to embrace the 'solution' and conclude (this phase of) our inquiry. In some cases the solution may elude us altogether until we look in other directions and modify our expectations. We may even find ourselves faced with a choice between a time-honoured and much valued feature of our existing theories (such as the principle that planetary motion is uniformly circular) and a radical departure (planetary motion is elliptical and its velocity is a function of the distance from the sun), the advantages and drawbacks of which may not be altogether clear at first. (Or compare the choice faced by physicists at the turn of the century between the advantages of a quantum treatment of certain phenomena and the belief that physical change must be continuous.)

Where there is more than one means available, or the one means available has a cost which may make us hesitate to draw our inquiries to a conclusion, we are faced with the need for a kind of practical thinking which Dewey called 'valuation' (or 'evaluation'). Inquiry typically is governed not only by matters which are taken as established fact, it is also governed by traits which are to be realized or avoided in the outcome. Matters which are taken as established fact may be explicitly judged to be so, or the inquiry may proceed unreflectively *as though* they had been judged to be so. Similarly, certain traits may be judged to be valuable or undesirable, or they may be taken unreflectively to be so. Judgments of fact made (implicitly or explicitly) during the inquiry may need to be revised before the inquiry can reach a satisfactory conclusion. Similarly, judgments of what is valuable (or otherwise) may need to be revised. Different ways (means) to institute unity in a problematic situation will each realize a different complex of traits thought to be valuable. It may not be possible to combine all the traits thought to be desirable and avoid all those thought to be undesirable. A choice has to be made; and if it is to be made reflectively, (e)valuation has to take place.

If science is, as Dewey insists, practical activity, and practical activity has the features Dewey attributes to it, science will inevitably from time to time face the prospect of having to evaluate and revalue the traits of the methods, theories and experimental techniques which it uses. This perspective on science is not unfamiliar. Thomas Kuhn (1973, p. 322), for example, has listed five high-level traits of theories – accuracy, consistency, scope, simplicity and fruitfulness – and insisted that the trade-off between these valued traits, when competing theories realize different traits to different degrees, cannot be settled *a priori*. This perspective is, however, unwelcome to many, and there are strong impulses either to deny that anything like this has to take place in natural science, or to deny, if it does take place, that it involves anything which is properly called 'value'. Value is widely assumed to be the expression of an individual's feelings, the very thing which science tries to leave behind. Surely if the aims of scientific inquiry are open in this way at crucial points to *choice*, we will have surrendered to the very thing Peirce feared, a kind of cognitive hedonism. For what could determine our choice other than a feeling of satisfaction?

For Dewey, both hedonism and the fear of it reflected in this argument embody a serious mistake about the empirical facts of human psychology. The error is to assume that our feelings are unchanged and unchangeable by any understanding of their consequences, are a 'quasi gaseous stuff' endowed 'with the power of triple-plate steel', as Dewey wrote in 1944 (PM, p. 281). We can, as rational reflective creatures, raise the question whether we should take satisfaction in something in which we find ourselves prone to take satisfaction.

> Nothing more contrary to common sense can be imagined than the notion that we are incapable of changing our desires and interests by means of learning what the consequences of acting upon them are, or as it is sometimes put, of *indulging* them. (TV, p. 31)

Evaluation is a process of adjusting the way we feel, what we desire, what it is that we will take satisfaction in. This idea of evaluation requires closer scrutiny, but consider first what follows if it is at all coherent to accept that this process can, does and should take place. By looking at the consequences of having what we in fact desire, we arrive at the distinction between what is desired and what is desirable. (A person may as a matter of fact have a desire to smoke three packets of cigarettes a day, but the long-term consequences of fulfilling this desire may make it undesirable to do so.) By looking at the consequences, short- and long-term, of taking satisfaction in a certain proposed solution to a problem, even a strictly theoretical problem, and seeing how that way of resolving the problem bears on the resolution of future difficulties, we arrive at the distinction between a resolution in which we take satisfaction and a satisfactory resolution.

We find, moreover, as our inquiries become more reflective, that we acquire control over the conditions in which our judgments of value (our 'valuations') take shape. A choice that has to be made *will* be made on the basis of how we feel about the matter. The problem is not to eliminate feeling but to school it properly. We can withhold judgment until we have knowledge of enough of the consequences of choosing one way or another to make a choice, which is not only satisfying but will (probably) be satisfactory. Experimental method is that method of inquiry which not only extends control over the conditions of observation, but also over conditions in which we frame our judgments of value. We cannot know if we have made a reasonable choice of values, Dewey taught, until we have explored the consequences of our choice.

Recent discussions in the philosophy of science have highlighted the extent to which the adoption of a theory or a whole explanatory framework often cannot be justified until much later in the history of science, when the theory or framework has proved to be degenerating or progressive. There inevitably has to be an element of wait and see. Dewey's position is simply to urge that the same attitude be adopted toward values, in other words that they be adopted hypothetically in much the way theories and explanatory frameworks are adopted, and tested by their consequences. But there is scope for more than a wait and see policy. One can experimentally explore the consequences of a value choice: one can judge that to make a proper assessment one needs to know what happens if. . . . One can judge, 'If I do X, I will have more data on which to judge.' (See M13, pp 10–20.)[10]

This last point reveals a second important strand to Dewey's opposition to the belief that science and value are – and should never be thought to be other than – wholly separate domains of concern. Not only must scientific activity confront questions of value, it is possible for scientific methods (specifically the experimental method) to make contributions to the determination of values generally. But one should not let the invocation of 'experimental method' obscure the sense in which values are 'determined' in judgment. Experiments are not to be used to 'discover' what is already there. Dewey explicitly repudiated 'the prevailing view . . . that goods, ends, "values" are all given, given in the sense of being completely there for knowledge, provided only we could get at them' (M11, p. 9).

Experimentation is not in this context an instrument of discovery, but an instrument of construction, [11] for (e)valuation has a quite radical role.

> At the risk of whatever shock, this doctrine should be exposed in all its nakedness. *To judge value is to engage in instituting a determinate value where none is given.* It is not necessary that antecedently given values should be the data of the valuation: *and where they are given data they are only terms in the determination of a not yet existing value.* (M8, p. 35)

The second sentence of this quotation (italics added) should not be read in isolation from the second clause of the third (italics added). One inquires into values because often those that are given, those which have guided practical judgment in the past, are not adequate and a revaluation is needed for adequate guidance in the present situation. The first clause of the third sentence refers to a special 'limit case' (cp. 'intellectual absraction', M13, p. 7), and to appreciate its implications, it will be useful to compare what Dewey says about perception.

Perception, we have seen Dewey insist,[12] is not an interior 'psychic' event, but an aspect of an integral organic *response* to environmental influences. What is peculiar about human perceptual responses is that the stimuli are treated as signs, as objects, as 'events with meanings'. This is perception as a cognitive event. If the signifying function is absent, as it is in infants and animals, there is still a non-cognitive event with its own peculiar qualities, qualities which are *had*, but not known. The corresponding aspect of human and animal behaviour, which is roughly characterized by the term 'motivation', has a similar structure. What motivates is not an isolated interior event standing in a logically external relation to a behaviour pattern which it produces, just as a perception is not an interior event standing in a logically external relation to the object which causes it. In each case there is a pattern of behaviour and the interior event is an abstraction from that pattern and is incapable of existing or being understood in isolation from the whole pattern.

The patterns of behaviour from which the study of motivation must start are those involving efforts to remain with, enhance, care for or preserve, and those involving efforts to flee, diminish, damage or destroy. Non-cognitive animal behaviour is characterized by these patterns just as it is by patterns of response to external stimuli. As perception acquires cognitive status when qualities of perceptual events are treated as signs, motivation acquires cognitive status when traits which are 'prized', or 'held dear'[13] or 'avoided' or 'rejected', come to be appreciated as signs of other things. When such traits are grasped in their connections to other things, the immediate response of prizing or avoiding is modified, and as events acquire cognitive status such traits acquire the status of values (valued things). This is why 'It is not necessary that antecedently given values should be the data of the valuation'.

What is being referred to here is the familiar phenomenon of finding that something in which one has taken innocent pleasure has injurious consequences, or is socially disapproved of, or interferes with what other people hold dear. On the other side one may discover that what one instinctively shunned has beneficial consequences, or arouses the admiration of other people or if experienced enough becomes intensely pleasurable. The upshot is that what may be called 'proto-values'[14] (marked by innocent or unreflective pursuit or avoidance) are converted into values. And values go on being reconverted in this way throughout the life of a human being, sometimes being reinforced, sometimes reversed altogether.

It needs to be stressed that the process of (e)valuation and revaluation is not typically smooth, and not *necessarily* progressive. People are moved to constitute or reconstitute values only because, as they confront new situations with a more comprehensive appreciation of the facts, they find that what motivates them pulls in conflicting directions. They face, in other words, indeterminate situations, situations calling for inquiry. Values are 'constituted' or 'constructed' through the process of inquiry as the responses of intelligence to objective problems. And as problems are objective,[15] whether a response constitutes a solution is also objective. But a solution has to contribute, where appropriate, to the continuum of inquiry, or it is not ultimately satisfactory, and it would be a mistake to assume that what constitutes an ultimately satisfactory solution can be (objectively) determined on the spot. The best one can do to construct values which will contribute to the continuum of inquiry, is to anticipate experimentally the consequences of adopting them.

We have seen that, according to Dewey, the truth of a factual judgment answers in an important way to the successful outcome of the practical activity in which it is (of necessity) embedded. The success of the outcome is determined by the values that are realized in that outcome. (When the activity is what we think of as theoretical science, the values in question will be the sort of things of which Kuhn gave five instances.) Values – whether theoretical, social or aesthetic – are not, however, independent objects which are waiting to be discovered. We have seen Dewey repudiate the view that values are 'given in the sense of being completely there for knowledge, provided only we could get at them'. Values are not even, strictly speaking, things; they are qualities that things acquire as a consequence of our interacting with them (M15, p. 20) and the interactions must involve the grasping of the distinctions and connections between things, i.e. must involve what is expressed (when it is expressed) in judgment. Knowing influences what is valued and what is valued shapes the outcome of practical activity. Yet it is the outcome for the sake of which we strive to know, strive to ascertain the facts, and the outcome is ultimately the criterion of our having stated the facts well or badly.

It might seem that a vicious circularity threatens the whole perspective on knowledge, value and practice which Dewey is trying to establish, but it must be remembered that facts and values are not all to be settled in a single inquiry, one which is cut off from previous inquiries and from inquiries to come. Humans start with unreflective impulses to prize certain events and to reject others (as well as with unreflective responses to external stimuli). There then begins a process whereby their unreflective impulses and responses are – in the light of the consequences which these impulses and responses are seen to have – transformed into values and meanings (valued events and meaningful events). These values are then brought into subsequent inquiries and exposed to revision as those inquiries proceed. There is no circularity, only a constant dialectical spiral of reassessment and revaluation as thought becomes more and more responsive to the relatedness of things.

Section VII.d: The combat of passion and reason

Dewey's account of value tries to combine three features which are ordinarily thought to pull in different directions. His account is rationalist, constructivist and experimentalist. The first of these is not Dewey's preferred label. He used cognates of 'intelligent' rather than cognates of 'rational', when setting out his position. But the unmistakable role which he assigns to cognition in the formation of values was vigorously resisted by those who would have insisted upon Hume's doctrine that reason has no other role than to serve the passions by identifying their objects and devising the means to their gratifications. D. W. Prall, for example, wrote about the process which Dewey called 'evaluation'. 'I can not help seeing here a suggestion that value is not the creation of irrational preference, but is somehow at bottom rational' (Prall, 1924, p. 628).

The role which Dewey assigned to intelligence, however, was not that traditionally assigned to reason, viz. the discovery (in the form of innate principles or transcendent ideas) of the ultimate guides of conduct. Intelligence through the exercise of judgement was to *constitute* values. Traditionally cognitive functions are stressed in order to pre-empt the claims of what we learn by experience (including experiment); when the stress is on construction, the roles of reason or experience appear highly problematic. If our values are made, they are acquired neither by reason nor by experience. However, Dewey, who took practice (with production as a paradigm) as the basis of all cognitive processes, had no trouble seeing how reason and experience could – and indeed had to – combine with and constrain constructive activity. One cannnot produce something which enriches life without learning by experiment the limits of one's materials and using intelligence to devise something within those limits.

The reluctance on the part of Dewey's contemporaries to comprehend, let alone accept, Dewey's position arose from two presuppositions, one about cognition, the other about motivation, which still stand in the way of a sympathetic reading of Dewey. The assumption about cognition centres on the function of judgment. Its role is supposed to be that of representing what is 'there', not participating in (or effecting in any way) the construction of something not already 'there'.[16] The second assumption, about motives, is one (we saw in the previous section) which Dewey regarded as wholly contrary to common sense. It is that our motivational impulses, like our perceptual experience (according to sense data theorists) have at their core a 'given' which remains what it is regardless of what we learn of its connections to other events, in particular its consequences. This doctrine has even more resilience than the corresponding epistemological doctrine regarding sense data. In denying that what were called 'proto-values' in the previous section deserved to be called 'values', Dewey was trying to crowd out this doctrine by terminological manoeuvres, just as he tried to crowd out the bare sensory given by defining 'objects' as 'events with meaning' (L1, p. 240).[17]

The two assumptions are interconnected parts of a single philosophic outlook, the essence of which is the separation of cognition from the influence of motivation, and motivation from the influence of cognition. The classic locus of this outlook is found in the philosophy of David Hume. It is important to appreciate exactly where Dewey and Hume part company, for Dewey's position is in some respects close enough to Hume's for Hume's arguments to overshoot Dewey's claims on behalf of the role of intelligence. At M8, p. 24, for example, we find Dewey endorsing Hume's doctrine that 'A passion is an original existence . . . and contains not any representative quality which renders it a copy of any other existence or modification' (Hume, 1739, p. 415). And where Hume insisted that (not reason but) only a contrary impulse could oppose any impulse of passion (ibid.), Dewey agreed.

> The conclusion is not that the emotional, passionate phase of action can be or should be eliminated in behalf of a bloodless reason. More 'passions', not fewer, is the answer. To check the influence of hate there must be sympathy, while to rationalize sympathy there are needed emotions of curiosity, caution, respect for the freedom of others. . . . (M14, p. 136)[18]

But when Hume insists that a passion contains no 'representative quality', this is part of a general argument for placing reason and passion, judgment and motivation, in such disparate categories that it can make no sense to talk of the former opposing or influencing the latter. 'Reason is the discovery of truth or falsehood'; what does not represent cannot be true or false, 'can never be an object of our reason' (Hume, 1739, p. 458). This is the burden of Hume's argument for his famous thesis that 'We speak not strictly and philosophically when we talk of the combat of passion and reason' (ibid., p. 415). Because our 'passions, volitions and actions' are original existences, not representations, none of them 'can be pronounced true or false, and be either contrary or conformable to reason (ibid., p. 458).

For Dewey, however, there is no sharp separation of things or events into original existences and representations. Things and events in nature – not just mental or linguistic things – can perform the function of representations. This, as we saw in Section IV.c, is an important feature of Dewey's approach to meaning, and, as we saw in Section VI.b, the crux of his dispute with Lovejoy over statements about the past. That passions, volitions and actions are events occurring in the natural world does not prevent them being treated by the mind as representative of their consequences.[19] The other side to this coin is that acts of representing are themselves original existences and, moreover, there is no reason why, if a passion or volition has a representative quality, the imaginatively controlled use of that passion or volition – in a 'rehearsal' of it and its natural consummation – should not retain both a representative quality and a motivating influence.

To appreciate the difference this makes, recall that for Hume thought has but two roles in influencing action . . . either it identifies for a passion the existence of its proper object, or it finds for a passion the means to exerting it (Hume, 1739, p. 459). Hume makes very little of the circumstance in which more than one passion or volition pull in opposite directions over the very same act. 'Reason' may alert not only a passion for pleasant and delicious taste to the presence of a pastry, but also aversion to obesity, tooth decay or heart disease. The means adopted to secure the satisfaction of some passion will likewise have other consequences – different means having different consequences – and these may excite all manner of attractions and aversions. To ignore 'the plural effects that flow from any act' (M14, p. 158) struck Dewey as not only presumptuous but perverse.

On Dewey's account deliberation is stimulated precisely by the problem of resolving conflicts that come to a head where there is more than one way to proceed and hence more than one set of consequences in the offing. 'We begin with the summary assertion that deliberation is a dramatic rehearsal (in imagination) of various competing possible lines of action. . . . Deliberation is an experiment in finding out what the various lines of possible action are really like' (M14, p. 132) What reason does for Hume can be typified in the situation where, finding that my soup tastes flat, and my eye falls upon the salt shaker, I represent to myself the consequences of putting salt on food, and straightaway my hand moves. There are here no competing possible lines of action, and hence, for Dewey, there is no deliberation.

> Deliberation means precisely that activity is disintegrated, and that its various elements hold one another up. While none has force enough to become the center of a re-directed activity, or to dominate a course of action, each has enough power to check others from exercising mastery. Activity does not cease in order to give way to reflection; activity is turned from execution into intra-organic channels, resulting in dramatic rehearsal. (M14, p. 133)

The following situation illustrates Dewey's account of deliberation: I wish to enlarge a room by removing a load-bearing interior wall. Due to prevailing circumstances, various ways of supporting the load will give different distributions of head room and different distributions of floor area clear of supporting columns. Under each alternative I will achieve a variety of features, some of which attract and encourage, some of which annoy and repel. As long as these features and my responses to them do not 'fit harmoniously together' (M14, p. 134) further variations are 'rehearsed', the deliberation goes on. When the factors come together and 'a unified preference' emerges 'out of competing preferences' (ibid.), choice has been made, the disintegrated activity is integrated, and the modification of the house proceeds.

Deliberation thus fits the definition of inquiry:[20] *Inquiry is the controlled or directed* (by dramatic rehearsal) *transformation of an indeterminate situation* (how to proceed with the project of removing a load-bearing wall) *into one so determinate in its constituent distinctions and relations* (a beam of precisely this size supported, exactly here and here, to be finished and decorated thus and so) *as to convert the elements of the original situation into a unified whole.*

There are two points to be stressed here. The first is that deliberative inquiry actively transforms the 'indeterminate', 'disintegrated' situation by coming up with a judgment embodied in a dramatic rehearsal of a plan in which the conflicting elements are unified. The second is that this process does not always leave the competing preferences as they are, but transforms *them* as well:

> . . . the object thought of may be one which stimulates by unifying, harmonizing, different competing tendencies. It may release an activity in which all are fulfilled, not indeed, in their original form, but in a 'sublimated' fashion, that is in a way which modifies the original direction of each by reducing it to a component along with others in an action of transformed quality. (M14, p. 135)

Our intellectual capacities, in other words, consist in more than the ability to produce representations; in producing representations (in some cases out of motivational material) they affect the original motivating factors. Thus hand in hand with Dewey's account of the function of intelligence (or 'reason') goes an account of the nature of the factors motivating us, both of which which diverge radically from that given by Hume.

The difference here boils down to the claim that until we have invested thought, we do not know precisely what we want.

> We have no direct consciousness of what we purpose to do. We can judge its nature, assign its meaning, only by following it into the situations whither it leads, noting the objects against which it runs

and seeing how they rebuff or unexpectedly encourage it. (M14, pp. 133–4)

Hume's reason 'is and ought only to be [thought to be] the slave of the passions' (Hume, 1739, p. 415), because his passions all have minds of their own (metaphorically speaking). They recognize their proper objects when exerted on those objects and will accept no substitutes.

This way of regarding human motivation leads on the one hand to the view which, we saw in the previous section, Dewey claimed was contrary to common sense, viz. that our desires are unaffected by our discovering what their consequences are. And on the other hand it expresses an aspect of the view of human beings as located on the margins of nature, constituted as individual selves prior to their entering into social relations.[21] But it is only through entering such relationships that humans derive their appreciations of the consequences of pursuing their desires.

Dewey's motivating impulses do not arise by themselves with clear conditions for their satisfaction, are not locks which will accept keys cut only to one pattern. This is no more than a psychological corollary of the account of practical reasoning given in Section VII.b. The question whether Hume has drawn the boundaries of reason too narrowly, whether his account ignores a perfectly intelligible motivating role, cannot be considered in isolation from the question whether he has presupposed excessively object-specific passions.

Section VII.e: Will and its weaknesses

Dewey cited Hume's claim that passions are original existences in support of a move to overturn an ancient doctrine that the experience of something as good is identical to the judgment of it as good. Rejecting this doctrine was part of Dewey's campaign to undermine 'intellectualist' assumptions in philosophy; some experiences, we have seen him insist, are merely *had* and not *known*. What Dewey (M8, p. 24) quotes from Descartes, as typifying the view he opposed, is this sentence from *The Principles of Philosophy:* 'When we are given news the mind first judges of it and if it is good it rejoices.'

This Cartesian account has an echo in the way Hume treats passions as 'secondary or reflective' (Hume, 1739, p. 256) impressions occasioned by sensory impressions or ideas. Belief or judgment for Hume boils down to the mind's entertaining ideas of a certain vividness ('the mind first judges') but this is followed in the case where passion is aroused not only by a further secondary impression ('the mind rejoices/sorrows') but a general movement whose character is determined by 'the general bent or tendency of it from the beginning to the end' (ibid., pp. 384–5). Dewey would have applauded as a step in the right direction the way

Hume ties the character of a passion to the tendency it has to produce a certain pattern of behaviour, but would have regarded the role of such dispositions in Hume's account far from satisfactory.

The idea that an external stimulus may trigger a quite determinate pattern of behaviour may apply to 'lower' animals – 'lower' by virtue of the uniformity and inflexibility of their behavioural responses – but in the case of higher animals, this account makes no allowance for the fact that, depending on the experience and present state of a creature, the same stimulus may on different occasions produce quite different responses. It is the pattern of the organism's behaviour which determines how it will respond to a stimulus, not the stimulus which determines the pattern.

The fact that the patterns of reponse of human beings can be broken down in reponse to adverse experience and restructured, had been one of the leading principles of Dewey's thought from at least the time of his treatment of the reflex arc concept. For a new pattern to emerge from the break-up of an old pattern, it is necessary for an animal to be capable of responding to the situation which triggered the old pattern in a way which does not conform to the old pattern, and around which a new pattern can form. Such 'pivots upon which the re-organization of activities turn' are what Dewey calls 'impulses' (M14, p. 67). The organization of a pattern of activity which can be modified in this way is called a 'habit':

> . . . the saw and hammer are means only when they are employed
> in some actual making . . . and eye, arm and hand are,
> correspondingly, means proper only when they are in active
> operation. And whenever they are in action they are cooperating
> with external materials and energies. Without support from beyond
> themselves the eye stares blankly and the hand moves fumblingly.
> They are means only when they enter into organization with things
> which independently accomplish definite results. These
> organizations are habits. (M14, p. 22)

Animals whose patterns of behaviour are rigid and not adaptable to circumstances are said to 'act on instinct'. Instinctive patterns have the feature of being initiated by specific triggers, and once triggered each step unfolds from the previous step by what can only be a genetically laid-down mechanism. Animals whose patterns of behaviour are flexible, and need the influence of circumstances in order to take a specific shape, still need to respond spontaneously in certain directions to specific things, otherwise the environment cannot interact with the nascent pattern to give it any more specific shape. Impulses, thus, are required not just to pivot revolutions in habits; they are needed to prompt the unfolding of the earliest habits. But it is a mistake to confuse impulse with instinct.[22]

What follows from the triggering of many of a human being's first ('instinctive') impulses is simply the occasion for more mature human beings around it to give the developing behaviour pattern the form which it is to take in that culture.

Habits should not be thought of as rigid patterns which simply repeat themselves on cue.

> Repetition is in no sense the essence of habit. Tendency to repeat acts is an incident of many habits but not of all. . . . The essence of habit is an acquired predisposition to *ways* or modes of response, not to partucular acts except as, under special conditions, these express a way of behaving. Habit means special sensitiveness or accessibility to certain classes or stimuli, standing predilections and aversions, rather than bare recurrence of specific acts. It means will. (M14, p. 32)

The grounds for saying that habit means will (habits '*are* will' – M14, p. 21) reside in the claim that human impulses are not object-specific. They cannot be what Hume called 'desires'; there is nothing specific which counts as their being exerted, as their fulfilment. And on the other hand, desires, according to Dewey, do not originate action. Like Newton's uniform rectilinear motion, nothing is needed to explain the continued activity of a living organism, only the redirection of that activity. 'When the push and drive of life meets no obstacles, there is nothing which we call desire. There is just life activity' (M14, p. 172). When this activity is obstructed desire arises and it subsides when the push and drive is no longer obstructed. The satisfaction or fulfilment of desire is the resumption of the activity obstructed, and is therefore determined by reference to the pattern of that activity.

It follows from this account of desire that for us, animals whose on-going activities are not all laid down by instinct, habits 'form our effective desires,' (M14, p. 21). For habits, being the shape of our behaviour patterns, 'are demands for certain kinds of activity' (ibid.) and hence are that by reference to which our desires are specified. It is in this sense that 'in any intelligible sense of will, they *are* will' (ibid.).

But the word 'habit' has connotations of shackles, as in 'bad habit', 'the smoking habit'. As with the connotation of predictable repetition, this is only a sometime feature of the concept Dewey is employing. His notion of habit has antecedents in Aquinas's '*habitas*' and before this in Aristotle's '*hexis*'. In explaining Aquinas's notion Anthony Kenny (1964, p. xxx) points out that whereas we tend to think of a habit of Φing as making it *difficult not to* Φ, Aquinas treated a *habitas* to Φ as making it *easy* to Φ. And this applies equally to Dewey's notion of habit. Of course if it is hard not to Φ, it is much easier to Φ, but it may only be easy to Φ unless some alternative is even easier. An obstruction in the path of Φing will elicit a desire which will only be fulfilled by resumed Φing. But if the pattern of unified activity of which Φing is a dominant element gives way to a pattern in which Φing has no place, the desire simply subsides or abates.

On Dewey's view the main engine of this process of creative reorganization of behaviour patterns, or habits, lies in the conflicts that arise when different patterns pull in different directions. We have observed that in setting out the doctrine which insists on a servile role for reason, Hume makes very little of conflict between passions or of its resolution. If there is conflict, presumably the stronger passions win out over the weaker. Somewhat later in the *Treatise*, however, Hume acknowledged one peculiar kind of conflict which may result in our 'correcting our sentiments' (Hume, 1739, p. 582). The strength of passion aroused by an object, Hume notes, varies with the nearness in time or space of the object. A person may find that a

> servant, if diligent and faithful, may excite stronger sentiments of love and kindness than *Marcus Brutus*, as represented in history; but we say not upon that account that the former character is more laudable than the latter. We know, that were we to approach equally near to that renown'd patriot, he wou'd command a much higher degree of affection and admiration. (Ibid., p. 582)

This method of correcting not only the sentiments but all impressions and ideas is crucial for the existence of a common language:

> Such corrections are common with regard to all the senses; and indeed 'twere impossible we cou'd ever make use of language, or communicate our sentiments to one another, did we not correct the momentary appearances of things, and overlook our present situation. (Ibid.)

On the surface this appears to be a concession to judgment which completely undermines Hume's claim about the impotency of reason. Here we appear to have judgment *adjusting* passion, toning down the passion aroused by an object near at hand, amplifying one whose object is remote. But Hume insists that his claim stands, for what effects this correction is not reason or judgment, but 'a general calm determination of the passions, founded on some distant view or reflexion' (ibid., p. 583) – in other words, other passions, 'certain calm desires and tendencies', are easily overlooked because they 'cause no disturbance in the soul' (ibid., p. 417).

If one is to participate in human society, one has to acquire at least the desire to judge how one *would feel if* one were not situated as one is. This desire does not guarantee one will *act* from such adjusted sentiments; 'reason requires such an impartial conduct, but . . .' 'tis seldom we can bring ourselves to it . . . our passions do not readily follow the determination of our judgment' (ibid.). Hume's 'distant view' provides a foundation for the notion that where values, desires or even 'the socially controlling'23 enter, objectivity is not automatically excluded. Although it is not clear exactly where this 'distant view' is to be taken from, it might well provide a foundation for a notion of objectivity which transcends any existing consensus. In this light, the stand which Dewey takes on this matter is interesting.

As a matter of fact, Dewey claims, people seldom consider how they *will feel* at some point in the future, or *would feel* in some other circumstance. And they are wise, he argues, not to try; for such feelings depend on external circumstances and developments in individual character which it is extremely difficult to assess (M14, pp. 140ff.). To have 'reason' to act on anything other than the strongest passion of the moment, it is not necessary to remove oneself from present circumstances to a situation which will never in fact be occupied, an 'objective standpoint', a 'distant view', where feelings, passions, pleasures and pains are judged in a 'proper perspective'. Because the thought of future consequences does not leave present feelings untouched, we do not need to think ourselves out of our present inclinations away from what pleases and pains us here and now. It is sufficient that 'We think, through imagination, of objects into which in the future some course of action will run, and we are *now* delighted or depressed, pleased or pained at what is presented' (M14, p. 140).

What divides Hume and Dewey here can be made clearer by reference to the curious duplicate model of the mind which Plato employs in the *Philebus* (38e–42c). When we survey some distant (future) pleasure or pain there is, Plato says, a scribe in our soul who writes down a true or false statement comparing pleasure with distress, distress with distress, or pleasure with pleasure (41e5). There is in addition a painter who paints pictures of what the scribe writes about. On the intellectualist assumptions, which Dewey worked to undermine, it is difficult to see why Plato included this second 'worker' in his model. The mind first judges and then rejoices (or sorrows): one only needs to 'paint a picture' to help those who are slow to form a judgment. But Plato recognized that we not only judge how we will feel (pleased, distressed) *when* . . ., but that we feel (pleased, distressed) *now* about the prospect of future events (39d5). The painter represents the way our *present feelings* stand as (true or false, accurate or inaccurate) representations of future events.24 Like Dewey, Plato saw non-cognitive, non-judgmental psychological events performing the role of representations.

Hume's model of the mind contains only the scribe and Hume is generally pessimistic about what effect the scribe's work can have on our actions. Dewey's model of mind is built around the painter. The problem as he saw it is to make us *feel here and now* (which is where and when actions have to be taken) in a manner which gives due weight to distant consequences, and which reconciles the conflicting elements in the widest possible manifold of feelings. What Dewey says about judgment (particularly value judgments in the sense for which he uses the word 'valuation') is initially puzzling precisely because he has fused the roles of painter and scribe by assuming the techniques for making distant objects *touch* us here and now will involve the painter in performing the distinctive tasks given to the scribe in Plato's model.

Approaching thought from this direction, which inevitably gives judgment a constitutive function, made Dewey prone to overlook cases which 'intellectualists' regard as highly typical. In a 1922 article, 'Valuation and Experimental Knowledge', Dewey set out 'six significations' of 'value' and then acknowledged in a footnote (M13, p. 7, n. 4) the criticism of one Dr Picard, which pointed to a seventh sense of 'value'. This was a case where judgment proclaimed a thing to have value, to be worthy of appreciation (hence Picard proposed to call these 'judgments of worth'), but nevertheless one went on disliking it. Judgment typically in Dewey's view did not operate this independently of how one felt, but he acknowledged that his overlooking of this case had led to misunderstanding of his position.

Dewey's claim about (valuation) judgments is that determinate liking, preference, or feeling is easily upset by perceiving the consequences of having such inclinations satisfied and that (valuation) judgment is the process whereby the indeterminate feeling or preference is made more stable and determinate. Picard's case of judgments of worth, Dewey acknowledged, raised two possible exceptions to (and thereby constituted a test of) the rule that judgment determines feeling (M13, pp. 26–7). In one case it appears that our mind is already made up, our feelings are in fact fully determinate and our judgment is a matter of going through the motions 'in deference to habit or social expectations'. In the other the judgment of worth stands as a hypothetical judgment of the form, 'So and so would have my admiration, if . . .'. Such a judgment might well prompt experimentation to see if the antecedent (the ulterior value) can be instated. I do not like opera, but I judge that I might well enjoy it, if I could develop the taste. . . . So I expose myself to opera until with enough experience I (perhaps) acquire the taste. 'Worth is the tribute paid by reason to value' (ibid.).

Such judgments of worth have their parallel in scientific pursuits. Standards of rigour, of observational adequacy, of experimental design, are subject to continual re-examination, and judgments about what would constitute better scientific practice are made and refined by criticism. Judgments of worth (by no means all of them infallible) play a part in the development of any science.

But notoriously, humans do not always make judgments of worth in order either to pay a tribute of lip service, or to express an open-minded preparedness to experiment. Some unfortunate souls find they have habits, if ill-formed, of preference for certain ultimate values, which do not sustain themselves far enough to yield action to secure the necessary means. There may be several reasons for this. People may rehearse the consequences of certain activities and may not apply the outcome to their particular case. Heavy smoking leads to lung cancer, but this may not affect smokers who keep the degree of *their* habits out of mind as thought moves from heavy smoking to cancer. Or the habit which presently governs a person's activity is able to crowd out the thought of the remote consequences, which should delight or depress, please or pain. A habit manifests itself not only in overt action but in how the imagination is directed and a habit presently governing a person's activity may 'keep imagination dwelling upon those objects which are congenial to it, which feed it, and which by feeding it intensify its force, until it crowds out all thought of other objects' (M14, p. 136, drawing openly on James). The rehearsal of the outcome may in that case be more like rehearsing a play. As Aristotle put it:

> those who have just begun to learn a science can string together its phrases, but do not yet know it; for it has to become part of themselves, and that takes time; so that we must suppose that the use of language by men in an incontinent state means no more than its utterance by actors on the stage. (1147ª21–5)

For deliberation (or 'reason') to affect what is done here and now, it must be applied to the present (perceptible) situation, the relevant description of which Aristotle placed as the last premise of a practical syllogism. It then follows that a man's deliberation may fail to influence his action for one of two reasons:

> Now the last premise being an opinion about a perceptible object, and being also what determines our actions, this a man either has not when he is in a state of passion, or has it in the sense in which having knowledge did not mean knowing but only talking, as a drunken man may utter the verses of Empedocles. (1147ᵇ7–10)

When Dewey (drawing on James) writes of passion crowding out thought of other objects, he converges with Aristotle who concluded that it is 'perceptual knowledge' which is 'dragged about [like a slave, 1145ᵇ25] as a result of the state of passion' (1147ᵇ14). In neither case is the meaning of present activities clearly recognized.

It will be urged, therefore, against Dewey – for it is a common theme with commentators on Aristotle – that he leaves no room for *genuine* cases of weakness of will. No one, under the approach shared by Dewey and Aristotle, ever acts in full knowledge of what he is doing, in a way which he judges not to be best (or which he does not want). As long as his judgment relating to his present circumstances is clouded, or his perception of it crowds out thought of its long-term consequences, judgment, reason, intelligence – clear and fully operative – never wrestles with passion and loses.

Now what is identified as 'the will' that is weak in these supposed *genuine* cases of weakness of will is the bare representation of some course of action as 'the best'. But neither Aristotle nor Dewey identifies the will with a bare representation of something as the best course of action. What fail, in what are commonly called cases of weakness of will, are, for both Aristotle and Dewey, habits (*hexeis*) which make it easy for the long-term consequences of an activity to affect the direction of its present course. When Aristotle and Dewey explain the failure of the long-term, or most the comprehensively integrated, objectives to guide the course of action by claiming that certain crucial perceptions are clouded or crowded out, it is because they recognize how perception and thought interact with the dispositions which govern our behaviour. What we see, what our imagination dwells upon, what it occurs to us to consider, are connected to what we are in the habit of doing, and what our thought represents to us determines which of our dispositions (passions) dominate our activity. We have seen that for Dewey a habit of overt action overlaps the habit of the imagination to dwell on objects congenial to it and 'means special sensitiveness or accessibility to certain classes of stimuli'. Or, as Aristotle put it, 'the eye of the soul acquires its formed state not without the aid of virtue (1144ª27) – i.e. not without a set of behavioural dispositions.

Within an Aristotelian framework of moral psychology (for that is what Dewey in effect adopts), weakness of will and the strife between passion and reason are cases where more intelligently guided habits are pitted against less intelligently guided habits. It is a struggle which makes sense because it does not match contestants from logically different categories. In Hume's framework much the same struggle takes place between logically compatible contestants, viz. passions, but because our intellectual abilities have been artificially restricted to the bare ability to represent, reason or intelligence is supposed to play only a subservient role in the outcome.

What sustains, ultimately, the belief that science and our intellectual efforts generally are (and must be thought to be) separate from that part of our life which expresses our values, aspirations and desires, is, Dewey would maintain, nothing more than an artificial separation of our images of the intellectual and the motivational. But our cognitive and affective lives are both rooted in our habits of response. The very operations which refine our scientific judgments in the direction of greater objectivity can, if we undertake the effort, refine our feelings in the same direction. The philosophical doctrine, which most obscures this, is that which teaches us that the elements of our experience, our perceptions and our inclinations do not alter their character as our experience grows. It is this doctrine which obscures the role intelligence has in constituting our values and the role our values have in constituting our intellectual achievements.

If we have made progress in science over the past few centuries, there is a sense in which this had in part to be moral progress, for morals are institutionalized habits, and scientists have had to refashion the practices and institutions which foster and sustain special sensitivities or accessibilities to certain classes of stimuli, as well as standing predilections and aversions. There is no reason why, Dewey argued, humans could not undertake the same reconstruction of their social and political institutions (including those devoted to scientific research) so that our intellectual efforts generally are harnessed to the enrichment of human life. There is an optimism here which will be stigmatized as 'utopian' and dismissed as absurd. But the belief that it is absurd rests in many cases on images of the character of human intelligence and human will, which are, if nothing else, highly questionable, and not by any means the only way we have of thinking of ourselves.

VIII

Art, Intelligence and Contemplation

Section VIII.a: Temporal quality

It was Dewey's aim not only to resist the autonomy of factual discourse by insisting on the importance of the practical context in which it is of necessity situated, but also to resist the elevation of purely theoretical activity to the status of an end in itself. Thus we saw in Section VII.b how Dewey urged us to keep before our minds the implications of both the methods and the results of natural scientific activity for the possibilities of social control. In the remainder of the chapter we considered assumptions about value and human motivation, which lead to the beliefs that values are not susceptible to objective methods of inquiry, and that to allow natural scientific inquiry to be influenced by our interests in social control will result in its corruption.

The central assumption here is that human motivation, and the self which it expresses, are antecedent to, rather than shaped by the natural (regarded as including the social) environment. Desires are conceived of in the same way as sense data to the extent that sense data are treated as externally related to one another and to the world, in which lies their causal origins. In other words, desires are regarded as externally related to one another and to the world on which they exert themselves. It followed, however, from the way Dewey conceived the relationship between means and ends in the continuum of (especially practical) inquiry that this conception of human motivation is ill founded.

At the end of this chapter we will see that Dewey's resistance to elevating knowledge of nature to the status of an end-in-itself is a particular instance of a general denial that any partial aspect of human life should be regarded as possessing this status. This denial arises from a development of Dewey's view of the reciprocal relationship of means and ends, a development which yields a general account of how the continuum of practical inquiry *should* develop, and of a general human need which it should be used to fulfil. This development will occupy Sections VIII.c and VIII.d, where the basic features of Dewey's approach to the place of art and aesthetic experience in human life will be explored. Before this is undertaken, however, it will be helpful to bring Dewey's philosophical psychology to bear on aesthetic experience and contrast it with a view which sees such experience as externally related to other experience and to the world.

When Dewey called into question the 'intellectualist' account of the relation between the judgment that something is good and the experience of it as good (as we saw him do at the beginning of the previous section), it was not to segregate judgment and experience into independent categories, but to portray accurately their proper functional relationship to each other. 'Prizing', 'esteeming', 'holding dear' can all refer to experiences which have virtually no cognitive component. When judgment ('appraisal', 'estimation') is integrated into such experience it transforms it, constituting it, or its object, as something *valued*. (Hence things and activities prized without appraisal or esteemed without estimation were referred to as 'proto-values' in Section VII.c.) This process, once underway, forms an important part of the 'continuum of inquiry'; as problematic experience reveals their inadequacies, values are continually 'transvalued'.[1]

Whether the fear expressed by D. W. Prall (which was quoted at the beginning of Section VII.d) is justified, i.e. whether on Dewey's account value 'is somehow at bottom rational', depends on whether one follows Dewey in assigning to cognition more than the limited role of representing independent existences (including perhaps objective standards of value). Prall argued strenuously against the idea that judgment might have a role in 'constituting' value, and if rationality is the limited faculty Prall conceived it to be, Dewey could hardly be convicted of making value 'at bottom rational'. But Prall was clearly exercised by wider issues, viz. whether values require, or necessarily involve, any investment of thought, and whether a person's values (the things that person values) can be criticized if they have involved a relatively poor investment of thought. The answer to both questions would, for Dewey, be 'yes', and Prall's arguments were intended to remove any support for such answers.

Prall maintained that value was constituted *only* by the 'motor-affective attitudes' of a person toward the thing or activity valued (M15, p. 343). Any judgment, any experimenting with new conditions or new habituations, which may lead to changes in the motor-affective attitude in question, all lay wholly outside the thing or activity which is valued or enjoyed. Prall's argument is a paradigm application of the logic of external relations;[2] the context (causal or any other sort) of a motor-affective attitude (a preference, an emotion, a desire, etc.) has no bearing on the nature or quality, let alone the worth, of such an attitude.

For Prall the motor-affective attitude which constituted a thing as valued placed a person in a dyadic relation of 'disinterested attentiveness' to the thing valued. The emotional content of this attentiveness, which he also referred to as 'contemplation', involved at least liking if not something stronger, 'loving, adoring, worshipping' (M15, p. 348). Dewey asked how this motor-affective attitude could differ from that of the liking of a pig for swill, how indeed it could be called contemplation unless thought, indeed judgment, were a constituent of the experience (M15, p. 24). Prall happily accepted the pig as an example, but suggested a cat in the sun or a ruminating cow were better examples (Prall, 1924, p. 626). He went on to cite various descriptions of heaven as 'thoughtless contemplation': Plato's *Phaedrus*, Aristotle's God,

> Montaigne's neat eulogy of the permanent pleasure of sex intercourse, Dr. Johnson's equally pat notion of the perfect life as driving with a pretty woman, and Browning's sentimental, but barbarous *Last Ride* all give us the same notion of heaven. It is a thoughtless place; there is no judging in heaven: the Last Judgment has been made. . . .
> Value occurs instantaneously. (Ibid., p. 627)

Prall allowed that he could not provide a demonstration of this claim, other than 'just this kind of careful indication' (ibid.).

Dewey clearly regarded all such accounts as based on a deep misunderstanding of the nature of experience. We can think about a moment of experience in isolation from all that went before and think of it stripped of all elements of anticipation, but this does not prove that experience can occur in such isolated moments or that the nature of such a moment can be adequately represented in this way. (Descartes similarly found he could clearly and distinctly think of his mind in isolation from his body, but this did not prove his mind could exist without his body or could be properly understood without reference to his body.)

Dewey did not respond directly to Prall (1924). He had, however, been working his Paul Carus Lectures into the book *Experience and Nature* during the latter part of his exchange with Prall and the general position Prall defended is attacked at several levels in that book. The most general level is metaphysical. In several places Dewey diagnosed the errors he was working to combat as having their origin in 'the denial of temporal quality'. The problems which constitute modern epistemology 'have a single origin in the dogma which denies temporal quality to reality as such' (L1, p. 120). The mind/body problem has a threefold root, one fold of which is 'the ignoring of temporal quality' (L1, p. 194).[3]

'Temporal quality' is what gets left out when the structure of things is portrayed as an '*order* of succession, an order convertible into one of coexistence' (L1, p. 202). The encouragement to think of time in this way comes, Dewey believed, from the success of mathematical representations of natural processes. These representations and the habit of looking at time as a mere order of successions is one of the most powerful theoretical instruments to emerge from the seventeenth-century revolution in science. But it proceeds (although this in no way vitiates it in terms of its own purposes) by ignoring an important feature of reality which is crucial particularly to the experience of more advanced living creatures.

By virtue of organic activities being organized into 'a *series* (as distinct from a *succession*)' (L1, p. 206) there is an immediate experience of temporally distant (future) affairs in activities which are preparatory or anticipatory. (Dewey, perhaps, should also have stressed here the immediate presence of past affairs in activities which are consummatory.) 'This series forms the immediate material of thought when social communication and discourse supervene' (ibid.). And thought extends the scope whereby the temporally distant can inform the temporally immediate.[4]

In identifying the issue as metaphysical Dewey was simply indicating the generality of the question of whether temporal quality could be discounted. To dispute questions at this level does not require reaching for an 'absolute standpoint',[5] but simply carrying on the sort of dispute which, as we saw in Section VI.d, Dewey had with Spaulding. Spaulding appealed to mathematical representations of time, where each instant is represented as independent of every other to support his 'logic of external relations'. But his argument consisted in advancing from what has been a successful way of abstracting from experience for certain purposes, to employing the resulting framework as a comprehensive representation of all that we have experienced, or could experience. Dewey, who at one time expressed hostility to any kind of metaphysical enterprise, had by 1915 softened his attitude and accepted that philosophers could advance hypotheses about 'ultimate, that is irreducible, traits of existence, the very existence with which scientific reflection is concerned' (M8, p. 6). In Spaulding's case the claims being made on behalf of mathematical representations were not nonsense, but based upon the error of trying to operate with an inadequate basis of irreducible (or 'generic' – see also L1, p. 52) traits.

That considerations of quantity and mathematical order are indispensable to the successful prosecution of researches into particular occurrences is a precious fact. It exhibits certain irreducible traits *of* the irreducible traits we have mentioned [namely, diverse existences, interaction, change], but it does not replace them. When

it tries to do so it cuts the ground out from under its own feet.
(M8, p. 7)

A candid examination of the present state of our scientific understanding of ourselves and our environment will reveal that unless we acknowledge the reality of temporal quality, we will make the place of mind and knowledge in nature incomprehensible.

In the case of Prall a further metaphysical point would have to be stressed. Prall took 'To be constitutive' to mean 'to go to make up as an essential element or part in a total situation' (Prall, 1924, p. 623). Dewey on the other hand took context as well as part to be in some cases constitutive, because one of the traits of existence he recognized was (as he put it in his definition of sentience (L1, p. 197) the possibility of an 'operative presence of the whole in the part. . . .' This is what temporal quality involves with respect to temporal parts and wholes, and because Prall recognized only the presence of the part in the whole, not the whole in the part, he could see no *constitutive* role for judgment, anticipation, past experience or context generally.

The issue at this level will inevitably appear highly general and abstract, but there are important concrete implications of the dispute when it is applied to the notion of value. Specifically, how much thought is to be invested in values? Prall at one point dropped the phrase 'learning to value justly' (M15, p. 343) and Dewey seized on it (M15, p. 26): how could Prall provide a basis for the clear implication of such a phrase, that some values can be unsatisfactory, and some more satisfactory than others? Prall's reply was simply that more satisfactory human values are those motor-affective attitudes formed by humans who are 'all a human being can come to be by training in perception and feeling' (Prall, 1924, p. 628). But while this allows, as Prall put it, 'the word *justice* to mean something here', it is far from clear why this training should not include the self-developing and satisfaction-modifying influence which Dewey took to be the role of intelligence.

Section VIII.b: Imagination in experience

Experience and Nature contained a response at a less abstract level to Prall's general position, specifically to the account of aesthetic experience, which he presupposed when he assigned an aesthetic character to value generally. (Cp. '[The cow] is having elementary esthetic enjoyment in each chew . . .' (Prall, 1924, p. 626).) If Dewey stressed the importance of a cognitive contribution to value – and aesthetic values were no exception, as we shall soon see – he was far from ignoring the importance of simple and immediate enjoyments. Philosophers, he remarked (L1, p. 69), have paid insufficient attention to the things which people *directly* enjoy, such as celebrations and conversations, spectacles and sports, anything which has 'the same quality of immediate and absorbing finality' (L1, p. 71). It is toward such activities, rather than toward what are thought of as simple bodily gratifications (creature comforts) or intellectual abstractions, that human consciousness most easily gravitates. This is not the sign of living in a complicated or decadent culture, it is equally true of primitive man. 'The body is decked before it is clothed. While homes are still hovels, temples and palaces are embellished. . . . Useful labour is, whenever possible, transformed by ceremonial and ritual accompaniments, subordinated to art that yields immediate enjoyment' (L1, p. 69).

What is particularly significant about the things which humans find absorbing is the demand on mental activity which these things often involve. Not always; it is possible to find the flickering of a log fire or the pounding of surf on rocks absorbing without in any way injecting what is commonly called 'imagination' into what one sees and hears. Nevertheless it is a psychological phenomenon which is given a prominent place in the way Dewey accounts for consciousness[6] that a mind that is not drawn by its objects continually to modify itself loses consciousness, and being absorbed in fire or surf will either release daydreams or empty the mind altogether. What holds conscious attention effortlessly must call upon the mind continually to supply anticipation and interpretation without taxing its resources by leaving too many salient features which it cannot relate to the rest of what it takes in. To find a street brawl or work on a construction site absorbing, one must be able to relate to one another the episodes one witnesses and see within them a unifying structure of reasons, causes and consequences. 'Consciousness so far as it is not dull ache and torpid comfort is a thing of the imagination' (L1, p. 71).

Dewey, we saw in Section VII.d, characterizes the activity of imagination in deliberation as 'dramatic rehearsal', and when speaking of the imagination as the activity which sustains consciousness also claims it is 'primarily dramatic' (L1, p. 77). Now it may well be an important and insufficiently appreciated fact of human experience that this ability to perceive imaginatively develops around the ability to use symbolic substitutes.[7] The way a child can hold the heel of its mother's shoe to its ear with the toe in front of its mouth and declare, 'I'm on the telephone', may not only be common, but necessary to cognitive development.

But the general function which Dewey attributes to 'imagination' – 'a *way* of seeing and feeling things as they compose an integral whole' (AE, p. 267) – extends to media where rehearsal in the sense of enactment is not a plausible preliminary. A piece of music has a development which must inform the hearing of each succeeding passage and shape the anticipation of what is immediately to come (even if what does come surprises the listener) if the mind is to be conscious and the listener *hear music*. These anticipations do not have to come from the ability to perform or rehearse a performance. They may arise simply from having been exposed to the music on previous occasions or from being familiar with a musical *genre*. A picture, even a non-representational composition, must, if it is to be appreciated, be taken in by a series of focusings on various portions in which subconfigurations as well as the whole modify and inform each other as they are taken in.[8]

These are largely non-cognitive responses, but to the extent that they form part of an appreciation of the music or the picture they will be drawn into, and to some extent controlled by cognitive responses. 'According to the [conception of consciousness stated here] every mode of awareness – as distinct from [mere] feeling in its immediate existence is exactly the same sort of thing, namely a remaking of the meanings of events' (L1, p. 240). 'Meanings', the material of cognition, are according to Dewey patterns of[9] 'using and interpreting things; interpretation being always an imputation of potentiality for some consequence' (L1, p. 147).

As we read a novel or watch a drama unfold on the stage we are presented with a succession of events. Unless these are taken in *as a series* we will be unable to follow the thread of the story. Clearly we cannot hold past events and potential developments actively in our memories or they will crowd out what is happening now. These past and potential developments which give significance to whatever is presently unfolding, have to suffuse the present, not crowd it out. What focuses our attention is the partial development of the wider integrated system of meanings which constitutes the plot, together with the setting, characters, emotional materials, etc. The last of these, it should be stressed, is by no means an optional extra. Consciousness and emotion emerged simultaneously in the account Dewey first developed in 1894–6[10] and remained for him two aspects of a unitary phenomenon. Imagination 'is a *way* of seeing *and feeling* things as they compose an integral whole' (italics added to AE, p. 267, which was quoted above). 'Psychologically, deep seated needs cannot be stirred to find fulfillment in perception without an emotion and affection that, in the end, constitute the unity of the experience' (AE, p. 257).[11]

These facts are used to illustrate a general claim about the relationship of mind to consciousness (L1, p. 231)[12] which is most plausible where what is called for is a response to things which clearly transcend the concrete affairs we confront. It is not two men who live respectively in Knightsbridge and Chelsea and who pay taxes who are duelling. It is Hamlet and Laertes; and the event absorbs our attention for that reason. The point that applies to all instances of conscious awareness is the need for a sustaining framework of subconsciously apprehended relationships suffusing present events, giving them their 'drift', but which at the same time demands the remaking of those relationships to 'give this system of meanings an unexpected turn, and constitute a suspended and still indeterminate meaning, which induces alertness, expectancy' (L1, p. 232).[13]

In other words, the things which humans find it worth seeing and hearing, just for the sake of seeing and hearing them, are more successful captivators of the conscious mind, and hence more often enjoyed and for longer periods, to the extent that they involve the perception of and the remaking of meanings. The attitude taken toward such things is 'aesthetic' but not necessarily in a eulogistic sense (L1, p. 70), and the principle just stated is not (yet) a canon of artistic or aesthetic merit; it is a fact of human psychology. It applies to the 'penny-dreadful of fiction' (ibid.) and the predictable development in a piece of popular music, as well as to Shakespeare's *Hamlet* and Schubert's 'Impromptus'.

The aesthetic, then, is to be found among those activities (specifically perceptual activities) which people are able to enjoy directly; it has to do with 'the delight that attends vision and hearing, an enhancement of the receptive appreciation and assimilation of objects of production' (L1, p. 267). Such experience can occur spontaneously without the intervention of human contrivance. But the control which imagination (in the stricter sense of dramatic rehearsal) gives humans over their experiences gives them the opportunity to arrange for, preserve and enhance opportunities for aesthetic experiences. Dramatic rehearsal is itself, apart from what instrumental value it has for planning future activities, an immediately enjoyed experience enhanced by the perceptions of meanings. But the instrumental aspect of activities and things is also opportunity for such experience.

> Even the utility of things, their capacity to be employed as means and agencies, is first of all not a relation, but a quality possessed; immediately possessed, it is as esthetic as any other quality. If labor transforms an orderly sequence into a means of attaining ends, this not only converts a casual ending into a fulfillment, but it also gives labor an immediate quality of finality and consummation. Art, even fine art, is long, as well as a joy. (L1, p. 91)

Now art should not be conflated with aesthetic experience, however closely they may be related. This conflation, Dewey claims, is the source of our contemporary muddled thinking about art. 'Art' has to do with the production of things or the control of events: 'the esthetic' has to do with receptive appreciation. Dewey approaches 'art' from the direction of its older classical sense (Latin: *ars, artes;* Greek: *techne*) where rather than leave our satisfactions and enjoyments to chance we exercise intelligent control over the circumstances of their occurrence. 'Art is the sole alternative to luck' (L1, p. 279).[14]

'Art' in this sense extends over more than the familiar stereotypes of painters, sculptors, poets, playwrights, composers or performing 'artists' such as actors, musicians or dancers, which are nowadays conjured up by the word. Aristotle defined a *techne*, as 'a productive habit (*hexis*) involving a course of reasoning' (1140ª10). The idea (as elaborated at 981ª19-b14, along lines set out by Plato at *Gorgias* 465a) is that a man with a *techne* can *explain* why he does what he does. He has a clear idea of what he is trying to do, why it is worth achieving and what had to be done to achieve it. An art in this sense covers the production of instruments, things which will be used to achieve other things, as well as things to be immediately enjoyed in their own right. Our stereotypes, however, cluster around the latter, specifically around those which will yield aesthetic experience; and do not necessarily involve – and even sometimes exclude – the application of explanatory principles in the course of achieving their ends. The 'arts' of our stereotypes involve a large measure of what Plato in particular sought to exclude from *techne*, the reliance on blind (in his case 'divine') inspiration. This older sense of 'art' is still sufficiently common for the newer sense to need on occasion to be marked by the phrase 'fine art' (or an upper-case initial letter, 'Art').

The muddled thinking, which Dewey complained about, centres on this distinction, which Dewey regarded with deep hostility. He traced the separation of the two (as well as the spectator model of knowledge)[15] back to the influence which the social structure of ancient Greece exerted on its intellectual thinkers. High social status was accorded to the man of leisure, free to behold and enjoy what servile workers laboured to produce (L1, p. 80). This refined appreciation of the efforts of others became the Greek model of the approach (akin to 'the superior attitude [of] the modern esthete' – L1, p. 76) which rational thought should adopt to the evidently more lofty objects of the understanding. The clean and idle hands of the gentlemen thus came to be incorporated in the stereotype of the knowledge state, and when in later centuries experience was claimed to be the foundation of knowledge, it was thought necessary for it to wash and fold its hands in order for its claims to be taken seriously. The Greeks, at least, had a sounder conception of experience. The notion of *empeiria* (from a verb meaning to attempt, to try, to make a trial of) was, as Dewey says, 'the outcome of accumulation of practical acts, sufferings and perception gradually built up into the skill of the carpenter, shoemaker, pilot, farmer, general and politician' (L1, p. 178).

There is, however, an oversimplification in Dewey's view of this part of the social history of ideas, enough to amount to distortion, even of the reading of the texts. It is not the case that for the Greeks 'experience is equivalent to art' (L1, p. 266). The two were sharply distinguished by both Plato (*Gorgias* 465a) and Aristotle (981ª29-b14). The sharp social division between labouring and genteel classes owes more to Hegel's famous dialectic of Lorship and Bondage[16] than it does to the social structure of fourth-century Athens. 'Artists' in classical times did not form a homogeneous class, but someone who could claim to possess a *techne* would not have been regarded as a labourer, as among the 'living tools' of *Politics* 1253[b]30, the 'artisans' of *Metaphysics* 981[b]5, 'who make but do not know what they make' in the way a fire makes ashes. While it may have been true that despised practitioners of the 'art' of sculpture[17] provided Greek thinkers with 'ready-made to hand and eye a realm of esthetic objects with traits of order and proportion, form and finality' (L1, p. 79), not by any means all practitioners of the (fine) arts – e.g. painting, music, dramatic poetry – had the status of the *banausoi*.

When one appreciates the social implications of the campaign which Dewey mounted against the distinction between exclusively 'fine' (in the sense of *fin*al) and exclusively 'useful' art, it becomes clear that the oversimplifications made about Greek society reflect worries about general tendencies in our own society. Such worries by their nature oversimplify matters in precisely the way Dewey's view of the social history of ideas is oversimplified. The worries themselves bring together a great deal of what animates the various doctrines which Dewey advanced, and fortunately the cogency of the worries, and of the criticisms they engender, does not rest on the detailed accuracy of Dewey's picture of the classical past.

Section VIII.c: Genuine instrumentality

On the surface Dewey's hostility to any absolute distinction between fine and useful art appears to be little more than a high-minded desire to bring refined and popular culture closer together, to 'democratize Art'. There is, to be sure, a tendency in our culture, which may perhaps have been even more pronounced in Dewey's day, to separate things which give absorbing satisfaction to our perceptual capacities from things which engage more than our perceptual capacities. We put the former in museums or use them as status symbols and sound investments (L1, p. 273), but do not connect their qualities to the perceptual satisfactions which everyday objects may or may not afford.

The result is impoverishment on both sides. So-called fine art becomes esoteric, and even the 'new training of modes of perception' (L1, p. 293) which it affords is not applied outside Sotheby's or the Tate. Little heed is paid to the immediate perceptual qualities of everyday objects unless they have been imported from another culture or originate in another period of our own history (L1, p. 283: cp. AE, Chapter 1). At the same time effort is invested in 'design' only where it is likely to affect the exchange value of commodities and vast areas of our artifact-structured environment are left offering little to satisfy the eyes and ears. Against this tendency it is salutary to proclaim, 'Any activity that is productive of objects whose perception is an immediate good and whose operation is a continual source of enjoyable perception of other events exhibits fineness of art' (L1, p. 274).

It is possible, Dewey admits, to draw some kind of distinction between fine and useful art. 'It is tempting to make a distinction of degree and say that a thing belongs to the sphere of use when perception of its meaning is incidental to something else; and that a thing belongs to fine art when its other uses are subordinate to its use in perception' (L1, p. 283). But, he insists, this distinction has no more than 'rough practical value'. What Dewey is resisting here is in part a certain conception of how human actions are related to their ends. One species of this conception is reflected in the idea that value is constituted solely in a contemplative 'aesthetic' response to some thing or activity. In general the conception takes it that human thought and action are external means to human satisfactions, that all desires and appetites are for a certain modification (viz. pleasurable) of the organs of sensory reception, that we act in order to attain a state of pleasant (or at least not unpleasant) stimulation, in other words act for 'the occurrence of an event having immediate and static qualities' (L1, p. 276).

This pattern reflects what our economic regime inflicts on a great many people, routine productive exertions undertaken as (or to give) the means to 'spasms of excited escape from the thraldom of enforced work'. 'The idea that work, productive activity, signifies action carried on for merely extraneous ends, and the idea that happiness signifies surrender of mind to the thrills and excitations of the body are one and the same idea' (L1, p. 271). And this idea is the antithesis of 'art'. 'Useful' when applied to 'art' places the stress on production, while 'fine' places it on consumption, but these are 'adjectives which, when they are prefixed to "art," corrupt and destroy its intrinsic significance'.

> For arts that are merely useful are not arts but routines; and arts that are merely final are not arts but passive amusements and distractions, different from other indulgent dissipations only in dependence upon a certain acquired refinement or 'cultivation.' (Ibid.)

Appeal to the 'intrinsic significance' of anything will naturally arouse suspicions. How, to begin with, can Dewey move from 'art' in roughly its classical sense (intelligent control as an alternative to luck) to insisting that art is not art unless it celebrates a perpetual union of the instrumental and the consummatory, the useful and the final? If 'art' extends over any intelligently applied body of techniques then sewage disposal, designing assembly lines and keeping business accounts are arts; and unless their practitioners are ineffective or inefficient, it is silly to complain that these are arts whose intrinsic significance has been corrupted. Surely the practitioners of useful arts do not have to give any thought to the final ends of their activities, they just have to produce or perform what is required of them – what other people have determined their aims to be – as intelligently and inventively as they can. It is the intelligence and inventiveness they put into realizing the end given to them, which means their efforts are not mere routine and their success not a matter of luck.

Nevertheless because of the multiple consequences of any means which one may choose to adopt, and because of the principle introduced in Section VII.b above, the reciprocal character of means and ends, intelligent practitioners of an ostensibly useful art who are seeking improved means to some end must also bear in mind how their original end may be enhanced or corrupted by what they choose. Merely to adopt some means because it *looks* like an improvement is to surrender an important part of intelligent practice to routine, the success of which can only be a matter of luck. 'It is right to object to much of current practice on the ground that it is routine' (ibid.), and even where a routine procedure may be modified to keep it productive of a goal which itself is only routinely determined, we still lack art in the full sense. If, instead of 'arbitrarily cut[ting] short our consideration of consequences', we 'honestly and fully faced' them (L1, p. 272), we would probably find reason for regarding our so-called useful arts detrimental.

> They are useful to make shoes, houses, motor cars, money and other
> things which *may* then be put to use; here inquiry and imagination
> stop. What they also *make* by way of narrowed, embittered and
> crippled life, of congested, hurried, confused and extravagant life,
> is left in oblivion. (L1, p. 272)

All this may be true, will come the reply, but to lay the blame for this on the separation of means and ends, the useful and final, is to obscure an important and perfectly serviceable category. Some things just *are* irreducibly instrumental, e.g. to the maintenance of life, to the elimination of discomfort, to the activities which we find absorbing in themselves. To which Dewey would reply that although the category is widely used, ingrained in our habits of thought, its serviceability is questionable, for it obscures from us our potentialities as creatures who simultaneously think and feel. The conception of means and ends in common use is an obstacle to clear thought about human fulfilment.

In Section VII.b two ways of understanding the relation of means to ends were outlined, *instrumental* – typified by the relation of 2 × 20p to a cup of coffee – and *constitutive* – typified by the relation of coffee beans to a cup of coffee. It is the domination over our thought of the former sense of means – 'things that are only external and accidental antecedents of the happening of something else' (L1, p. 274) – which

Dewey deplores, and he quotes from Aristotle's *Politics* to illustrate what he does not like: 'When there is one thing that is means and another thing that is end, there is *nothing common* between them, except in so far as the one, the means, produces, and the other, the end, receives the product' (L1, p. 227, quoting 1328a29–31).[18] What is wrong with this concept is not that it is false or inapplicable, but that it so dominates our thinking that it obscures the other, the constitutive, relation, which is, Dewey believes, more properly that of means to ends, a relation in which means constitute 'a genuine instrumentality' (L1, p. 276). He cites (ibid.), as proper examples of the relation, paints and skill in relation to a picture; tone and susceptibility of ear in relation to music ('because they constitute, make, are, music'); flour, water, yeast to bread; sound institutions of government to the prosperous life of the community ('because they are integrated portions of that life').[19]

Dewey indulges here in a piece of hyperbole which does not serve to clarify his position; he says 'external and accidental antecedents' 'are not means at all' (L1, p. 274). But a more cautious account of his position is that external means always present us with an unfinished task, with a problem, '*the* problem of experience' (L1, p. 277), the problem of how to convert such external means or instruments into something which is in Dewey's view more worthy of the name 'means'.

There is no particular significance in the fact that Dewey's star examples of 'genuine means' exist contemporaneously with their ends, while what he decries (external antecedents, relations of succession) do not coexist with their ends. The former are simply the most readily grasped examples of the relationship which he prizes, organic unity ('A genuine instrumentality *for* is always an organ *of* an end' (L1, p. 276)). It is possible, we have seen, to have an organic unity over time; a piece of music, the plot of a story, must have a temporal structure, must be unified by a temporal quality, which gives its episodes more coherence than simply one thing following another ('bare succession in time') – there has to be 'a deposit at each stage and point entering cumulatively and constitutively into the outcome' (ibid.).

This last phrase comes from one of several not altogether successful attempts on Dewey's part to explain his special means/end relation. 'Means are always at least causal conditions' (L1, p. 275). What more is required? – 'being freely used, because of perceived connections with chosen consequences' (ibid.). But someone may freely insert two coins into a vending machine because of a perceived connection between doing that and the choice of having a cup of coffee. The labourer freely toils because he perceives a connection between toil and his wage. How can Dewey cite (ibid.) this man's toil in relation to his wage or livelihood as a misapplication of the notion of means? True, the man is in a sense coerced in that he must toil to receive a wage, but so is a painter under an 'enforced necessity' to apply paint to a surface if she wants to produce a picture. The labourer seems to have an even greater degree of freedom than the painter: 'He might – and frequently does – equally well or ill – perform any one of a hundred other tasks as a condition of receiving payment' (ibid.).

To explain Dewey's position using the notions of 'perceived connection' and 'freedom' vs. 'coercion' requires some care. One possible avenue of approach lies in the contrast which Dewey draws between human and non-human existence:

> . . . in nature, outside of man, except when events eventuate in
> 'development' or 'evolution' (in which a cumulative carrying
> forward of consequences of past histories in new efficiencies occurs)
> antecedent events are external transitive conditions of the occurrence
> of an event having immediate and static qualities. (L1, p. 276)

Non-human animals (which develop and whose species evolve) can only act out of blind habit (instinctive or acquired) to satisfy their needs. Their 'acts have no meaning'; they do not perceive any connection between what they do and the satisfactions (immediate and static qualities) which they receive. Humans begin on this level, pushed by blind appetite down channels of action cut by their previous responses when interacting with the environment. They make use of things and events, but their interactions are not with 'objects, or things-with-meanings'.

What makes the crucial difference for human beings is that they have acquired the ability to perceive the consequences (and hence the meanings) of events.

> When appetite is perceived in its meanings, in the consequences it
> induces, and these consequences are experimented with in reflective
> imagination, some being seen to be consistent with one another, and
> hence capable of co-existence and of serially ordered achievement,
> others being incompatible, forbidding conjunction at one time, and
> getting in one another's way serially – when this estate is attained,
> we live on the human plane, responding to things in their meanings.
> (L1, p. 278)

The tasks assigned to 'reflective imagination' reveal that it is an important misunderstanding of Dewey's position to think that an animal which responds to the perceptible signs, of whatever will satisfy its appetite, perceives the meanings (consequences) of those signs, or the meanings of its appetites, or the meanings of the exertions which those signs prompt it to undertake (such as following, stalking, pouncing, killing and eating). As long as *one* appetite produces *one* pattern of response to a class of similar signs, the animal cannot be said to perceive *meanings*. The plural, which Dewey frequently uses, is significant. What is required to reach the human plane is (1) the ability to respond in *several* ways to an impulse (of appetite or whatever); (2) the ability to rehearse the consequences of *each* channel of response, without actually responding; (3) the ability to see how *each of these* sets of consequences will close or leave open channels for the exercise of *other* appetites ('some being seen to be consistent with one another, and hence capable of co-existence . . . others being incompatible . . . getting in one another's way'); (4) the ability to coordinate *several* possible channels of response into a single complex response ('serially ordered achievement').

There are two features sufficiently general to merit being called 'logical features' of what it is which an animal on the human plane must be able to perceive in the consequences of its responses, viz. compatibility and incompatibility relations. From the latter, it must make selections so that its end, what it aims at, is articulated by the former sort of relations. Even if an animal's total pattern of response over some period fits together coherently so that it prospers, we remain reluctant, because of what we know of animal abilities in general, to say that its responses are governed by the perception of the harmony in that pattern. (If tempted, we will avoid doing so directly by personifying nature; in human affairs similar circumstances will prompt us to personify providence.) It is for this reason that Dewey would say that such an animal did not perceive the meaning of its actions or appetites.

Now the elements that go into a set of responses, when those responses are governed by the perception in each of them of their contribution to a unitary pattern, are the *means* (in the sense of constituents) of the achievement of that pattern as an end. This is the means/end relationship in Dewey's favoured sense. It is clear why Dewey's illustrations of this favoured sense feature wholes and constituent parts, and why 'external' characterizes the notion which he opposes; for a constituent is internal to the unity to which it contributes. The labourer's toil (his job) is not means to a livelihood if it does not enter into a life in which that occupation was selected from among many possible ones to harmonize with a conception of what it is to have a life or livelihood that will be worth a human's (that particular human's) living it.

The freedom which human beings have over their (genuine) means is the freedom which arises from possessing a wider view of what they are doing and of its consequences. This wider view will make available to them more possible avenues of response than are open to creatures which are blind to their situation. It will also present avenues as closed (by reason of unwelcome remote consequences) which creatures unable to see as far (and as wide, i.e. the variety of possibilities, which remote consequences will influence) will regard as open channels for their impulses. Even it if seems that thereby foresight (insight into meanings) narrows scope for action it remains a liberating capacity, for whoever possesses it is less forced into 'servile submission to accident' (L1, p. 279), less coerced by fortune, possesses an alternative to luck.

Section VIII.d: The characteristic human need

The suspicion which a phrase like 'intrinsic significance' arouses is that we are having the meanings of our words twisted and stretched. This is undeniably what Dewey is perpetrating. Behind the 'intrinsic significance of "art" ' is the notion of 'genuine instrumentality', which Dewey would like to see supplant the more familiar notion. Ordinary linguistic practice, however, obscures some matters as well as embodying clarity about others; and it reinforces baseless prejudice as well as preserving a kind of wisdom. There is not much to be gained by arguing over meanings, intrinsic or otherwise. But there is at stake here an idea and an ideal.

The idea lies at the heart of Dewey's main doctrines. It is that some of the things which we do, and some of the things we interact with, are distinguished by their role in wider unities which we set ourselves to realize. These wider comprehensive unities, what Dewey calls 'ends-in-view', inform our perception of events or things and change them, both *for us* (alter our perceptions of them and the satisfactions we take in or from them) and *in themselves*, for, we have seen,[20] our altered perceptions alter their potentialities for physical interactions. Dewey illustrates with the familiar example of building a house. The house as end-in-view informs 'each stage of the process [of building]; it is present as the *meaning* of the materials used and the acts done' (L1, p. 280). As meaning (pattern of using and interpreting – which is evidently bound up with the perception of potential consequences), the end-in-view guides the next stage and possibly also the development of the idea of the end-in-view.[21]

One important consequence of this idea is contained in the ideal, which was referred to above. The perceptions of things as constituents of wider unities not only can and do inform our satisfactions, it is right and proper that they should do so. We have it in our power to transform our situation so that more of the bare external relations of uniform succession are transformed into means in the favoured sense. This takes place when they are incorporated in our wider purposes, and our success in achieving this may well be helped by an understanding of the causal mechanisms underlying such bare relations, as when someone comes to an understanding of the mechanisms that link coins to coffee in a vending machine so as to be able to repair or design such a machine, or comes in an analogous way to understand a natural process. But until taken up into our purposes and projects, the results of our efforts to understand yield meanings but not means in the favoured sense. For it is not enough to find a meaning 'determined in terms of consequences hastily snatched at and torn loose from their connnections'; for that will only prevent 'the formation of wider and more enduring ideas . . . that unite wide and enduring scope with richness of distinctions' (L1, p. 278).

The ideal at stake is the proper understanding of what it is for human beings to be free, to rise above and take control of their situations. It is not advanced by a starry-eyed optimist. 'It is part of wisdom to recognize how sparse and insecure are such accomplishments in comparison with experience in which physical and animal nature largely have their own way' (ibid.). But it does not follow that the ideal is not worth pursuing. Nor is the ideal one which is too vague to apply to concrete situations. Dewey's comparison of the conditions of wage-earners (the degree of control they have over their lives)[22] to existence on an animal level and his linking of means, conceived of as external relations of succession, to the dignity (or lack of it) of labour, are thinly veiled political statements. Whether or not one sympathizes with Dewey's politics, these implications of his philosophic position reveal by contrast that those who cannot view things and events in the world except in their individual separateness, who profess not to see any connections but those of contiguity and regular succession, for whom context makes no difference to perception or satisfaction, hold a position which lends strength to the counsels of complacency. For they render invisible the basis of Dewey's criticism of an 'economic régime' (L1, p. 275) which is still with us.

At the bottom is an issue not of fact but of the status of fact. For Dewey claims:

> The characteristic human need is for possession and appreciation of the meaning of things, and this need is ignored and unsatisfied in the traditional notion of the useful. We identify utility with the external relationship that some events and acts bear to other things that are their products, and thus leave out the only thing that is essential to the idea of utility, inherent place and bearing in experience. (L1, p. 272)

There is no doubt that people do on occasion express the desire to 'understand the meaning' of various things or events and that also on occasion they are satisfied; they come to *feel* the inherent place and bearing of events or acts. But from many familiar philosophic perspectives these phenomena appear to be fabrics woven from subjective attitudes and responses and draped over an experience whose events in themselves lack meanings, lack any unities that would give them an inherent place and bearing. To see in this fabric a 'characteristic human need' is from this perspective vastly to overrate what is only the whim of a number of over-sensitive souls. That many people do not (any longer, if they ever did) appear to feel this need is not a condemnation of our culture, its opportunities and its educational institutions, but evidence that 'need' is a misnomer.

The view of experience and of nature, which supports this hard line, goes hand in hand with a policy of confining the notion of meaning to the 'formal mode of speech'. Meaning belongs to linguistic entities (or according to some views to psychical or intentional entities) not to the material mode of speech, not to things spoken or thought about. Dewey's approach, we have seen,[23] has no respect for this policy, for it is a crippling restriction on our thinking about the possible ways in which one thing may signify another. No attention is paid by the hard liners to the aspect of meaning which Dewey labels 'sense' as opposed to 'signification'.[24] Signifying comes to be treated exclusively on the model of assigning an arbitrary (conventional) sign to some object, as though the only way one experience could signify another is like the red light signifying danger. There can be thus no connection between sign and object of the kind which Dewey would classify as genuinely instrumental; neither is a constituent of the other, and both are constituents of a whole (social practice) only because of an adventitious association made somewhere in human history. And with our thinking about the sign relation restricted in this way we are led by the spirit of Hume to see relationships between events as wholly and irreducibly external.

As a consequence we find inexplicable the familiar experience of having a relationship, which has hitherto been for us no more than external, receive an explanation and come to be understandable. And we come to doubt that this experience is anything more than an illusion, for if Hume is right there is nothing for humans to understand. But our faith in our own intellectual experience is made vulnerable because we are blinded[25] to the way in which placing an object of 'crude macroscopic experience – the sun, earth, plants and animals of common everyday life' (L1, p. 16) – in a wider context alters the meaning of that object.

> But when the secondary objects, the refined objects, are employed
> as a method or road for coming at them [i.e. the primary objects,
> their] qualities cease to be isolated details; they get the meaning
> contained in a whole system of related objects; they are rendered
> continuous with the rest of nature and take on the import of the
> things they are now seen to be continuous with. (Ibid.)

By 'secondary objects', 'refined objects', Dewey means the objects ostensibly referred to in our scientific theories. 'They *explain* the primary objects [of crude macroscopic experience], they enable us to grasp them with *understanding*, instead of just having sense-contact with them' (ibid.). They are instruments; but by now it is clear just how far Dewey's 'instrumentalism' is from the positivist doctrine which trades under the same name. Positivist instrumentalism is based on the concept of instrument as externally related to its end. Dewey's cognitive instruments are 'genuine instruments', constituents of that to which they stand as means, viz. understanding. His doctrine expresses the drive to understand things in terms of organic interrelatedness, which characterized his thinking and personality from the start of his career.

It follows from this account that there should be something closely akin to aesthetic experience in scientific thought and Dewey does not overlook what amounts to a confirmation of one aspect of his general approach.

> The thinker has his esthetic moment when his ideas cease to be mere ideas and become the corporate meaning of objects. The artist has his problems and thinks as he works, but his thought is more immediately embodied in the object. Because of this comparative remoteness of his end, the scientific worker operates with symbols, words and mathematical signs. The artist does his thinking in the very qualitative media he works in, and the terms lie so close to the object that he is producing that they merge directly into it. (AE, pp. 15–16)

And Aristotle was no doubt under the influence of this cognitively generated quasi-aesthetic experience when he characterized the activity of a person who had achieved understanding as 'contemplating' (*theorein*) the objects of this understanding – the same verb which characterizes the activity of a spectator in relation to a drama or to a work of art generally (see 1122ᵇ14–24).

What is to be contemplated is fairly clear from the account which Aristotle gives of the articulation of a demonstrative science (*episteme*, body of understanding). It is a structure of links between the terms which occur in propositions, so that the propositions can be deductively strung together. The exercise of the contemplative understanding of some object must consist in dwelling upon it with the thought of it informed by its place in that structure.

About the conduct of the activity which *generates* this body of understanding, Aristotle leaves little more than scattered hints, but one suggestion that he recognized its productive nature is contained in an otherwise obscure classification of the premises of a syllogism as the matter ('that from which') of the conclusion (195ᵇ12; 94ᵇ25–34). This should not be thought of as a production of a conclusion from two or more premises found lying about. For in the *Posterior Analytics* Aristotle describes the problem of the scientific investigator as that of finding middle terms which can be used to form a chain of essentially linked connections between the terms of a true, but not self-explanatory, proposition, so as to permit a series of deductive steps which will constitute an explanation of that proposition. The search, in other words, is for a kind of intellectual material out of which to constitute the proposition to be explained.

Dewey's account of the reasoning that takes place in the 'art of thinking', the product of which is knowledge, is strikingly similar.

> Premises are the analysis of a conclusion into its logically justifying grounds; there are no premises till there is a conclusion.[26]
> Conclusion and premise are reached by a procedure comparable to the use of boards and nails in making a box; or of paint and canvas in making a picture. (L1, pp. 283–4)

Section VIII.e: Nothing in nature is exclusively final

Aristotle, notoriously, regarded the demonstrative explanation as something to be appreciated quite independently of the work undertaken to produce the intellectual product, which serves as the vehicle of the understanding. He held this as part of the general outlook which left productive activity without any claim to constitute living well or flourishing, for to count as flourishing an activity had to be done entirely for its own sake, not for the sake of something else (e.g. a product). This line of reasoning not only treats production as merely useful, it runs contrary to a part of Dewey's doctrine which regards the exclusively final as contrary to the 'intrinsic significance of "art" '. This in turn reflects a general hostility on Dewey's part to any category comprising things or events exclusively final (cp. 'nothing in nature is exclusively final' – L1, p. 99). But although Dewey's case against art which is merely useful has been laid out, it has not touched the Aristotelian attitude toward the products of the art of thinking, nor the formally similar attitude of the 'modern esthete' toward the products of what are commonly called the fine arts.

Aristotle's argument is based on what is essentially the same distinction in the narrower field of human action and in the wider field of happening in general. In the narrower field he distinguished activity (*praxis*) from production (*poiesis*) (1094a3–6); the former appears to be a species of actualization (*energeia*), while the latter is clearly a species of change (*kinesis*) (1174a14–1175a3. Production and change are distinguished by having an end which is not realized until the happening in question is no longer taking place. Actualization and activity, on the other hand, have ends which are realized during the whole of the time they take place. Thus building a temple (production) and recovering from a disease (change) have as their ends a temple and health, but these are not realized until the building and the recovering are over and done with, no longer taking place; until then we cannot say that a temple had been built or a recovery has taken place. Seeing something (actualization) and taking part in public life (activity), however, are such that at any point during the time they take place we can say that the object has been seen, the person has taken part in public life.

Aristotle held that to be a component of living well or flourishing, an action would have to be done for its own sake, and no production is undertaken for its own sake, but for the sake of something that comes into being when it is no longer taking place. On the other hand the exercise of sensory capacities, participation in public life and the exercise of the intellect (in contemplating the objects of nature, of mathematics or of reality as such) are all actions which can be done for their own sake, for they have the 'ends', which define what they are, 'within them', i.e. fully realized the whole of the time they take place.

This line of reasoning and its conclusions reflect from Dewey's perspective not only the general social disdain in which Greek aristocrats and their intellectual spokesmen held the labouring class, they manifest that neglect of temporal quality to which he traced many of our modern philosophic problems.[27] Aristotle, whose thinking is profoundly permeated by the concept of organic unity applied to things (plants, animals, artifacts) whose parts exist simultaneously, seems not to have been able to apply the concept as readily to temporal wholes, to series such as productions. Applying the notion of temporal quality, and the unity it bestows, to production puts Dewey in a postion to undermine the sharp distinction between actualization and change (particularly if the change is a development).

There is a sense in which activity takes place during the whole of a production, activity that could be undertaken for its own sake as well as for the sake of the product. (Someone may write murder mysteries because she enjoys writing them, not just to receive the royalties.) And the product, the end-in-view, we have seen, informs every stage and procedure of a production such as building a house. The end-in-view is present at each stage of the process; it is present as the *meaning* of the materials used and acts done (L1, p. 280). But this response only attacks yet again the idea of exclusively useful action, urging us to bear in mind that it may (ideally should) also be final. This does not yet show why there cannot be things and activities which are exclusively final, which exist or take place for the sake of their being perceived, for the aesthetic experience which they yield.

Labour, we have seen,[28] can acquire that 'immediate quality of finality and consummation' which constitutes an experience as aesthetic. This applies to the 'labour' of the scientific theorist, who also, we have just seen, 'has his esthetic moment' (AE, p. 15). But the fact that productive activity of all kinds affords aesthetic experience still leaves what appears to be a sharp and apparently viable distinction between those labourers whose products are readily accessible material for the aesthetic experiences of others and those whose products can only be appreciated by people capable of the same productive feats. It is possible for people who produce theories, pieces of machinery, or market gardens to find that in their efforts the elements of their actions which are regular or repetitious and elements which are novel or contingent 'sustain and inform each other' (L1, p. 271). But they have not failed if these traits do not sustain and inform each other in the eyes of those who behold their works.

We saw at the beginning of Section VIII.c that Dewey was prepared to allow 'rough practical value' to the idea that 'a thing belongs to fine art when its other uses are subordinate to its use in perception' (L1, p. 283). 'Other uses' here include more than the nominal or adventitious functions which, say, a fine (to behold) chest of drawers may perform, e.g. holding clothes, barricading a door. Dewey points out the role of the 'fine arts' in experimenting with perceptible material to yield 'new training of modes of perception' (L1, p. 293).[29] This, as he notes, by no means assigns to fine art the role of producing 'final goods' for this is an instrumental (educative) role. 'This is a genuine service; but only an age of combined confusion and conceit will arrogate to works that perform this special utility the exclusive name of fine art' (ibid.).

Education might in any case be dismissed as not really part of the 'intrinsic significance of (fine) art'. On the other hand, if it is permissible to appeal to what constitutes an artistic achievement as Great Art, in order to draw conclusions about the intrinsic significance of (fine) art, it might be argued that an educative role of some kind is part of the intrinsic significance of (fine) art. Dewey argues that the so-called 'eternal' quality which Great Art is supposed to possess is nothing more than 'its renewed instrumentality for further consummatory experiences' (L1, p. 274). This does not mean merely that more than one person living in more than one age or culture should be able to experience the same or a similar absorbingly final perception of the object. Given the dependence of aesthetic experience on the 'perception of meanings' it is virtually impossible that people in widely differing times and places should interact with such an object in the same or closely similar ways. What the object must be is 'indefinitely instrumental to *new* satisfying events' (ibid.), capable of acting as the cause of the perception of new meanings.

This feature of what constitutes an object as *distinctively* fine art carries over to those more ephemeral objects, performances. Even before the advent of recording techniques, a performance of a play or a piece of music need not have been an event which was exclusively the terminus of causal influences, the consequences of a variety of factors but with no consequences of its own. A performance can set a bench-mark for future interpretations of a play or a piece of music. A performance can alter the perceptions of its audience, who will thereafter experience performances of that play or piece of music, and possibly others, in quite different ways: '. . . a genuinely esthetic object is not exclusively consummatory, but is causally productive as well' (ibid.).

Very well, what constitutes Greatness of Art suggests that fine art can aspire to be more than final, more than something the function of which is only to afford aesthetic experience. But is there anything wrong with things or activities which do not achieve greatness, which perhaps are no more than entertaining? Entertainment may not be what we normally think of as the sole function of fine art, but it may be that in pursuing the argument we have been too quick to let our thinking about fine – in the sense of final – art be directed towards fine – in the sense of noble – art. Dewey's philosophic position is as hostile to the whole category of the purely fine as it is to the merely useful. But in this case is there more than a snobbishness about some people's simple pleasures in unedifying entertainment?

To see what more might lie behind Dewey's hostility to the exclusively final, it is intructive to turn again to Aristotle's philosophy and consider the precarious position of any activity which is both instrumental and final, when it stands alongside a category of activities which are exclusively final. The three examples of Aristotelian actualizations mentioned above, sense perception,[30] participation in public life and contemplation, answer to the three main candidates which Aristotle considers for what might constitute a fulfilled, flourishing, 'happy' (*eudaimon*) human life. The serious consideration which Aristotle gave to the second of these reveals the inadequacy of any representation of Athenian society of Aristotle's days as divided into active producers and indolent consumers.

But, as he recognized, acting in concert with other people, deliberating, taking and giving counsel, issuing orders and arranging affairs, is done in order to provide *for* something. This something can only be a human life that counts as fulfilled, blessed, *eudaimon*. So action of this sort cannot itself constitute the answer to what human flourishing consists in, for ultimately it is specified as an instrument for achieving just that. Confronted by this argument, and probably not at all reluctant (in the light of his profession) to accept the conclusion, Aristotle turned (1145a7–11) to the exercise of philosophical wisdom in contemplation (*theoria*) as the activity that must constitute human flourishing, as the activity for which political and practical wisdom arranges affairs so that it might take place.

Aristotle's conclusion (ibid., and in *Nicomachean Ethics* X.6–8) that only intellectual contemplation can constitute a truly flourishing human life seems unjustifiably narrow. But it is clear from this attempt to justify the conclusion that it is not sufficient to hold (as we have seen Dewey urge) that activities, which Aristotle would classify as productions, in fact have the logical features of actions and therefore can be done for their own sake *as well as* for the sake of something else. For Aristotle is ultimately drawn by the assumption that for an activity to constitute a life of human flourishing it must be done for its own sake and for the sake of *nothing else*. One might stop Aristotle's argument simply by denying this assumption; but the very possibility that there is a specific category of activity which can be engaged in for its own sake, and only for its own sake, is a category of activity which is in an important respect beyond criticism, and for that reason dangerous.

When an activity is regarded as done for its own sake and for the sake of nothing else, the means chosen for its realization, the manner of its conduct, and the impact which it has elsewhere can be criticized only as these bear on whether more or less of that activity can be engaged in. The disquieting implications of such a category emerge in the criticisms of Aristotle's doctrine of the role of philosophic contemplation in a truly flourishing human life, which centre on the fantasy of a man who commits serious crimes in order to provide himself with what is necessary to conduct pure scientific research.[31] (Pure scientific research being a not implausible modern gloss on 'philosophic wisdom', any benefit for humanity which might arise from the man's activity is strictly irrelevant.) The only basis for criticizing such a person is that, if his crimes are discovered, he might then be prevented from carrying out his research. But if he can get away with it . . . ?

A central concern of much moral philosophy revolves around the problem (going back to the story of Gyges in Book II of Plato's *Republic*) of what argument can be mounted to dissuade a man who has the means (the power or cunning) to indulge himself at the expense of other people. That answer is that nothing can be said if the man regards whatever it is he proposes to indulge in as something to be done for its own sake and not for the sake of anything else. For unless one can appeal to the effects which the proposed indulgence will have on a wider range of concerns, unless one can consider how the act bears on other things also desired for their own (although not necessarily *just* for their own) sakes, there are no places where rational leverage can be applied to the man's course of action.

Dewey takes the course of denying that there are any activities which may be regarded as done for their own sake and not for the sake of anything else. To reconcile us to what might seem (and would certainly have seemed to Aristotle) a vicious infinite regress, Dewey claims that all intelligently guided human activity, i.e. all activity that is art and is not a matter of blind impulse and routine habit, is a process of bringing unity and thereby meaning to what would be unconnected tendencies and possibilities in things and events. Like an Aristotelian activity or actualization, this process does not need to stop as soon as it is realized, it can continue as long as human ingenuity and endurance can sustain it.

IX

Ideals

Section IX.a: Public and private

The 'thoroughly reciprocal character of means and ends' meant, we saw in Section VII.b, that not only do ends constrain and provide the standard of adequacy for means, but means, as they are hit upon, refine and enlarge ends (or 'ends-in-view'). In the previous chapter we saw Dewey go beyond this claim to urge us to seek means in order to refine and expand our ends, and to treat our ends as open in this way so that our means could become constituents of our ends, i.e. 'genuine instruments'. The answer to the question why we should do this lies in the thought traced out in Section VIII.c, that doing so is part of what enables human beings to escape the contingencies of their existence, and thereby to act freely.

It might well be difficult, however, to recognize that what is at stake is the question of freedom. It is easy enough to grasp how hitting upon new means, conceived of as 'external' instruments, may be said to increase our freedom. We are, as a result of such innovations, better able to get what we want. But the claim, that inquiry into ends-in-view (and values) is an indispensable part of increasing our freedom, seems to be unsupportable. In part this is the effect of familiar images of the nature of inquiry into matters of fact (which yield new means and instruments) and here issues about the nature of inquiry explored in Chapters V and VI will in Section IX.c below bear in an important way on the argument.

But the main source of the feeling that this claim is unsupportable lies in a set of assumptions exposed and called into question in a variety of contexts in the preceding chapters. It is a consequence of these assumptions that individual human selves and their ends, what they desire, are givens, and these givens function as absolute constraints on inquiries rather than as features, as much in need of reconstruction as any other features of the problematic situations, which arise in human life. Before looking for the last time at this set of assumptions in the final two sections, this chapter will consider how in Dewey's view these assumptions give rise to distorted conceptions of our relationships as individuals to our institutions of government and of their (supposed) democratic character.

Under these distortions it is probably easier for us to follow Aristotle when he dismisses political action as the supreme end in life (that which by itself constitutes human flourishing) than it is to see why excelling in political (or military) affairs should be a candidate in the first place. To most citizens in our culture, political affairs are at best that part of the external trappings (indispensable conditions) needed to have their lives free of nuisance and interference from inconsiderate fellow citizens and predatory foreigners. Some people make a living as elected officials or civil servants and some no doubt find this rewarding, but to suggest such people are in an ideal position to fulfil themselves as human beings or that organized society exists for the sake of political activity is no more convincing than the same claim made about philosophers and their activity. Aristotle at least saw through the first claim:

> But the action of the statesman . . . aims – beyond the political action itself – at acquiring power and honours; or if [the action of the statesman aims] at happiness (*eudaimonia*), for himself and his fellow citizens, this happiness is different from political action, and evidently sought as something different. (1177b12–15)

Political ambition for some people, however, is more than just the pursuit of one among many possible careers. Participation in decision making affords a sense of freedom which is not available to those who have decisions made over their heads. Prominence in public life affords recognition and respect (fearful, if not admiring) from one's fellow human beings. It is for these sorts of reasons that political activity presented itself to Aristotle as a plausible candidate for the supreme end in life. But the difficulty is to see how concrete political action could be directed at nothing other than political action.

Surely it is the mark of despotism to wield power for *no* other aim than to enjoy the exercise and to maintain or enhance the opportunity to carry on wielding power. This may be what motivates individual politicians, but when their power depends on the consent of the governed, they, ostensibly at least, have to direct their policies to something else, economic prosperity or social stability, some goal wider than merely holding on to power. Even a despot, if he does not use his position to afford himself gratifications other than those that arise directly from wielding power, is hard for us to understand. And if people think of themselves as fortunate to live in what is commonly known as a 'democracy', it is not because it affords them the opportunity to partici-

205

pate in the formation of common objectives (for at most it affords the opportunity to select a few people who will do that for them), nor because of the (thoroughly diluted) respect accorded to 'citizens'. It is rather because it seems the best way to provide themselves with the means to pursue their individual ideas of happiness without finding that other individuals have appropriated all necessary means for themselves.

Few people perform the one public office which all citizens in a 'political democracy' hold, viz. 'elector',[1] with the idea that it is part of what makes life worth living. (Far too many, indeed, fail to perform the office at all.) The reasons they, as their leaders put it, 'cherish' the institutions of democracy are something like this: history has taught us that unless there are some socially accepted constraints (requiring mechanisms to enforce), individuals, each in pursuit of his or her irreducibly different ideas of what counts as a fulfilled life, are likely to cross and conflict with one another. Thus they find that they must have some form of recognized government. Moreover, leaving institutions of government in the hands of people, who do not have to answer for what they do, leads to abuse. People all too readily find that such positions of authority give them an advantage over others when it comes to obtaining the means to pursue their own particular ideas of what it is to flourish, and those not 'in power' find their own pursuits handicapped. The only way so far found to prevent such abuse is to make the institutions of government answer ultimately to everyone. Hence 'democracy', an instrument often inefficient and sometimes inconvenient, for resolving conflicts between – and sometimes enhancing through cooperative action – individual pursuits of a satisfying life.

Dewey sounds at times lukewarm about this conception of democracy – 'political democracy' – calling it 'not the most inspiring of the different meanings of democracy' (L2, p. 286). It is not that he disputed the lessons supposedly learned from history. He endorsed as a 'well attested conclusion from historical facts' (L2, p. 327) the belief that government will not serve well the interests of a public unless its members share at least in selecting the most important officials who will embody the government. It is rather that the presuppositions behind the rationale just given are distortions of important facts, distortions which carry into our concrete democratic practices. It should be clear in the light of the previous chapter that the way the foregoing rationale for democracy ends up treating public, particularly democratic, institutions as *external* means adopted to secure the end of a fulfilled life will not meet with much enthusiasm from Dewey. His own idea of democracy makes it much more integral to what is involved in human flourishing than Aristotle concluded political activity could be. But his perspective on democratic practice is only available once the presuppositions, which are built into our usual justifications of democracy, are rooted out and discarded.

The central error is that, which in Dewey's view also plagues our understanding of language, of knowledge and of human motivation, the error of thinking that human beings are what they are quite independently of living in association with other human beings, are creatures who only enter into association as a means of getting what they are quite capable of wanting regardless of whether they live socially or in isolation. The root of the misconception, Dewey would argue, runs deeper than merely to the level of our thinking about human nature; it runs down to our thinking about things in general, in particular about their being what they are as well as knowable/intelligible in isolation from other things. Dewey at least felt it necessary to take the development of his 1927 treatise on *The Public and its Problems* back to the level of the general traits of existence which he had identified as the proper study of metaphysics.[2] All things in nature act in conjunction or association with other things and such actions have results. (Cp. the irreducible traits of 'diverse existence, interaction and change' (M8, p. 6).) This he claims is a matter of 'actual and ascertainable fact' (L12, p. 257). These 'facts', as we will see, produce not only engineering problems, but political problems as well. Genuine facts yield real problems, which in turn call for intelligent responses employing the best intellectual instruments (including scientific method) available, and hand in hand with the objectivity of problems goes the objectivity of solutions.[3]

Humans act in association with one another as naturally as do any other things in nature (L2, p. 330). When humans act in *human* association with one another they do so with certain results in view, but there are also consequences which they do not intend or foresee. Human society has its origin in forms of association in which participants do not act with results in view, but simply react to one another. However, language[4] makes it possible for interactive reactions to be transformed into cooperative actions with common ends-in-view. The perception of the consequences of cooperative action, Dewey holds, constitutes such consequences as a common interest. Sometimes the consequences are confined only to those who share in a cooperative transaction: sometimes they affect people who are not directly engaged. People who are not directly engaged in some activity thus also have the basis of an interest in that activity. Dewey ties the distinction between *private* and *public* onto this distinction between people who are *directly*, and people who are *indirectly*, affected by, or have an interest in, some cooperative activity. To constitute a public the people in some group have to be 'indirectly and seriously affected for good or evil' (L2, p. 257).

The distinction between public and private, it should be observed, is not the same as that between social and individual. Many social activities (i.e. those without serious indirect consequences) are private and some individual actions are of public concern. The distinction, moreover, has several grades of actuality. Where there is a body of people who are unaware of serious indirect consequences which affect them, they constitute a potential public. Where they are aware, but lack any institutional means to control such consequences, they constitute an 'inchoate public' (see L2, p. 317). Where they possess any form of organization which allows some degree of regulation of the indirect consequences of (private) activities, they constitute a public, whose form is determined by that organization. The organization they have is 'political'; the institutional means at their disposal constitutes a 'government'; and the public thereby becomes a form of political state (L2, p. 257).

One should be cautious (particularly in using this last word in the sense given to it by Dewey's analysis) not to think only in terms of the sovereign states which divide up the political map of the world. The way Dewey has defined 'public' does not readily lend itself to partitioning either the earth's surface or the earth's human population. 'Publics' are not a tidy way to package political phenomena. Interests do not define a single public, for not everyone is affected indirectly and seriously for good or evil by the same sets of private activities. It would follow from this that there may be more than one public within what is recognized as a sovereign state or local administrative district, as well as the possibility that 'natural publics' do not coincide with the populations within administrative boundaries, either because they spread far more widely or because they form a relatively insulated sub-group within the population determined by such a boundary.

'A public' has been defined in terms of indirect consequences, but what public we define depends on what consequences we have in mind, and 'state' if it follows 'public' will also depend on what consequences we have in mind. The transactions between individual doctors and their patients have consequences, e.g. on public confidence in medical practitioners in general. To the extent that professional bodies like the American Medical Association or its British counterpart regulate these transactions they serve as the relevant 'state'. To the extent that patients generally are affected by these regulations, but have no hold on the institutional means which control those consequences, they are an 'inchoate' part of a public.

This conceptual untidiness is not really an embarrassment to Dewey; it is rather a way of stating what he sees to be the general form of the political problems which face us. Industrialization, urbanization and mass communication have resulted in a network of important interconnections between people which reach beyond the confines of any one local community and across national boundaries. That Dewey's analysis makes national boundaries appear much less significant than they do in newspapers is a welcome consequence to a man who recommends that 'The secondary and provisional character of national sovereignty in respect to the fuller, freer, and more fruitful association and intercourse of all human beings with one another must be instilled as a working disposition of mind' (M9, p. 105).

But what is the theoretical status of Dewey's definitions of 'public' and 'state', if they only serve to blur what otherwise appear to be sharp distinctions within the phenomena? Dewey refers to his definitions as a 'hypothesis' and he draws a number of consequences which are supposed to confirm it (L2, pp. 265f.). He does not, however, make much effort to compare the explanatory power of his 'hypothesis' with that of possible competitors; its function is not primarily 'explanatory' in the sense usual in natural science, but rather to aid clear thinking in a practical framework.

The organizational means for the (public) regulation of the indirect consequences of (private) activities need not have come into being as a response to the perceived need to regulate anything. They may have arisen quite accidentally, perhaps through the efforts of robber barons to extort an easy living some generations ago, or through social customs which grew up interwoven with a body of religious beliefs, and they may be maintained through any manner of collusion or false consciousness. But once an institution, which makes it possible to regulate indirect consequences, is in place it may be brought under criticism and efforts made to improve its functioning. Other human instruments arise naturally (e.g. the stone that serves to bash something) and once adopted as instruments they can be criticized, improved, refined or redesigned.

Drawing the line between public and private in the way Dewey does is designed to facilitate clear thinking regarding the criticism and reform of political institutions. His functional account yields a *formal* criterion for a good state, according to which a state is to be judged by 'the degree of organization of the public which is attained, and the degree in which its officers are so constituted as to perform their function of caring for public interests' (L2, p. 256). To stress the purely formal nature of this criterion Dewey goes on immediately to deny that there is any *a priori* rule for bringing a good state into existence and to deny that the public/private distinction *can* be drawn in the same way in different ages and cultures. The formal nature of this criterion dictates that all concrete political problems are to be approached in the spirit of what Dewey conceives to be experimental practice in natural science.

> In concrete fact, in actual and concrete organization and structure, there is no form of state which can be said to be the best; not at least till history is ended, and one can survey all its varied forms. The formation of states must be an experimental process. (L2, p. 256)

And further on: 'The line of demarcation between actions left to private initiative and management and those regulated by the state has to be discovered experimentally' (L2, p. 275).

The foundation of this experimentalism rests on Dewey's conception of human intelligence as the ability to adapt means and ends to one another. 'Experimentation' here does not mean haphazard trial and error, but the interaction between a general conception and its application to hitherto unexperienced situations, which will very likely call for its modification and development. This is what happens to a scientific idea and Dewey sees no reason why the ideal which governs a practice should not undergo the same kind of development.

Section IX.b: Community

Dewey's account of what constitutes a division between the private and the public and his formal criterion of the good state will remain precisely that, purely formal, until supplemented by an account (having also, of course, the status of a hypothesis) of the ideal of practice which determines what constitutes a successful, and what an unsuccessful, experiment. As a preliminary to considering what Dewey has to say on this point, consider what follows from the general form which Dewey's account gives to the political problems which confront us.

It appears that there is a conceptual difficulty with the notion of 'public', viz. how to individuate publics, how to count them, discern the limits of their extent.

> It is not that there is no public, no large body of persons having a
> common interest in the consequences of social transactions. There
> is too much public, a public too diffused and scattered and too
> intricate in composition. And there are too many publics, for
> consequences are multitudinous beyond comparison, and each one
> of them crosses the others and generates its own group of persons
> especially affected with little to hold these different publics together
> in an integrated whole. (L2, p. 320)

But this is at bottom a family of practical problems. The challenge is to determine what publics need to be represented, and how they could best be served by institutions of government.

A consequence of putting such a plethora of problems into this single form is that it becomes possible to argue that the common form of solution to these problems is 'more democracy'. In one sense of 'democracy' (the one Dewey finds not the most inspiring (L2, p. 282)) this follows from the way Dewey has defined 'a public'. An unperceived common interest in the indirect consequences of some (private) activity constitutes only a potential public. A perceived interest of this kind without the means to regulate affairs in the light of that perception constitutes a body of persons only as an inchoate public. To have form a public must have some institutional means, however ill-adapted, to regulate the activities which affect their interests. These institutions may involve each member of the public in every decision taken, but more commonly decisions will be taken by official representatives of the public on its behalf. In either case we have what Dewey is prepared to call a form of 'political democracy', and the degree of political democracy is a measure of the form or formlessness of a public. Dewey's theoretical framework, thus, bestows on a wide variety of concrete political problems a form which ostensibly calls for democratic institutions for their solutions.

The reason that a devoted believer in democracy should not rest content with this conclusion is that it is far from sufficiently specific. It is not enough to wheel out old forms of 'democracy' to meet new problems. 'Democratic' institutions have arisen historically, like other forms of government, as a product of social forces generated by changes in the material bases of social life.[5] The democratic institutions which we have and the way we think and operate within them are as likely to represent adjustments to historical circumstances no longer relevant to the public interests in question, as they are to offer us as members of a public the means to control effectively the indirect consequences of people's (private) activities. What is needed is constant ('experimental') rethinking and reworking of our institutions. And to assess the success or otherwise of our thought and work, we need the guidance not of a rigidly formulated end-in-view, for this would be directly contrary to Dewey's approach to practical reasoning,[6] but some form of ideal nevertheless. Here Dewey offers what he must regard as one of the *more* inspiring of the different meanings of 'democracy', an ideal he labels variously that of 'social democracy' or 'community'.

Dewey's formulation of this ideal comes in two parts. One applies to the relations which hold between individuals and the social groups to which they belong, and here 'it consists in having a responsible share according to capacity in forming and directing the activities of the groups to which one belongs and participating according to need in the values which the groups sustain' (L2, pp. 327–8).[7] The question to pose when applying this part of the criterion is, 'How numerous and varied are the interests which are consciously shared?' (M9, p. 89). Because human society is not in Dewey's view a matter merely of interactions between individuals and cannot be understood without examining how groups of people interact with each other *as groups*, there is a second part to this ideal which calls for 'different groups to interact flexibly and fully in connection with other groups' (L2, p. 328). Here the question to pose when applying the criterion is, 'How full and free is the interplay with other forms of association?' (M9, p. 89).

211

This is a species of ethical ideal belonging to that family of ethical theories which, like Aristotle's, is based upon a conception of what it is for human beings to live well and flourish in a distinctively human fashion. The ethical roots of the ideal are clear, for when Dewey presents his two criteria, he immediately applies them to explain what is wrong with associations of criminals.

> If we apply these considerations to, say, a criminal band, we find that the ties which consciously hold the members together are few in number, reducible almost to a common interest in plunder; and that they are of such a nature as to isolate the group from other groups with respect to give and take of the values of life. (M9, p. 89; cp. 'robber band', L2, p. 328)

The ethical roots of this ideal are firmly planted in the recognition of the social nature of human beings and the way humans need to be assimilated into a social environment. Humans are indeed born free of social chains, but physically helpless and totally dependent on other members of their species for an unusually prolonged period (M9, p. 50). In exchange for a degree of independence, humans accept from their social environment dispositions which shape their perceptions, beliefs, inferences, desires and patterns of activity. They receive these for the most part unreflectively, without intending, or making any effort, to acquire them.

Inasmuch as humans enter into social relations unreflectively, slot themselves into niches prepared by their culture, and conform to the tacitly acquired norms which define those niches, their behaviour is on the same level as that of any other association between natural bodies, e.g. 'the interplay of iron and the oxygen of water' (L2, p. 330). It is only when activities are assigned signs and symbols and can be reflected upon, 'viewed as from without, arrested for consideration and esteem', can they be regulated, made objects of 'recollection and foresight' (L2, p. 331). It is only at this reflective level that activities involving human beings are conducted on a distinctively human level; so long as a person's behaviour is governed by dispositions, unreflectively acquired and followed, it remains at the level of a pigeon or a rat.

And it is only on the reflective level that association between biological individuals becomes distinctively human association. One human may employ recollection and foresight to manipulate affairs on the basis of established relations and procedures ('established meanings' as Dewey would call them) and his individual interactions with others thereby move toward the distinctively human plane. But activity does not become distinctively human simply by virtue of acquiring a social dimension; to become distinctively human, the goals and methods involved (those consciously adopted, i.e. reflecting awareness of meanings) must be shared. When all who participate in social activity perceive common meanings in their activities and are pursuing a shared goal, 'there is generated what, metaphorically, may be termed a general will and social consciousness: desires and choice on the part of individuals in behalf of activities that, by means of symbols, are communicable and shared by all concerned' (L2, p. 331).

This situation does not obtain in a group where one member is aware of what events mean and manipulates them in furtherance of personal (private) interests and goals. It does not obtain if, when two members of a group come into conflict, one is able to dominate or suppress the other, force the other to surrender his or her interests. To the extent that neither of these takes place within a group, associated life therein constitutes community life. But this will be only a limited form of community life for its members if, when the activities of one such group intersect and possibly conflict with those of another, one group has a better hold on what events mean and manipulates them for its interests, or there is no basis for harmonizing and sharing recognized purposes and established meanings between the groups.

A conflict, a lack of intergroup or intragroup harmony, is a problem, but it is a *problem in these terms* (i.e. how both parties are to harmonize as opposed to how one party might dominate or suppress the other) only if the individuals involved in the conflict are able to share openly and equitably in the development of the common purposes and meanings necessary to the resolution of the conflict, the solution of the problem. This means that individuals from each group will have to be treated equally although not necessarily identically.

> Equality does not signify that kind of mathematical or physical equivalence in virtue of which any one element may be substituted for another. It denotes effective regard for whatever is distinctive and unique in each, irrespective of physical and psychological inequalities. It [namely equality] is not a natural possession, but is a fruit of the community when its action is directed by its character as a community. (L2, pp. 329–30)

Section IX.c: Faith in science

It needs to be stressed that this spells out an ideal, that is something toward which existing things may move, *but* may not necessarily, or will in fact not ever, reach. Dewey indeed suggests the latter is the case for the democratic ideal: 'democracy in this sense is not a fact and never will be' (L2, p. 328). The point of being as clear as we can about ideals is that, faced with a choice, we can try to assess which of our options is likely, as far as we can judge consequences, to leave us better off.

Dewey is not urging us to dismantle our existing institutions wholesale and replace them by a system of fluid (loosely knit and transient) communes or cooperatives, which would expend enormous time and energy in earnest deliberation to ensure that all with an interest in some matter are heard and accommodated. This would be to submit needlessly to the tyranny of an idea, and would evidently be ignoring the central principle of Dewey's account of practical reasoning, which is to match ends to existing means, as well as to judge means by ideal ends. The recommendation is rather that we progressively reconstruct our existing institutions so that they reveal to us the means by which this ideal might be realized – and thereby reveal to us what the ideal means.

But why this ideal rather than some other? Because, Dewey contends, it is in some sense the only ideal. It is not one among several possible 'principles of associated life. It is the idea of community life itself' (L2, p. 328). It is possible to motivate this claim by taking the same sort of steps which, according to Bernard Williams, lead to the 'absolute conception of reality'. Williams, we saw in Section V.c, traced the source of his conception of 'what is there *anyway*' to conflicts between ways of representing the world. To resolve such conflicts requires a form of representation comprehensive enough to include each conflicting representation as a partial viewpoint, revealing thereby how far each of the originally conflicting representations can be used to guide our anticipations of nature.

The ideal of community likewise can be traced to a need to resolve conflict, only this time conflicts of interests, i.e. from the need to find a framework of purposes which incorporate each conflicting interest, and revealing thereby how far each may be reasonably pursued. The ideal of community thus arises naturally from the discovery, perhaps made accidentally, that interests and purposes *can* be harmonized, for there are clearly cases where cooperation is not only possible but more beneficial to potentially conflicting parties than is combat. But what reason have we for thinking that human conflict generally is resolvable? Does it make any sense to hope for something we might call 'The Great Community' in which the 'pulls and responses of different groups reinforce one another and their values accord' (L2, p. 328)?

It was far from clear that Williams's characterization of his 'absolute conception' (as 'a reality which exists independently . . . of any thought or experience') was well motivated by the problem of resolving conflicts between representations, but given the general problem, precisely the same question can be posed: What reason have we for thinking that conflicting representations, conflicting human beliefs about the natural world, can in general be reconciled? Assuming we are not exaggerating the extent to which we have succeeded in reconciling conflicting representations (because the hegemony of our scientific outlook hides from view representations which have not been accommodated so much as suppressed), we still have no *a priori* guarantee that it will be possible to go on doing this. We have had a few centuries of notable scientific achievements, in which we have built powerful intellectual instruments for relating a wide variety of experienced phenomena. But have we anything more than *faith*, the same sort of faith which sustains religious believers, that representations of the natural world *ought* in the end to form a unity, that they *can* without arbitrary imposition of authority be integrated into a single framework of perspectives?

Have we, on the other hand, any reason to think we would not achieve similar results if we followed the advice, which Dewey repeatedly urged, and applied to our social problems the methods and techniques which have proved so powerful in investigating natural phenomena? It is widely believed that we do have reason. The phenomena studied by natural science and our lack of 'subjective' involvement in those phenomena mark out the natural world as a particularly appropriate field for the application of what has come to be known as 'scientific method'. Human interests, moreover, arise from the irreducibly individual natures of human subjects; human experience, human subjectivity, is precisely what science has to purge from its representations in order to come to grips with its subject matter.

These widely held beliefs, however, have the consequence that human beings are in an important sense a phenomenon apart from nature. The consequence is drawn explicitly in Williams's account. The 'absolute conception' is of 'a reality which exists independently . . . of any thought or experience'. Cultural as well as psychological phenomena come to have a highly problematic status[8] and this consequence is supported by the fact that linguistic meanings, *the* fundamental cultural phenomena, have been shown by Quine to be indeterminate. Reality must not only be independent of experience, it must, if Williams's argument is cogent, be in all respects fully determinate. But does our scientific activity really require *this* conception of reality, *this* conception of its object?

What theoretical scientists increasingly do is to try to devise representations which relate what are becoming more and more *experimental* phenomena, the stable products of premeditated intervention in the natural world; while their experimentally oriented colleagues use existing representations to devise more such interventions. As the union of mathematical representations and experimental methods, which is what characterizes 'modern' science, continues to prosper, the immediate material, for which explanations are sought, and which tests hypotheses, is more and more becoming material that is not *found* in nature. Instead it is the product of human ingenuity responding to what Dewey characterized as indeterminate situations by applying technology to transform them into situations which are determinate.

215

The indeterminateness may not be something that is there *anyway*, it may require the experience of a human being ill-equipped to deal with the situation for its indeterminateness to be realized, just as colours require creatures with certain perceptual equipment to be realized, but it does not follow that it is not an 'objective' feature of the situation. If human beings and human thought are natural phenomena, then the qualities of experience both before and after the application of reflective thought are natural qualities.

A naturalistic metaphysics is bound to consider reflection as itself a natural event occurring *within* nature because of traits of the latter. . . . Yet philosophers, and strangely enough philosophers who call themselves realists, have constantly held that the traits which are characteristic of thinking, namely uncertainty, ambiguity, alternatives, inquiring, search, selection, experimental reshaping of external conditions, do not possess the same existential character as do the objects of valid knowledge. . . . The world must actually be such as to generate ignorance and inquiry, doubt and hypothesis, trial and temporal conclusions; . . . the ultimate evidence of genuine hazard, contingency, irregularity and indeterminateness in nature is thus found in the occurrence of thinking. (L1, pp. 62–3)

True, the *ideal* toward which science works is determinateness in the situations which engage its experimental and theoretical practices, but must the world already *be* determinate for science to proceed as it does? To infer that it must is to make the move Dewey characterized as *the* philosophic fallacy and to make it in a form which Dewey claimed is characteristic of idealism, viz. 'The conversion of the logic of reflection into an ontology' (L1, p. 61).

Nevertheless, the attraction of this move, fallacious or not, is very powerful. Humans seem to need a kind of faith in order to participate in any large enterprise like political reform or scientific research. (The latter is, after all, an attempt to reform existing beliefs and intellectual practices.) One must, of course, believe that the world is capable of being made more like the ideal toward which the enterprise is working. But faith often seems drawn to attach itself to something else as well. A mere possibility does not seem enough to anchor commitment; the ideal has not merely to be a possibility but in some sense an actuality. Dewey remarked on how some ' "idealists" cannot trust their ideal till they have converted it into existence' (L1, p. 320). His own early philosophic position had been founded on precisely the move from the realiz*able* to the already realiz*ed* (E1, p. 141). At a much later stage in his career (1934) he advanced the suggestion that 'God' should be understood as a word for 'the unity of all ideal ends arousing us to desire and action' (CF, p. 42). He acknowledged that this sense of the word would not

216

answer to its use in conventional religious contexts, for although in such contexts the word 'God' does tend to represent such a unity of ideals, it is also taken to designate an actually existing Entity.

> Now the ideals that move human beings have various material embodiments. Historical personages in their divine attributes are materializations of the ends that enlist devotion and inspire endeavor. They are symbolic of the reality of ends moving us in many forms of experience. The ideal values that are thus symbolized also mark human experience in science and art and the various modes of human association. . . . (CF, p. 41)

What, Dewey goes on to ask, is lost if we admit that such materializations are merely symbolic and that 'ideals have authoritative claim upon conduct just because they are ideal' (ibid.)? Well, ideals, which we must make determinate as we go along, do not have what we think of as authority; authority tells us what to do, how we should think. And we also lose, it appears, authority in the sense of compulsion, 'since all that an Existence can add is force to establish, to punish, and to reward' (CF, p. 44). A mere ideal, it seems, we can take or leave; an existence can inflict itself on us if we are foolish enough to ignore it.[9]

This is why Williams did not feel able to leave the 'absolute conception' as vague as 'whatever it is that these representations represent'. It has to have enough content to perform the authoritative role of mediating between competing conceptions, and the 'basic dilemma'[10] then faced was over how any particular conception could acquire sufficient authority to perform this function. But the conception of reality as entirely divorced from experience does not contribute to solving the original problem, which is how to relate apparently conflicting experience so as to resolve conflict; experience has no place in a concept of a world as independent of all experience. There is, however, at least some content in 'what it is that these representations represent'. For the experiences are already classified as possibly partial representations of something which ideally ought to have a unified representation. Here is a challenge; to accept it is to accept the authority of an ideal and to be prepared, through the attempt to realize the ideal, to find out precisely what that ideal demands.

But surely the existence of a world independent of our knowledge and experience is not *just* an ideal in which we have something akin to a religious faith? Yes, but that is not what is being claimed and not what is at issue. The issue is what we can *say* about this world – this world, which clearly sets constraints on what we can successfully do within it and on what we can justifiably think about it. Is it coherent to think we can describe it in a way which leaves out the facts that description is based on experience and experience by its nature is partial, is perspectival, and, insofar as it is representative, is a representation needing to be related to other representations? Is it coherent to think we can describe the world, in Thomas Nagel's phrase, 'from no point of view' (Nagel, 1979, p. 212) and that this is the aim of natural science? Is there not a highly questionable step from recognizing that science aims to transcend particular viewpoints to the claim that science seeks (again Nagel's phrase) 'The View from Nowhere'?[11] What is *not specific to one* particular point of view, but can be used from *many* points of view, is not *severed from all* points of view. What is maximally comprehensive does not obliterate whatever it is that it comprehends.

What is at issue is not what we might at some remote point in the future achieve, but the direction of our present intellectual endeavours, the character of what we think have been our most important recent intellectual achievements and the prospects we have for similar achievements in other areas. It is true that science has set to one side the so-called secondary qualities as well as the qualities that depend on our emotional responses to things.[12] But does this reflect anything more than that science like every human practice is a system of selective responses made for particular purposes? Are such qualities not, as Dewey insisted they were, objective natural phenomena which can be related to other objective natural phenomena? If on the other hand linguistic meaning and cultural phenomena generally are to be treated as non-natural, as ultimately unsuited to objective treatment, what authority can Dewey's ideal of community have? For it is based on communication of objectively shared meanings and values. If, however, science has not been permanently divesting itself of human involvement in the phenomena it treats, but has been merely selecting and refining human experience in order to make important but by no means fully comprehensive steps at relating phenomena experienced under different conditions (from 'different perspectives'), then we might hope that by similar honest effort we can make progress relating different interests formed under different conditions into a set of values that would constitute the basis for community life.

Section IX.d: Unfinished selves

It appears, however, that even if the material which science must use to work toward its ideal is irreducibly *human* experience, it is still a material quite unlike that from which we would have to forge the ideal of community. Beliefs and intellectual practices can be shown to be mistaken. The world will frustrate certain beliefs and, unless they are abandoned, will in time destroy those who hold them. Yes, and the world will frustrate certain interests and, unless they are abandoned, will in time ruin those who pursue them.

Nevertheless, is it not the case that when two beliefs come into conflict, at least one must be wrong; but when two interests of values come into conflict we have no basis on which to say one must be wrong? No, this is far from the complete picture. The incorporation of apparently conflicting beliefs into a comprehensive framework which resolves these conflicts may neither leave those beliefs quite what they were before this took place, nor wholly negate them. Each may have something of epistemic value which the other lacked, and yet each stand to be corrected, improved in the light of the resolution. In a similar way a conflict of interests which is resolved in the spirit of Dewey's ideal of community may neither result in the total frustration of one set of interests, nor leave interests unmodified. Human interests (as well as beliefs) are such that they can develop by being brought into contact with other interests (beliefs) and made not only to harmonize, but to find avenues of fulfilment (meanings) which would otherwise not be available.

But what if these new avenues of fulfilment hold no interest for those who will have to modify their aims and values, if they are to participate in those of a wider community? What if a person simply does not care about other people and their interests, does not care if interests can be harmonized, cares only to use what opportunities, strength and guile at his or her disposal in pursuit of private interests? Such a person has, Dewey would argue, a narrow and inflexible conception of self. But does not arguing that self-regarding motives should give way to other-regarding motives expose us to the tyranny of a social morality? No, this suggestion is based on a false dilemma, and misses Dewey's point. The choice is not between a self-regarding person and an other-regarding person, but between a person whose regard for self is regard for something narrow, trivial, transient and exclusive (L7, p. 296), and a person whose regard for self is for something wide and inclusive enough to embrace the interests of other people and permanent and significant enough to flourish only in an environment sustained by shared values and cooperative action.

But what foundation can there be for the implied criticism, 'narrow, trivial', etc.? People just have to be taken as they come and their irreducibly different ideas of what their fulfilment consists in have to be respected. This is the foundation of any democratic ethic which will not expose us to the danger of a social tyranny. Now this argument is in Dewey's view rooted in an idea of human individuality which, however widespread and influential, is false and stands in the way of clear thinking about the ideals which should govern our relations with one another. The idea, 'social atomism', had its origin in the particular historical circumstances which in the seventeenth and eighteenth centuries gave rise to our present institutions and conceptions of political democracy.

Forms of association which existed three to four centuries ago restricted trade and shackled inquiry; those who struggled against these restrictions formulated their opposition to existing institutions (which were defended as part of the order of nature) by appeal to the 'sacred authority resident in the protesting individual', and thus gave rise to 'a theory which endowed singular persons in isolation from any associations, except those which they deliberately formed for their own ends, with native or natural rights' (L2, p. 289). There is no logical reason, Dewey believed, why the political appeal should have been to the individual's rights rather than to the right of 'some primary groupings', except that similar battles were being fought on several fronts, religious and intellectual as well as commercial and political, and the individual was the lowest common denominator for the protesters on all fronts to make common cause. Thus arose the belief in 'the naked individual' to whom 'all associations [were] foreign to his nature and rights save as they proceeded from his own voluntary choice, and guaranteed his own private ends' (L2, p. 290).

It would be a mistake to infer from these quoted remarks, or from other numerous passages in which Dewey attacks this traditional form of individualism and its associated conception of natural rights, that his attitude was anti-individualistic or that he did not believe people should have rights. What he attacked he saw as misconception, which stood in the way of people understanding the nature of their individuality, and as dogmas which were used to defend vested interests. The notion of natural right, as associated with the 'naked individual', obscures the social origin and function of rights.

> Absolute rights, if we mean by absolute those not relative to any social order and hence exempt from any social restriction, there are none. . . . the more we emphasize the free right of an individual to his property, the more we emphasize what society has done for him: the avenues it has opened to him for acquiring; the safeguards it has put about him for keeping. . . . The only fundamental anarchy is that which regards rights as private monopolies, ignoring their social origin and intent. (M5, p. 395)

Rights, which would be specified independently of any social context, would establish a line between private and public which could be drawn in advance of knowing the historical circumstances in which it was to operate. As we saw in Section IX.b above, Dewey denied this could be done. This does not mean that a line between private and public does not need to be drawn or that individuals should not possess rights, merely that it should be recognized that obligations go with rights; and the lines they set up between the activities of different individuals, and between their activities and those of public officials, may need to be redrawn as circumstances change or as we come to understand circumstances better.

The interests of individuals, specifically the tastes and desires which form the basis of interests, are similarly not something which they bring with them when they enter society. It is a mistake even to think that human motivation is naturally self-regarding, and that it is only as a result of social conditioning that humans acquire other-regarding motivations. Dewey drew repeatedly in this connection (M5, p. 341; L7, p. 293) on William James, who made the point (1890, I, p. 320) that natural desires are neither self-directed nor other-directed, but are *object*-directed. 'Primitive selfishness' (such as children exhibit) is not concern for self (which children need to be taught as much as they need to be taught a concern for others) but absorption in the object of desire. Moral education consists in part in making humans aware of the effects on themselves and others of their 'instinctive' pursuits.

The conception of the 'naked individual' is maintained by this and a number of other 'fictions of psychology', the chief among which is a belief that conduct proceeds from conditions which lie within focal attention. For the liberal tradition which fostered the idea, ' "Mind" was "consciousness," and the latter was a clear, transparent, self-revealing medium in which wants, efforts and purposes were exposed without distortion' (L2, p. 299), whereas in fact 'the underlying and generative conditions of concrete behaviour are social as well as organic; much more social than organic as far as the manifestation of *differential* wants, purposes and methods of operation is concerned' (ibid). What people actually want is a product of the way their informed natural impulses are shaped by their culture, and as the exercise of shrewdness and calculation in pursuit of one's objectives depends in part on social conditions:

> The idea of a natural individual in his isolation possessed of full-fledged wants, of energies to be expended according to his own volition and of a ready-made faculty of foresight and prudent calculation is as much a fiction in psychology as the doctrine of the individual in possession of antecedent political rights is one in politics. (Ibid.)

Even where people profess to have taken on board the flaws in the conception of the 'naked individual', the force of its central assumption, that selves are prior to, and not the product of, their social environment, can be felt. It is on this assumption that the common defence of democracy outlined in Section IX.a above is based: democratic institutions are held to be the best available 'external' means for as many people as possible to pursue their irreducibly individual conceptions of their own self-fulfilment without getting too much in each other's way. It is not acknowledged that the selves who 'use' political institutions in this way have at their disposal an instrument which can to a degree reshape the conditions of the formation of selves (themselves and other selves). This external means is potentially a 'genuine instrument'.[13] It can function as a constituent in the pursuit of self-fulfilment, if it is employed intelligently to discover and make available further means to – and at the same time discover and elaborate the nature of – the ends which humans can pursue.

But this requires entering into cooperative deliberation and activity with the idea that one's conception of one's self-fulfilment is subject to enlargement – enlargement which may include projects for better equipping others to pursue their fulfilment – and is also subject to judicious pruning of pursuits (and perhaps also of the exercise of privileges) which narrow oneself and hinder the pursuits of others. Here we confront the militantly self-regarding person who simply does not care for an enlarged self, not at any rate a self enlarged to include satisfaction taken in the self-fulfilment of other people. And the feeling that this person is unanswerable derives its force in part from not recognizing that this conception of a self not open to certain forms of development is, like every other, not a given of nature, but the product of social influences.

Another part of the feeling that such a person is unanswerable, however, derives from the lack of a conviction that there is any sound intellectual basis for judging one conception of self, self-fulfilment, interests or what is desirable, to be worse than any others. This reflects in some measure a very proper reluctance to prejudge people whom we may not fully understand, or to pre-empt in any way the plurality of ends, which Dewey hopes will be sustained and mutually strengthened, as we work to realize the ideal of community. But pluralism does not entail that 'fundamental anarchy' in which each person has a right to pursue what he or she can get away with, untouched and untouchable by criticism. Yet we seem to be without a basis on which to mount such criticism.

Here our (mis)conceptions of the intellectual achievements, which we have made in understanding nature, stand in the way. We are persuaded that to enter science we must leave everything that is human at the door. We forget that to advance our understanding we must reform our habits, try to appreciate the peculiarities and limitations of our individual experience, work to explore the conditions which generate those limitations, and endeavour to transcend them in theories which systematically relate to one another as many such peculiarities as possible. Who does not undertake to criticize the habits of selection and the comprehensiveness of the forms of representation in use in science does not engage in its advancement.

Presenting the aim and end-product of science as a representation of the world as it is *anyway*, 'a view from nowhere', not only obscures the function of criticism and intelligent control in scientific work, it pushes experience in general beyond the reach of objective intellectual treatment.

'Perspectives' cease to be aspects of objective reality and come to have the status of subjective realms, related to one another and to the world only problematically.[14] Insulated as they are from connection to objective affairs, such subjective realms are the natural homes of selves who do not need to act through, develop by, or derive their character from participation in objective affairs.

Section IX.e: Freedom

Above all the idea of a 'fixed, ready-made, finished self' (L7, p. 306) stands in the way of clear understanding about aims and ideals. We become confused, for example, about what a benevolent regard for others requires of us. The individualism of 'classic Liberalism' has bequeathed to us an opposition between self-regarding and other-regarding, egoism and altruism, neither of which is satisfactory and between which we should not feel we have to choose.

> In a justly organized social order, the very relations which persons bear to one another demand of the one carrying on a line of business the kind of conduct which meets the needs of others, while they also enable him to express and fulfill the capacities of his own being. Services, in other words, would be reciprocal and cooperative in their effect. (L7, pp. 299–300)

Total sacrifice of self-interest to the interests of others is not necessarily a virtue and hardly an ideal. Even where ostensible service to others brings self-fulfilment, it should meet the genuine needs of others. Giving people what they want is not necessarily giving them what they need. What they need may be the opportunity to achieve something for themselves rather than being given it.

Dewey illustrates the pitfalls of 'abstract altruism' with the example of parents who 'justify an unjustifiable interference' in the affairs of their children 'on the grounds of kindly parental feeling'. The moral is that '*intelligent* regard' for the welfare of their children will realize 'the need for growing freedom with growing maturity' (L7, p. 301). The generalized lesson is that 'overt acts of charity and benevolence' are not essential to morals but only demanded by special circumstances. What is essential 'is found in a constantly expanding and changing sense of what the concrete realities of human relations call for' (L7, p. 302).

Freedom is another ideal we misunderstand if we let our thinking be governed by the assumption that selves are ready-made. Proceeding from this assumption, 'classic Liberalism' treated freedom as following naturally upon the removal of external obstructions which existing institutions place in the way of the ' "free" play of the native equipment of individuals' (L3, p. 100). Dewey contrasts this view with that of 'institutional idealism'. Hegel is the chief representative of this antithesis of liberalism, but its foundations were laid by Spinoza even before classic Liberalism had fully developed. Spinoza held that 'man in his original estate possesses a very limited amount of power' (L3, p. 101). A man who 'acts upon his private impulse, appetite or want and upon his private judgement about the aims and measures of conduct' finds the act he has initiated 'immediately caught in an infinite and intricate network of *inter*actions'. What people actually *do* on this basis is so much the result of the 'blind and partial action of other parts of nature' (L3, p. 102) that such actions can hardly be said to be the expression of freedom.

To free themselves people must come to understand the order and system of laws which condition their acts and must align their actions to this order and system. However:

> No individual can overcome his tendencies to act as a mere part in isolation. Theoretic insight into the constitution of the whole is neither complete nor firm; it gives way under the pressure of immediate circumstances. Nothing is of as much importance to a reasonable creature in sustaining effectively his actual – or forceful – reasonableness as another reasonable being. (L3, p. 102)

Spinoza's ideal product of the understanding was a rigorous geometric system and his world was correspondingly rigidly deterministic, so that transcending private impulse and private judgment appears ultimately to be nothing less than surrender to, submission under, and submergence in the whole (Nature or God).

Hegel incorporated and restated these fundamental ideas in a framework which was articulated around an unfolding development, which manifested itself serially in history, but was still based on a timeless 'logical' necessity. The primary embodiment of this unfolding development of reasonableness and greater freedom was not the burden of individuals but of the institutions in which they participated. The net result stood in stark opposition to the Liberal tradition.

> Freedom is a growth, an attainment, not an original possession, and it is attained by idealization of institutions and law and the active participation of individuals in their loyal maintenance, not by their abolition or reduction in the interests of personal judgements and wants. (L3, p. 103)

Dewey's position evidently owes a great deal to this 'institutional idealism'. The idea that freedom is growth is a consequence of his own position: 'Our idea compels us. . . . to seek freedom in something which comes to be, in a certain kind of growth' (L3, p. 109). The institutional idealist at least avoids the mistake of thinking that if human beings are to have something called freedom, they must have possession of it from the start. But if they avoid this form of '*the* philosophic fallacy' (of converting eventual function into antecedent existence), they commit it in a different form. Like the teleological theory of mind which regards all that happened before the appearance of mind on earth as preparation for that appearance, history is explained (and thus in a sense caused) by its culmination. A genuine emergence of freedom in the world, like the genuine emergence of mind,[15] requires taking the reality of growth seriously. Those who feel the need to explain by reference either to antecedent or to consequence fail to do this:

> . . . the notion of growth makes it easy, I think, to detect the fallacy residing in both views: namely, the breaking up of a continuity of historical change into two separate parts, together with the necessity which follows from the breaking-in-two for some device by which to bring them together again.
>
> The reality *is* the growth-process itself. . . . The real existence is the history in its entirety, the history as just what it is. The operations of splitting it up into two parts and then having to unite them again by appeal to causative power are equally arbitrary and gratuitous. (L1, p. 210)

Dewey's departure from institutional idealism on this abstract meta-physical level corresponds to a concrete difference in the attitude to be taken by individuals to social institutions. The predominant message of institutional idealism to individuals is the need to submerge themselves in institutions which transcend their individual peculiarities. Dewey's message is that although a degree of submersion of private impulse and private judgment is required, this is only a preliminary to making intelligent contributions to the development of such forms of 'objective mind'.[16] Development is a fact, but it is neither driven nor is its character guaranteed by any kind of necessity, logical or otherwise. What drives the development of institutions for better or worse is the reflective or unreflective actions of individuals.

Unreflective action, like the uncontrolled influence of the natural environment, is a matter of chance. It no more expresses freedom than does servile submission to existing custom. One should not, on the other hand, exaggerate the control individuals, even those working in full cooperation, can have over the institutions which shape their social environment. Any form of 'objective mind', any system of meanings, is wider than the field of consciousness; no form of mind is completely open and accessible to those who participate in it. All that can be attempted is the experimental exploration of modes of representation, forms of communication, which will cast light on the submerged features and permit a degree of control and reformation.

Institutional idealism not only overlooks the function of individuals in generating institutional innovation, it ultimately gives rise to an idea of freedom as one-sided as that of classic Liberalism. Dewey sets this danger in contrast to that of Liberalism by illustrating two flawed approaches to the education of children. The first would 'humour all . . . choices' children make, making it easy for them to do what they please, cooperating in bringing their preferences to fulfilment, allowing their blind impulses to set into habits. Such children would be 'free' in the Liberalist sense, but this is clearly a limited and accidental sense, because this 'freedom' is conditioned by a special environment which when it is no longer sustained will not leave them free, but lacking in the ability to reshape their own preferences, lacking a varied and flexible capacity of choice.

The opposite error, reflecting the attitude of an institutional idealist toward recalcitrant individuals, would be to inhibit or interfere with all spontaneous preference, constantly 'disciplining' children by circumstances which block their spontaneous preferences. This environment deprives children of the exercise of power and not only leads to apathy, it gives them no way to develop thoughtful autonomous preferences.

> 'Discipline' is indeed necessary as a preliminary to any freedom that is more than unrestrained outward power. But our dominant conception of discipline is a travesty; there is only one genuine discipline, namely, that which takes effect in producing habits of observation and judgement that insure intelligent desires. (L3, p. 107)

These educational environments model social environments, for which indeed they are often used to 'prepare' people. Neither educational environment equips people to become free; and the corresponding social environments could not be claimed to be inhabited by liberated human beings. The first, because it pays insufficient attention to the control of self needed to gain insight into alternatives, and thereby restricts the range of choice of individuals. The second, because it pays insufficient attention to the experience of the control of things, and thereby removes the power to act. It is these two things, freedom as power and freedom as choice, which Dewey believes have to be combined in an adequate account of freedom; and they have to be combined by exercising each to make possible the increase of the other in a 'widening spiral' (L3, p. 104). This is why it is a consequence of his account that freedom is 'a certain kind of growth', the very growth that should define the educational process.

> Even our deliberate education, our schools, are conducted so as to indoctrinate certain beliefs rather than to promote habits of thought. If that is true of them, what is not true of the other social institutions as to their effect upon thought? . . .

226

I shall begin to believe that we care more for freedom than we do for imposing our own beliefs upon others in order to subject them to our will, when I see that the main purpose of our schools and other institutions is to develop powers of unremitting and discriminating observation and judgment. (L3, p. 113)

Freedom is not unimpeded scope for spontaneous action, for this provides no opportunity for the intelligent development of varied interests. Nor is it the submergence of spontaneity in the loyal maintenance of existing institutions, for this surrenders the power to control a crucial aspect of the (social) environment. Freedom is the power to use foresight and insight to shape spontaneous action into enduring fulfilments and to shape both the natural and social environment into the means for those fulfilments. If spontaneity is not to dissipate itself in channels of blindly formed habits laid down and reinforced by the social environment, a plurality of ends-in-view, flexibly formed and intelligently managed so as not to cross one another, will have to be established. Freedom requires spontaneity, which in turn requires pluralism, which can only be sustained by cooperative action; in other words, the idea of community. And the overarching aim of a community and of the individuals in it, by which they can judge their efforts as failures or as successes? 'We set up this and that end to be reached, but *the* end [of self-development] is growth itself. To make an end a final goal is but to arrest growth' (L7, p. 306).

There has been growth; it has been accidental and precarious, but it is a reality. There should be growth; it will take the intelligent mastery of ourselves and our social environments to ensure that the growth which has taken place and the possibility for further growth are not obliterated by the same blind chance which produced it in the first place, but growth is the ideal. The character of the permanent deposit which Hegelianism left in Dewey's thought can perhaps best be seen in this instrumentalist identification of the real and the ideal.

Notes

Chapter I: Legacies

1 The most comprehensive biography of Dewey is by Dykhuizen (1973).

2 By virtue of being thirteen years Dewey's junior and having a longer life, ninety-eight years as opposed to Dewey's ninety-two, Russell held his position for two decades longer than Dewey.

3 Dewey recognized this and advanced perspectives on the history of philosophy from which he hoped his own position would stand in a more favourable light and those he opposed would appear benighted. These perspectives, like those they seek to supplant, tend to be oversimplified. An illustration occurs in Section VIII.b: otherwise this aspect of Dewey's arguments will not be considered here.

4 A notable example is Putnam (1981), which discusses Dewey's position on values under the label 'objective relativism' (pp. 162, 167–8). Dewey's phrase 'warranted assertability' (if not his spelling) has resurfaced in recent discussion of realism, as the anti-realist's label for the goal of scientific inquiry. See, for example, Smart (1986). (Dewey's spelling, 'assertibility', will be retained here.)

5 And moreover: 'are waiting at the end of the road which, for example, Foucault and Deleuze are currently traveling' (ibid.).

6 It is not always remembered that the Vienna Circle was itself split over the issue of foundations and whether a correspondence or coherence approach to truth should prevail. See Hempel (1935).

7 R. W. Sleeper makes very similar points. See Sleeper (1985).

8 In 1930 Dewey recalled how in the early 1880s Hegel's thought had 'supplied a demand for unification that was doubtless an intense emotional craving . . . that only an intellectualized subject matter would satisfy' (L5, p. 153).

9 '. . . of whom', Dewey wrote in 1886, 'the author would not speak without expressing his deep, almost reverential, gratitude' (E1, p. 153).

10 Kant distinguished between 'transcendental' and 'transcendent'. The former respects the limits of experience, the latter 'takes away these limits or even commands us actually to transgress them' (Kant, 1781–7, A296/B353).

11 Green, who died in his mid-forties, was born in 1836, just three years before

228

Peirce. Dewey was exposed to Green's thought during his postgraduate studies at Johns Hopkins by C. S. Morris, the teacher to whom he was closest. (He subsequently took up his first university post at Michigan under Morris.) Peirce also held a teaching position at Johns Hopkins during Dewey's postgraduate studies there, but it was only somewhat later, after he fell under the influence of William James, that Dewey came to appreciate and admire Peirce's philosophy.

12 The careful circumlocution 'which may be described indifferently as . . . realised in . . . or rendered possible by' is a sign of the precarious nearness of this philosophy to that of Spinoza.

13 Thus Pierce: 'Here we see how superficially the just-mentioned theory of reality is laid over the body of [Berkeley's] thought. That *an object's independence of our thought about it* is constituted by its connection with experience in general, he has never conceived. On the contrary, that, according to him is effected by its being in the mind of God. . . . it places reality wholly out of the mind in the cause of sensations . . .' (8.30).

14 See Section V.b below.

15 See Section V.a below.

16 Note, however, that by this stage in Dewey's career the structure of experience is tied very closely to functions realized as empirical events: 'But no one can deny that inference from one thing to another is itself an empirical event, and that just as soon as such inference occurs, even in the simplest form of anticipation and prevision, a world exists like in kind to that of the adult' (M8, p. 95).

17 More recently a philosopher, on whom reading Kant has left a mark, put the point this way. 'Thus [the sceptic's] doubts are unreal, not simply because they are logically irresoluble doubts, but because they amount to the rejection of the whole conceptual scheme within which alone such doubts make sense' (Strawson, 1959, p. 35).

18 In his 1930 intellectual autobiography Dewey credited James's *Principles* with being the 'one specifiable philosophic factor which entered into my thinking so as to give it new direction and quality' (L5, p. 157). The influence James had on Dewey will be treated further in the chapter which follows.

19 Cp. 'To the infant, sounds, sights, touches, *and* pains, form probably one unanalyzed bloom of confusion.* (*The ordinary treatment of this is to call it the result of the *fusion* of a lot of sensations, in themselves separate. This is pure mythology . . .)' (ibid., p. 496 and note).

20 For a criticism of the way John Mackie applied this tactic to insulate ontological claims from epistemological questions and to hide his own epistemological assumptions, see Tiles (1985).

21 'Genetic fallacy' like 'naturalistic fallacy' is a protean concept. At its least precise it is simply a term of abuse for the sort of approach which Dewey urges. Abraham Edel, himself feeling vulnerable to this sort of attack, identifies it thus: 'To substitute the sociological or the historical for the analytic and the logical is a genetic fallacy' (Edel, 1987, p. 827). Under a more careful, less rhetorically motivated definition, we will find Dewey in effect warning us off 'genetic fallacies' as *the* central errors of philosophy. See below, note 26.

22 Cp. L1, pp. 294ff. on the 'superior reality of "causes" ', and note 26 below.

23 A well-known article on 'the naturalistic fallacy' (Frankena, 1939, p. 50) begins by remarking on this feature of ' "thought and expression" in the twentieth century'.

24 He cites the psychologist's fallacy, for example, in 1894 at E4, p. 154. See note 25 to Chapter II.

25 See Section II.e below.

26 There is a corresponding mistake identified in *Experience and Nature*, the doctrine of 'the superior reality of causes' (see L1, pp. 194ff., and the previous section on 'the materialistic fallacy') which treats effects or 'eventual functions' as reducible to their causes or antecedent conditions. A close look at these two mistakes, '*the* philosophic fallacy' and 'the superior reality of causes', reveals them to be the two forms of the 'genetic fallacy' as it is defined in A. Flew, ed., *A Dictionary of Philosophy* (Flew, 1979): 'The mistake of arguing that because something is now such and such, therefore it must already have been such and such at an earlier stage: or because it was such and such then, therefore it must be the same now.'

27 See Sections IV.a and IV.b below.

28 See Section IV.e below.

29 It is the notion of universal found at the beginning of Aristotle's *Physics:* 'Thus we must advance from universals to particulars: for it is a whole that is more knowable to sense-perception, and a universal is a kind of whole, comprehending many things within it, like parts. Much the same thing happens in the relation of the name to a formula. A name, e.g. 'circle' means vaguely a sort of whole: its definition analyses this into particulars. Similarly a child begins by calling all men father, and all women mother, but later on distinguishes each of them' (184^a23-^b13).

30 Not only Russell, but also, for example, Lovejoy and the 'new realists', on which see Chapter VI.

31 As this doctrine applies to perception it would be wholly in the spirit of Dewey's approach to attempt to supplant the habit of using the word 'data' to refer to the elements of sense experience, because the etymology (*do, dare*) masks what is crucial: they are not *given*, they are *taken*, Far better would be to adopt the participle from *capto, capare* (the root of 'perceive') and speak of sense 'capta'.

32 See Section V.a below, and further on the comparison with Wittgenstein in Section IV.e below.

Chapter II: Sensation, emotion and reflex action

1 'As an example, I would say that the problem of "sense data," which occupies such a great bulk in recent British thinking, has to my mind no significance other than as a survival of an old and outworn psychological doctrine, – although those who deal with the problem are for the most part among those who stoutly assert the complete irrelevance of psychology to philosophy' (L5, p. 158).

2 See Section I.d above.

3 Dewey encountered the new 'experimental psychology' in the person of one

of its chief American exponents, G. Stanley Hall, who taught the subject in the philosophy department at Johns Hopkins while Dewey was a graduate student there. Dewey's first teaching responsibilities included psychology, traditionally a branch of philosophy, and his first published book, his *Psychology*, 1887 (E2), was a text to be used in that connection. For an excellent account of Dewey's early career from the standpoint of an intellectual historian see Coughlan (1973).

4 Green's 'concrete whole', see Section I.b above.

5 This is a form of words used six years later by Dewey as he advanced (in a course syllabus) the reflex arc as the physiological key to unlocking the structure of the universe. See E3, p. 214.

6 Green, for example, held the view (not unlike that urged by Quine) that the difference between analytic and synthetic judgments was relative to an individual's knowledge. See Green (1885, II, pp. 61–2).

7 Relating Kant's transcendental ego (the 'I' which functions as the basic condition of the possibility of experience) to the self encountered empirically was a problem with which post-Kantians had not made much satisfactory progress. Dewey wrote, 'With this falls, as a matter of course, the supposed two-fold character of man's nature . . . the distinction is now transferred to the two ways of looking at the same material, and no longer concerns two distinct materials' (E1, p. 148).

8 See Schilpp (1939, pp. 17–18) and below Section IV.a on 'Hegel's idea of cultural institutions as an "objective mind" . . . .'.

9 The text of Dewey's *Psychology* in E2 is the third 1891 edition. A careful record of the earlier variants will be found in hardback editions of E2.

10 The close connection between self and activity remained an important part of Dewey's thinking. Thus we read at L7, p. 288, 'It is not too much to say that the key to a correct theory of morality is recognition of the *essential unity of the self and its acts*, if the latter have any moral significance: while errors in theory arise as soon as the self and acts (and their consequences) are separated from each other, and moral worth is attributed to one more than to the other.'

11 Feeling is the subject of the middle portion, which is itself less than half the size of the space occupied by the treatment of knowledge.

12 And his daughters' biographical chapter (Schilpp, 1939, p. 23) cites the chapters in James 'dealing with conception, discrimination and comparison, and reasoning'. These are respectively Chapters XII, XIII and XXII.

13 Those who think of pragmatism as a set of doctrines about truth and meaning, and have absorbed the analytic attitude which treats such doctrines as independent of conceptions of the human mind and its activity, readily miss the extent to which pragmatist doctrines are plausible only under a conception of human beings as active, productive, creatures and human thought as primarily goal-directed. Just as it would be foolish to try to understand James's doctrines on truth in isolation from what he wrote in his *Principles*, it is equally foolish to ignore the philosophical psychology in Peirce's early series of articles published in the *Journal of Speculative Philosophy*, 1868–9, i.e. 5.213–357.

14 As early as 1884, and because a Danish physiologist, C. Lange, published a similar theory in 1885, this became known as the James-Lange theory.

15 As he explained in the note (E4, p. 171, n. 19) cited in the previous section.

16 '*The principle of serviceable associated Habits*, – Certain complex actions are of direct or indirect service under certain states of the mind, in order to relieve or gratify certain sensations, desires, &c.: and whenever the same state of mind is induced, however feebly, there is a tendency through the force of habit and association for the same movements to be performed though they may not then be of the least use' (Darwin, 1873, p. 29).

17 At E2, p. 301, he writes of reflex action as important 'because it forms the physical basis of sensuous impulse', where 'Sensuous impulse may be defined as *the felt pressure of a state of consciousness arising from some bodily condition to express itself in producing [sic] some physical change*' (E2, p. 300).

18 More about how an object such as a bear comes to be constituted as an 'objective or ideal content' appears in Dewey's treatment of the reflex arc concept, and will be taken up in the next section.

19 Dewey's development of this claim concentrates on emotions arising as competing patterns of behaviour are held in tension, and this appears to work only for distressing emotions such as fear or anxiety. To apply this claim to emotions like joy or elation, Dewey would have to appeal to the experience of releasing a prior tension. This is the approach he takes to laughter (as the 'expression of emotion') at E4, pp. 157–8. (I am grateful to Karen Hutchinson for pointing out the need for this note.)

20 Sense as distinct from signification will be discussed below in Sections III.c and III.d.

21 To those who would not relinquish 'consciousness' to Dewey's treatment, he eventually conceded 'consciousness' in an 'anoetic sense'. He clung, however, to his claim regarding consciousness in a 'noetic' sense. See L1, pp. 199, 226, and Section III.b below.

22 Cp. 'Immediately, every perceptual awareness may be termed indifferently emotion, sensation, thought, desire: not that it *is* immediately any one of these things, or all of them combined, but that when it is taken in some *reference*, to conditions or to consequences or to both, it has, in that contextual reference, the distinctive properties of emotion, sensation, thought or desire' (L1, pp. 230–1).

23 Cp. 'The very meaning of habit is limitation to a certain average range of fluctuation' (E4, p. 163).

24 The key to the way Dewey is viewing the reflex arc concept is the pattern of functional differentiation within an organic whole. This was made explicit in an article published in 1928. 'The beginning is with action in which the entire organism is involved, and the mechanism of reflexes is evolved as a specialized differentiation with an inclusive whole of behavior. The assumption that the nature of behavior is exemplified in a simple reflex is a typical case of the fallacy of neglecting development, historical career. In consequence an account of the mechanism of a particular moment of behavior is converted into an account of behavior in its entirety. Only in this fashion is the role of the mental in action relegated to the realm of fiction' (L3, p. 33).

25 In a republication of the article on the reflex arc in 1931 (*Philosophy and*

Civilization, New York, G. Putnam's Sons, p. 237), Dewey altered 'virtually' to 'actually'.

26 'The very word "expression" names the facts not as they are, but in their second intention. To an onlooker my angry movements are expressions – signs, indications: but surely not to me. To rate such movements as primarily expressive is to fall into the psychologist's fallacy: it is to confuse the standpoint of the observer and explainer with that of the fact observed' (E4. p. 154).

Chapter III: The emergence of mind and qualities

1 The distinction between primary and secondary qualities is John Locke's (Locke, 1690, II xxiii 9). Locke spoke of 'three sorts' of ideas *'that make our complex ones of corporeal substances'*, the third of which were the powers of a body to affect or be affected by other bodies. Dewey often follows Santayana in speaking of 'tertiary qualities', by which are meant those associated with human moods, such as 'cheerful' sunshine or a 'depressing' scene. These should not be confused with Locke's third sort. Dewey at one point suggested introducing the notion of 'quaternary qualities, meaning the qualities that custom prescribes as properly belonging to objects in virtue of their being factors in a social life' (M6, p. 21).

2 This image was attributed to Heinrich Hertz by Ludwig Boltzman in a passage in a letter to *Nature*, 28 February 1895, which appears as the motto of Chapter 2 of van Fraassen (1980). 'The rigour of science requires that we distinguish well the undraped figure of nature itself from the gay-coloured vesture with which we clothe it at our pleasure.' (Cp. Blackburn, 1984, pp. 145ff.)

3 The reference is possibly to James (1890, II, p. 451), which says that in abstraction from bodily symptoms *'we find we have nothing left behind*, out of which an emotion can be constituted'.

4 The concept of *situation* subsequently became central to Dewey's analysis of the process of meeting and resolving a problem, i.e. of what he understood by 'inquiry'. See LTE (Chapters IV, VI *et seq*).

5 Cp. Section I.b on Green's system of related appearances, Section I.c where Dewey is quoted as saying against Russell, 'particulars can be identified *as* particulars only in a relational complex' (M8, p. 90), and Section II.b on the role of the synthetic activity of mind in constituting experience as of an objective world.

6 This point is made with great clarity and thoroughness in Burnyeat (1979). On p. 111 Burnyeat cites the following criticism of Russell's reasoning given in 1913 by Dawes Hicks. 'The reasoning would only be valid on the assumption that if the table is really coloured, the real colour *must* appear the same in darkness and in day-light, through a pair of blue spectacles and without them, in artificial light and in the sun's rays – an assumption which, on the view I am taking, is at once to be dismissed as untenable.' To explain the attraction of the reasoning which requires this implausible assumption Burnyeat appeals to something very close to what Dewey referred to as the

notion of a 'spectator outside the world' (M10, pp. 26; cp. p. 41). See below Section V.e, especially note 27.

7 See Section II.b above.

8 See Section II.d above.

9 See note 21 to Chapter II.

10 On how Dewey saw himself as responding to Aristotelian currents in James, see Section II.c. A hierarchy of forms of being is an idea which extends from Aristotle and the Stoics down to the present. (A modern version appears in an analogy drawn in mathematical terms in Medawar (1969, p. 16, n. 8).) It is worth observing that although traditional hierarchies are strictly cumulative in that every capacity possessed by lower forms is supposed to be possessed by higher forms, Dewey's argument does not require this, but allows, for example, that what are traditionally regarded as 'lower' forms, plants, may possesses capacities (to photosynthesize) which are not possessed by 'higher' forms.

11 Indeed the pressure to embrace this kind of panpsychism could be traced to the influence of '*the* philosophic fallacy'. See Section I.e above.

12 See the end of Section II.a above.

13 Cp. 'Discrimination, not integration, is the real problem' (E4, p. 179).

14 Cp. the phenomenon which Dewey called 'mediation', Section II.e.

15 See L1 (pp. 92, 119–20, 194). Temporal quality is an important factor in Dewey's account of art and its appreciation. See Section VIII.a below.

16 See Section II.e on 'mediation'.

17 See L1 (pp. 213–15).

18 Cp. including 'oral and written speech . . . gestures . . . rites, ceremonies, monuments and the products of industrial and fine arts' (LTE, p. 46). Cp. also 'But if "language" is used to signify all kinds of signs and symbols, then assuredly there is no thought without language; while signs and symbols depend for their meaning upon the contextual situation in which they appear and are used' (L6, p. 4).

19 See above, note 4.

20 I.e., *recognized*, known again – on the difference between knowledge and recognition, see L1 (pp. 247–8).

21 Dewey quotes from Darwin (1873, pp. 249–50), adding the italics (E4, p. 153, n. 1): 'A man, for instance, may know that his life is in extremest peril, and may strongly desire to save it: yet as Louis XVI said when surrounded by a fierce mob, "Am I afraid? Feel my pulse." So a man may intensely hate another, *but until his bodily frame is affected* he cannot be said to be enraged.'

22 See the first note to this chapter.

23 See Chapter II, note 21.

24 'Apart from sentiency and life, the career of an event can indeed be fully described without any reference to its having red as a quality, – though even in this case, since description is an event which happens only through mental events, dependence upon an overt or actualized quality of red is required in order to delimit the phenomenon of which a mathematical-mechanical statement is made. Qualities actually become specifically effective however in psychophysical situations. Where animal susceptibility exists, a red or an odor or sound may instigate a determinate mode of action; it has selective

power in maintenance of a certain pattern of energy-organization. So striking is this fact that we might even define the difference between an inanimate body and a vital and psychophysical one, by saying that the latter responds to qualities while the former does not' (L1, p. 205).

25 Cp. Hofstadter and Dennett (1981, p. 409): 'it sounds like a blatant contradiction – and indeed, that is [Nagel's] point. He doesn't want to know what it's like *for him* to be a bat. He wants to know *objectively* what it is *subjectively* like.'

26 Cp. E2, p. 216, and L1, p. 222.

Chapter IV: Language and self

1 But recall the limitations of the fringe/focus metaphor; see the end of Section II.d above.

2 'The deification of the subconscious is legitimate only for those who never indulge in it – animals and thoroughly healthy naïve children – if there be any such' (L1, p. 228).

3 See Section I.e above.

4 See Section V.b below.

5 See Sections IX.a and IX.b below.

6 See Section V.e below.

7 See Section III.c as well as Section II.e on 'mediation'.

8 This is an outlook which in recent times has acquired the name 'methodological individualism'.

9 See Section I.b above.

10 See note 18 to Chapter III.

11 This particularly fine statement of the sort of conception of experience which Dewey opposed from his earliest period, comes from a criticism of Dewey's 1896 *Mind* articles by Shadworth Hodgson. See E1 (p. xliv).

12 See Section II.c above.

13 See Harrison (1979, pp. 185–8).

14 See Harrison (1979, pp. 190–1).

15 See above Section I.e and Chapter II, note 26.

16 'Language is specifically a mode of interaction of at least two beings, a speaker and a hearer: it presupposes an organic group to which these creatures belong, and from whom they have acquired their habits of speech' (L1, p. 145).

17 See L1, p. 137, for a comparison between the effects of introducing language and those of introducing money.

18 On the relation of Quine's indeterminacy thesis to the Löwenheim-Skolem Theorem, see Quine (1969, pp. 58ff.).

19 These connotations are deliberate, for Dewey regarded 'concerted action' and 'shared experience' as possessing great intrinsic value. 'For there is no mode of action as fulfilling and as rewarding as is concerted consensus of action. It brings with it the sense of sharing and merging in a whole' (L1, p. 145). 'Shared experience is the greatest human good' (L1, p. 157).

20 'The most useful doll I ever saw was a large cucumber in the hands of a little Amazonian-Indian girl; she nursed it and washed it and rocked it to sleep in

the hammock, and talked to it all day long – there was no part in life which the cucumber did not play' (James, 1890, II, pp. 303–4).

21 See Section IV.b above.

22 For further on this claim see Sections VII.d and VIII.b below.

23 L1, pp. 198–9; see Section III.c above.

24 L1, p. 147; see Section IV.d above.

25 Compare the first three essays in E1 with the remark quoted from Dewey's critique of Lotze at the beginning of Section I.d and the two parts of his treatment of Russell.

26 See Section II.e above.

27 See note 21 to Chapter II.

28 For Dewey's claim that this metaphor yields an artificial notion of consciousness', see L1 (p. 235). For an endorsement of the image, see Popper (1972, pp. 341ff.).

Chapter V: Truth and inquiry

1 'Truths already possessed may have practical or moral certainty, but logically they never lose a hypothetic quality, they are true *if*: certain other things present themselves' (L1, p. 123).

2 One can find precursors of the phrase earlier in Dewey's writings, e.g. 1905: 'critically assured presence with respect to further experiences' (M3, p. 176).

3 See Section III.c above.

4 By 'the logical standpoint' Dewey meant the standpoint from which one investigated 'controlled inquiry' (LTE, p. 280). Dewey always resisted confining the scope of logic to the study of pure forms of discourse. This, he argued (ibid.), was an arbitrary restriction grounded on nothing more than the personal interest of certain logicians.

5 See Section I.e above.

6 In a critique of Dewey's account of judgments of practice Ralph Barton Perry (Perry, 1917, pp. 361–2, 366–70) cites Schiller as someone who claims that all judgments are practical, and H. Rickert as someone who reduces the factual to the practical. Someone named Westermarck is cited as advancing views similar to Dewey's but less 'sophisticated and circumspect'.

7 Dewey appeals to this principle to answer Russell's complaint that James's pragmatism had addressed the truth of theories and overlooked the truths of fact. 'Facts may be facts, and yet not be the facts *of* the inquiry in hand. In all scientific inquiry, however, to call them facts or data or truths of fact signifies that they are taken as the *relevant* facts of the inference to be made. *If* (as this would seem to indicate) they are then implicated, however indirectly, in a proposition about what is to be done (if only as to some inference to be made) they themselves are theoretical in logical quality' (M8, pp. 22–3).

8 'Pragmatism' was taken over by James as a mark of respect for his friend Peirce. But Peirce disliked the nominalist direction in which James took pragmatism and adopted 'pragmaticism', a word he hoped would be 'ugly enough to be safe from kidnappers' (5.414).

9 Cp. Peirce, 5.552: 'Mr. Ferdinand C. S. Schiller informs us that he and James

have made up their minds that the true is simply the satisfactory. No doubt: but to say "satisfactory" is not to complete any predicate whatever. Satisfactory to what end?' Russell, otherwise hostile to Dewey, could see from this that Dewey's form of pragmatism was 'not one intended to be used for the support of ancient superstitions or for bolstering up common prejudices' (Russell, 1919, p. 240).

10 Thus (M8, p. 57): 'there is no reason in the world why the practical activity of some men should not be predominantly directed into the pursuits connected with discovery. The extent in which they actually are so directed depends upon social conditions'.

11 As with arguments drawn from this book by Williams and criticized in Section III.a, the claims and arguments considered in this chapter are those which Williams advances as plausible and attractive independently of views which he attributes to Descartes.

12 Since Dewey and Williams conceive of our attempts to make intellectual advance in quite different ways, the different spellings – Williams's 'enquiry' and Dewey's 'inquiry' – will be retained to help mark the difference.

13 This roundabout way of describing the goal is in part a response to difficulties made notorious by Gettier (1963). There is no reason to discuss these difficulties here.

14 He did, however, at one point explain that his analysis of 'warranted assertibility' (his name for the 'end of inquiry') was offered as a 'definition of knowledge in the honorific sense according to which only *true* beliefs are knowledge' (PM, p. 332).

15 On mediation, see M8 (p. 52, n. 16), and Section II.e above.

16 See, for example, L1 (p. 316), and note 14 above.

17 Russell interpreted Dewey – correctly it would seem – as holding that 'The essence of knowledge is *inference*' (Russell, 1919, p. 240).

18 For evidence of the consistency with which Dewey treated the goal of thinking as bringing about unification, see the opening paragraph of Section I.c above.

19 See below Chapter VI, note 2.

20 Cp. '. . . this unity is unification of just those data and considerations which in that situation are confused and incoherent. The fallacy of unlimited universalization is found when it is asserted, without any such limiting conditions, that the goal of thinking, particularly of philosophic thought, is to bring all things whatsoever into a single coherent and all inclusive whole. Then the idea of unity which has value and import under specifiable conditions is employed with such an unlimited extension that it loses its meaning' (L6, p. 8).

21 See Section I.e above.

22 Cp. Jardine (1986, pp. 28–9) on the domination of one 'inquiry series' over another.

23 'This element of direction by an idea of value applies to science as well as anywhere else, for in every scientific undertaking, there is passed a constant succession of estimates; such as "it is worth treating these facts as data or evidence; it is advisable to try this experiment; to make that observation; to

entertain such and such a hypothesis; to perform this calculation," etc.' (L4, p. 209).

24 In L6, pp. 3ff.: see Section I.e above.

25 'I start and am flustered by a noise heard. Empirically that noise is fearsome: it *really* is, not merely phenomenally or subjectively so. That *is what* it is experienced as being. But, when I experience the noise as a *known* thing, I find it to be innocent of harm. It is the tapping of a shade against the window, owing to movements of the wind. The experience has changed – not that truth has changed, but just and only the concrete reality experienced has changed' (M3, p. 160).

26 See Section I.e above. The form of *the* fallacy lying behind the spectator model is the error of 'intellectualism', of treating all experience as cognitive *au fond*, when the cognitive elements are products either of inquiry or of the more primitive ways of responding to problems and conflicts in experience. On 'intellectualism' see Section II.d above.

27 With some diffidence ('To say that a philosopher is in the grip of an inappropriate picture of perception makes it sound as if something rather disreputable is going on . . . it seems not only rude but unnecessary . . .'), Burnyeat (1979, p. 87) suggests that a similar image, that of seeing things through an open window, has dominated and distorted epistemology from the time of Plato. What Burnyeat suggests is wholly in the spirit of Dewey (although Dewey is nowhere mentioned) and makes clear that what Dewey derides as 'spectatorship' has by no means gone out of fashion.

28 For an excellent discussion of the *tuche* vs. *techne* theme in Greek thought, see Nussbaum (1986, especially pp. 89–99). This theme will resurface in Chapter VIII and it is important to say in the light of the main thesis of Nussbaum's book that Dewey's philosophy in no way involves the hope for the total elimination of 'luck' from human experience. We are simply invited to recognize that, to maintain a *human* life, we have to work constantly to bring our changing circumstances under control.

29 See Section V.b above.

30 See Chapter II above.

31 See Section III.b above.

32 It was argued in Section III.e (following the direction of Dewey's thought) that this involves an incoherent use of the notion of viewpoint.

33 See Section III.a above.

34 See Section IV.b above.

Chapter VI: Dewey and the realists

1 See Section V.a above.

2 It is noteworthy how close to Dewey's is Peirce's attitude to statements about the past. 'History would not have the character of a true science if it were not permissible to hope that further evidences may be forthcoming in the future by which the hypotheses of the critics may be tested. . . . a theory, which goes beyond what may be verified to any degree of approximation by future discoveries is, in so far, metaphysical gabble' (5.541).

Peirce illustrates with an attractive example. The biographical tradition has it that Aristotle was *traulos*, i.e. unable to pronounce the letter *r*. Can we ever hope to confirm or contradict this proposition? Peirce suggests that it is not beyond possibility that the sound waves made by Aristotle's voice may somehow have recorded themselves and in a hundred centuries of scientific progress we may have further evidence one way or the other. 'If not, it were better to hand the reports over to the poets to make something pretty of, and thus turn them to some human use' (5.542).

Lovejoy would doubtless have pressed on Peirce the same distinction between the means of verification and the meaning of the judgment, which he pressed on Dewey. Peirce's reply is unequivocal: the claim that Aristotle was *traulos* 'means nothing unless it be that Aristotle having been brought, directly or indirectly, to our experience, *will be* found, if found at all, to be incapable of pronouncing the R' (5.543).

Part of Peirce's defence of his position, a distinction between the *proposition* and the *assertion* of the proposition, was clearly taken up by Dewey in his *Logic* (See LTE, p. 120, and Section V.b above.) Assertion, according to Peirce, involves taking responsibility for the proposition in an act which is not unlike promising. But just as one cannot promise what the past shall have been, 'there can be no meaning in making oneself responsible for a past event independent of its future ascertainment. But to assert a proposition is to make oneself responsible for its truth. Consequently, the only meaning which an assertion of a past fact can have is that, if in the future the truth be ascertained, so [namely, as the proposition represents] it shall be ascertained to be. There seems to be no escape from this' (5.543). It is unlikely that Dewey was influenced by this particular part of Peirce in his debate with Lovejoy, for it remained unpublished for over a decade after that debate was carried out.

3 Dewey's recapitulation of 'the burden of my theme' at M15, pp. 35–6, has roughly these two parts.

4 See Berlin (1950, pp. 39ff.).

5 In this respect Dewey is again very close to Peirce, for Peirce's doctrine that belief involves expectation also clashes with the same central assumption. Peirce considers a natural challenge to his claim about the relation between belief and expectation, which arises in the case of 'direct perceptual facts. I lay down a wafer, before me. I look at it, and say to myself, "that wafer looks red." What element of expectation is there in the belief that the wafer *looks* red at this moment?' (5.542). But judgment (or the act of asserting) takes time, and its reference is to the state of the percept at the time it begins to be made. By the time the judgment (or assertion) has been made, it is already about the past. 'The judgment, then, can only mean that so far as the character of the percept can ever be ascertained, it will be ascertained that the wafer looked red' (5.544).

6 See Section IV.c above.

7 See Section IV.d above, and cp. Peirce's entry for 'represent' in Baldwin's *Dictionary*: 'To stand for, that is, to be in such a relation to another that for certain purposes it is treated by some mind as if it were that other' (2.273). The theses recapitulated in the next sentence are discussed in Sections IV.a, IV.b and III.c above.

8 'A sign, or *representamen*, is something which stands to somebody for something in some respect or capacity. It addresses somebody, that is, creates in the mind of that person an equivalent, or perhaps more developed sign. That sign, which it creates I call the *interpretant* of the first sign. The sign stands for something, its *object*. It stands for that object, not in all respects, but in reference to . . . the *ground* of the representamen' (Peirce, 2.228).

9 At the end of the sixth meditation Descartes is prepared to distinguish the dreaming from the waking state by the 'notable difference between the two, inasmuch as our memory can never connect our dreams one with the other, or with the whole course of our lives, as it unites events which happen to us while we are awake' (Descartes, 1641, p. 199). But before he can use interpretants in this way, he needs the assurance of a benevolent God that the signs constituting his experience correspond to (unknown) objects which are not accessible in that experience, and are (like the unknown soldier) known only to God.

10 See Section III.e above.

11 See Sections III.c and III.d above.

12 In order to distinguish bare perceptual-motor events from the cases where the sign function of perceptual events is 'telescoped' into what they are, the phrase 'as such' will be used to mark the 'bare events' in the text to follow.

13 See also Section V.e above.

14 See Section III.a above.

15 See Chapter V, note 25.

16 Dewey, however, was more than half serious about the basis of this burlesque. He was fond of insisting that coming to know is a change in a natural (i.e. physical) relationship involving physiological changes in the organism and a change in some objects in the organism's environment (see Section V.e above): '. . . the problem of how a mind can know an external world or even know that there is such a thing, is like the problem of how an animal eats things external to itself' (L1, p. 212). Cp. M10 (p. 24).

17 It would perhaps be better in the light of the doctrines (from a slightly later period in Dewey's life) which were surveyed in Chapter IV to say 'containing at least a "proto-self" '.

18 See Section I.b above.

19 *Journal of Philosophy*, Vol. 8, 1911, pp. 574–9, page references will be to its reprinting in M6. Some years later the Six Realists brought out a book, *The New Realism*, New York, Macmillan, 1922. The Six and their sympathizers, including McGilvary and Dewey's colleague at Columbia, J. E. Woodbridge, are known to students of the history of this period as the 'new realists'. Lovejoy belonged to a group of more traditional (re)presentational realists, who rallied in reaction to the 'new realism' under the banner of 'critical realism'.

20 'Demonstrably false' is probably too strong; certainly there is no prima facie case that external relations alone are adequate to treat such phenomena.

21 See, for example, Dummett (1973).

22 The appeal to external relations, which is implicit in presentative realism, was already in Dewey's sights when he took aim at the assumption of 'ubiquity'. See M6, (p. 114).

23 For a version of this line of argument in Dewey's early writings, see E1, (pp. 148–9).

Chapter VII: Objectivity, value and motivation

1 This is Dewey in 1941 quoting in abridged form from a reply which he wrote to Russell a few years earlier (Schilpp, 1939, p. 572) and which, he felt, Russell (1940, Chapter 23) had still not sufficiently acknowledged. Cp. 'For irrespective of whether a satisfaction is conscious, a satisfaction or non-satisfaction is an objective thing with objective conditions. It means fulfill-ment of the demands of objective factors. . . . satisfaction is not subjective, private or personal: it is conditioned by objective partialities and defections and made real by objective situations and completions' (L1, p. 59).
2 See Section V.c above, and note 20 to Chapter V.
3 The wording of this note influenced the wording of the second claim about statements about the past which was put in Dewey's mouth at the end of Section VI.a: '(2) We should not pretend that we can divide a problem(atic proposition) about the past into object and subject matter without referring to a context of inquiry, which is determined by the goal (objective) of giving settled and definite form to some objective.' The present chapter has the task of unpacking this claim.
4 These interpretations will be found reprinted in Rorty (1980). They are J. L. Ackrill, 'Aristotle on *Eudaimonia*', for which see pp. 18f., and David Wiggins, 'Deliberation and Practical Reason', for which see pp. 222ff. Isolated passages in Aristotle present difficulties for this interpretation. One such from the *Politics* will be found to figure in Dewey's argument in Section VIII.c below.
5 It will be noted below in this section that this cuts across a usage Dewey recommended in L1 (Chapter 9). The underlying issue is crucially important and will be discussed at length in Sections VIII.c and VIII.d below.
6 It is not, however, a wholly empty platitude, for creatures which cannot have aspirations for their lives as wholes, only desires for the moment, have no use for a concept of *eudaimonia*.
7 Wealth is disqualified by Aristotle as being something which can properly qualify only as a means, not as an ultimate end (1096^{a}5–10).
8 'It is . . . . no doubt true that men act, especially in the action of inquiry, *as if* their sole purpose were to produce a certain state of feeling, in the sense that when that state of feeling is attained, there is no further effort. It was upon that proposition that I originally based pragmaticism, laying it down in the article that in November 1877 prepared the ground for my argument for the pramaticistic doctrine. In the case of inquiry, I called that state of feeling "firm belief" and said, "As soon as a firm belief is reached we are entirely satisfied, whether the belief be true or false," and went on to show how the action of experience consequently was to create the conception of real truth' (Peirce, 5.563).

My paper of November 1877, setting out from the proposition that the agitation of a question ceases when satisfaction is attained with the settlement of belief, . . . goes on to consider how the conception of truth gradually develops from that principle under the action of experience, beginning with willful belief, or self-mendacity, the most degraded of all intellectual conditions; thence rising to the imposition of belief by the authority of organized society; then to the idea of a settlement of opinion as the result of a fermentation of ideas; and finally reaching the idea of truth as overwhelmingly forced upon the mind in experience as the effect of an independent reality' (5.564).

9 This is a description which, like Peirce's 'fixed belief', applies to all inquiry regardless of how refined or unrefined are the means of inquiry. As beliefs for Peirce are habits (Section V.b above), and are 'unfixed' when in the course of experience their smooth and coordinated functioning is interrupted, Peirce's 'fixed belief' is in fact very close to what Dewey means by 'unification'.

10 Experimentation, as an activity in which people come to know, was often cited by Dewey as proof that coming to know changes things, for to experiment one must actively exercise control over the physical conditions of observation. This will seem unconvincing to anyone who treats the change in cognitive state, however that is conceived, as logically external to the physical events which preceded it, even if they were causally responsible for it.

11 Cp. the title of Chapter 10 of the *Quest for Certainty* (L4), 'The Construction of Good'.

12 This and the next three sentences summarize material covered in Chapter III.

13 These are terms which Dewey uses to cover non-cognitive as well as cognitive patterns of behaviour. (Cp. M13, p. 11.)

14 This is not a term Dewey used, but it may help to clarify his position.

15 See Section VII.a above and especially note 1.

16 Ralph Barton Perry (one of 'the Six' – see Section VI.d above) made in criticism of Dewey a painstaking survey of all the roles which judgment might play where values are concerned (Perry, 1917, pp. 591–4) and found no constitutive role. His procedure, however, as Dewey pointed out (M11, pp. 4–5), simply ignored the question of whether when, for example, confronting the fact that I dislike ill-health (a fact which, we may grant for the sake of argument, is not constituted by judgment) I may raise the question of whether I *should* in my present circumstances go on disliking it. Here judgment does play a role in instating a new value or in reinstating the existing value.

17 Early in the 1940s Philip Blaire Rice advanced a view of values which professed general agreement with Dewey's position, but Dewey took strong exception to the way Rice tried to make immediate satisfaction into a piece of evidence for the value of an experience (Rice, 1943a, p. 639). No immediate satisfaction, Dewey insisted (PM, pp. 271–2), can provide evidence for its *own* value. The question whether something found immediately satisfying should be regarded as satisfactory depends entirely on connections it has to *other* events.

18 Cp. 'The intellect is always inspired by some impulse. Even the most case-hardened scientific specialist, the most abstract philosopher, is moved by some passion' (M14, pp. 177–8).

19 Cp. '. . . it is evident that "passions" and pains and pleasures may be used as *evidences* of something beyond themselves (as may the fact of being more than five feet high) and so get a representative or cognitive status' (M8, p. 24, n. 8).

20 See LTE (pp. 104–5), and Sections V.b and V.c above.

21 See Sections IV.a and IV.b above.

22 Dewey's conscious identification of the two terms – see M14, p. 74n – does not help the clarity of his position. The danger (to which Dewey is alive – see M14, p. 69) is that the specific form which a culture places on the outcome of an impulse will come to seem as unalterable as our biochemistry, simply because the difference between a determinate and inflexible instinct and an unspecific and plastic impulse will have been blurred.

23 See Section VII.b above.

24 Plato consistently associated the plastic and dramatic arts with the manipulation of emotional material, 'feeling' – cp. *Republic* X.

Chapter VIII: Art, intelligence and contemplation

1 See M8, (p. 47) where Nietzsche's word is deliberately employed.

2 See Section VI.d. Prall (1923) denied that Picard's notion of worth (Section VII.e) could be classed as a species of value and went on to castigate Dewey for the use he made of the notion. Picard had, Prall noted, used his concept to mount a criticism of an account of value given by Ralph Barton Perry, one of the six 'new realists'.

3 The other two, 'the denial of quality in general' and 'the superior reality of causes', were discussed in Sections III.a and I.e, respectively.

4 The background to this and the connection to the distinction between sense and signification are discussed in Sections III.c and III.d above.

5 See Section V.c above. Dewey's ambivalent attitude toward metaphysics arises from the way aspirations to portray things from the absolute standpoint cling to the word 'metaphysics' in the way they cling to the cognates of 'true'. Within the spirit of his own anti-absolutist philosophy Dewey is free to propound and defend highly general hypotheses about the nature of what there is. And indeed he is more or less forced to by the way (what he would see as) less adequate theses of this sort obstruct his own philosophy.

6 See L1 (p. 233) and above, Chapters II–IV, especially Sections II.e and IV.e.

7 See Section IV.d above.

8 See AE (pp. 173–6) for a good discussion of this.

9 Dewey says 'rules for' here, but as he clearly does not mean that what is perceived has to possess the form of a verbal instruction, it is best not to introduce an irrelevance.

10 See Sections II.d and II.e above.

11 The passage continues, '. . . the emotion aroused attends the subject-matter that is perceived, thus differing from crude emotion because it is attached to the movement of the subject-matter toward consummation. To limit esthetic emotion to the pleasure attending the act of contemplation is to exclude all that is most characteristic of it'. Cp. '. . . results . . . in a thoroughly anæmic conception of art' (AE, p. 253). Dewey's declared target here is Kant's

Critique of Judgement, but Prall's position does not differ in this respect from Kant's.

12 See Section IV.a above.

13 The passage continues, 'It is this double relationship of continuation, promotion, carrying forward, and of arrest, deviation, need of supplementation, which defines that focalization of meanings which is consciousness, awareness, perception. Every case of consciousness is dramatic; drama is an enhancement of the conditions of consciousness.' This claim clearly involves a generalization of the notion of 'drama' from that of 'enactment' to that of 'the effects which one commonly tries to achieve with enactment'. In this sense, one might describe the distribution of lighting in a room as 'dramatic'. (Such effects, Dewey would maintain, depend on drawing the affected person into a form of active participation, even if not one that, strictly speaking, involves a kind of 'acting out' of what produced the effect.) It is likely that in the earlier chapter (L1, p. 77) where Dewey characterized imagination as 'primarily dramatic', he was already pushing the word 'dramatic' toward this generalized sense.

14 See Section V.e above, and cp. Aristotle's *Politics*, 'the most artful (*technikotatoi*) [activities] are those which involve the least amount of luck' (1258^{b}33).

15 See Section V.e above.

16 See Hegel (1807, B, IV, A).

17 There was a stigma attaching to occupations which involved the use of the body, so that there is circumstantial evidence that amongst what we think of as the fine arts, painting had a higher status than sculpture. See Arendt (1958, p. 82n). Aristotle says (1258^{b}35) 'that the most servile [occupations involve] the most use of the body'. But the pejorative connotations of '*banausikos*' (from *baunos*, forge; cp. English 'banausic') may well not derive from the involvement of bodily activity as such, but from the degradation the body underwent (see Aristotle, op. cit.) or from the lack of freedom and self-sufficiency which such occupations involved (see Arendt, op. cit.). Aristotle (1277^{b}5) suggests it was not labour as such which was ungentlemanly, but for whom it was done: 'it is not proper for the good man . . . or the good citizen to learn manual skills except for his own private use occasionally'.

18 Somewhat more literally the passage reads, 'Whenever one thing is for the sake of (*heneken*) something and another that which it is for the sake of, there is nothing in common in their case except the making and the taking'. (Aristotle illustrates by citing the relationship between a builder, or his tools, and the house he builds. The point of the passage is that property, including livestock and slaves, is not a part of the *polis* in the way the citizens are.) Commonly, however, in Aristotle's writings the whole stands as the end (*telos*) or as the for-the-sake-of-which (*to heneka*) of its constituent parts. Cp. Chapter VII, note 4.

19 Dewey seems curiously reluctant to acknowledge the presence of his favoured notion in Aristotle. Another of his examples, virtue as a constituent of happiness, is Aristotelian, as is the principle, which he calls a 'trite saying', 'that a hand is not a hand except as an organ of the living body' (ibid.).

20 Section V.e above.

21 See Section VI.b above.

22 'Plato defined a slave as one who accepts from another the purposes which control his conduct' (M9, p. 90).

23 See Sections IV.e and VI.b above.

24 See Sections III.c and III.d above.

25 We are blinded (by our philosophic persuasions) rather than inherently unable to see; for Aristotle, at least, was able to see that understanding proceeds according to (*kata*) the whole (*holon*) and to see the role of the universal (*katholou*) in explanation. Cp. Plato, *Philebus* 18d.

26 Cp. there are no means until there are ends-in-view.

27 See Section VIII.a above.

28 See L1 (p. 91) and Section VIII.b above.

29 The independence needed by 'artists' to undertake this experimental work is the source of the popular association of 'creative art' with 'self-expression' (L1, p. 272) and the difficulty determining initially what counts as a successful experiment leads to the common confusion of 'self-expression' with 'self-exposure' (AE, p. 62).

30 Sense perception is the basis of pleasure. With regard to this candidate, the first lines of the *Metaphysics* observe that we humans take delight in the use of our senses (particularly vision). Normally we use our perceptual capacities in order to act (*prattein – praxis*), but there is delight 'even when we are not going to do anything', because the use of this sense is instrumental in knowing; it makes (*poiein – poiesis*) us familiar with things and reveals distinctions (980ª22–27). But a life consisting *only* in delight taken in the exercise of the senses, when not informed by the purposes of acting or knowing, would not be above the level of an animal capable only of the sense of touch, and not worthy of a human being. (When Aristotle condemns the life of pleasure, it is particularly the pleasures of touch he has in mind.)

It should be remarked, therefore (even if Dewey does not himself contribute to this error), that it would be mistaken to think that the pleasure which Greeks took in the 'artistic products' of their culture was akin to blind sensual gratification. That sort of pleasure was dismissed by Aristotle, and it is clear from the *Poetics* he would not have regarded the satisfactions afforded by dramatic poetry as on this level. The material of dramatic poetry in particular was said to be human action (*praxeis*, 1148ª1) and the satisfaction taken in it was informed by the meanings derived from interacting with other people. Other art forms, if to a less obvious degree, also derive their meanings from the action and appearance of human beings with and before others of their community. Aristotle could well have explained the difference between the self-indulgent life of *sensual* pleasure, which he dismissed, and the role which the *sensuous* has in art and life generally by employing Dewey's distinction between the two: 'those gratifications to which the name sensual rather than sensuous is given . . . are pleasing endings that occur in what is not informed with the meaning of materials and acts integrated into them' (L1, p. 281).

31 See Anscombe (1965, pp. 70f.). It should be noted how this point bears on the issue which in Section VI.b was seen to divide Dewey and Peirce, viz. the claim of pure science to be an end not answering to what Dewey called 'the socially controlling'.

Chapter IX: Ideals

1 One can, as Dewey observes (L2, p. 282), perform this public office in the two ways open to anyone filling a public office, either with only one's own interest in view or with that of the community in view.

2 See Section VIII.a. As we saw in Section VIII.d, philosophic views of nature and of language, which are metaphysical in scope, undermine the foundation for claims on behalf of what Dewey believes to be 'the characteristic human need'.

3 See Section VII.a, especially note 1.

4 In the general sense in which Dewey uses the term, see note 18 to Chapter III.

5 Perhaps to distance himself from the Marxist version of this claim, Dewey misquotes Carlyle ('no admirer of democracy'), 'Invent the printing press and democracy is inevitable', adding railways, the telegraph, mass production and urbanization to the list of significant material factors (L2, p. 304. Carlyle, it appears (L2, p. 481), actually said: 'Invent writing and democracy is inevitable.'

6 See Section VII.b above.

7 When it comes to having a say in affairs, Dewey seems prepared to subscribe to 'from each according to his ability', and when it comes to sharing in the benefits of the group's activities, it seems to be a case of 'to each according to his needs'.

8 See Williams (1978, pp. 297–303) and Section V.e above.

9 Thus John Mackie, who identifies 'objective' with 'existent', reads the element of compulsion into Plato's Form of the Good: 'something's being good both tells the person who knows this to pursue it and makes him pursue it' (Mackie, 1977, p. 40).

10 See Williams (1978, p. 65) and Section V.c above.

11 This phrase is the title of Nagel's recent book (Nagel, 1986), which develops this theme.

12 See Section III.a above.

13 See Section VIII.c above.

14 Nagel's position on subjectivity, which was criticized in III.e, is sustained crucially by his belief that objectivity requires 'the view from nowhere'; see note 11 above.

15 See Section III.a above.

16 See Section IV.a above.

References

I. Dewey's works

Where possible references are given by series, volume number and page to the *Works of John Dewey*, where the series is indicated as follows.

E *John Dewey, The Early Works, 1882–1898*, in five volumes, 1969–72.
M *John Dewey, The Middle Works, 1899–1924*, in fifteen volumes, 1976–83.
L *John Dewey, The Later Works, 1925–1953*, up to volume 8, 1981–.

All edited by Jo Ann Boydston, and published by Southern Illinois University Press, Carbondale and Edwardsville, Illinois.

This has only been possible as far as the eighth volume of *The Later Works*. For references to Dewey's works later than 1933, the following abbreviations have been used:

AE   *Art as Experience*, New York, G. Putnam & Sons, 1934, seventh impression, 1958.
CF   *A Common Faith*, New Haven, Connecticut, Yale University Press, 1934, paperback edition 1960.
ENF *On Experience, Nature and Freedom*, edited by Richard J. Bernstein, Indianapolis, Indiana, Bobbs-Merrill Company, 1960.
LTE *Logic, the Theory of Inquiry*, New York, Henry Holt & Company, 1938.
PM   *Problems of Men*, New York, Philosophical Library, 1946.
TV   *Theory of Valuation (International Encyclopedia of Unified Science*, II, 4) Chicago, University of Chicago Press, 1939.

II. Other works

Where two dates appear, the first refers to the date of the original publication and the second to the edition consulted if that is not the same as the first.

Ackrill, J. L. (1974) 'Aristotle on *Eudaimonia*', in Rorty (1980), pp. 18–33.
Anscombe, Elizabeth, (1958), 'Modern Moral Philosophy', in *Ethics and Politics, Collected Papers, Vol. III*, Oxford, Basil Blackwell, 1981, pp. 26–42.

Anscombe, Elizabeth (1965), 'Thought and Action in Aristotle', in *From Parmenides to Wittgenstein, Collected Philosophical Papers, Vol. 1*, Oxford, Basil Blackwell, 1981, pp. 66–77.

Arendt, Hannah (1958), *The Human Condition*, Chicago, University of Chicago Press.

Aristotle. References are given by Bekker line number. The translations used are from *The Complete Works of Aristotle*, edited by Jonatham Barnes, Princeton, New Jersey, Princeton University Press, 1984, except for a few occasions, when I modified the translation in the light of my own understanding of the Greek text.

Bennett, Jonathan (1976), *Linguistic Behaviour*, Cambridge, Cambridge University Press.

Berlin, Isaiah (1950), 'Empirical Propositions and Hypothetical Statements', in *Concepts and Categories*, edited by Henry Hardy, Oxford, Oxford University Press, 1980.

Blackburn, Simon (1984) *Spreading the Word*, Oxford, Oxford University Press.

Bradley, F. H. (1897), *Appearance and Reality*, second edition, London, Swan Sonnenschein.

Burnyeat, M. F. (1979), 'Conflicting Appearances', *Proceedings of the British Academy*, Vol. LXV, pp. 69–111.

Coughlan, Neil (1973), *Young John Dewey*, Chicago, University of Chicago Press.

Darwin, Charles (1873), *The Expression of the Emotions in Man and Animals*, second edition, London, John Murray, 1901.

Davidson, Donald (1980), *Essays on Action and Events*, Oxford, Clarendon Press.

Davidson, Donald (1984), *Inquiries into Truth and Interpretation*, Oxford, Clarendon Press.

Descartes, René (1641), *Meditations on First Philosophy*, in *Philosophical Works of Descartes*, translated by E. S. Haldane and G. R. T. Ross, New York, Dover, 1955.

Dummett, Michael (1973), 'The Philosophical Basis of Intuitionistic Logic', in *Truth and Other Enigmas*, London, Duckworth, 1978, pp. 215–47.

Dykhuizen, George (1973), *The Life and Mind of John Dewey*, Carbondale and Edwardsville, Illinois, Southern Illinois University Press.

Edel, Abraham (1987). 'Naturalism and the Concept of Moral Change', *Proceedings and Addresses of the American Philosophical Association*, Vol. 60, No. 5, pp. 823–40.

Flew, Antony, ed. (1979), *A Dictionary of Philosophy*, London, Pan Books.

Frankena, William (1939), 'The Naturalistic Fallacy', in P. Foot, ed., *Theories of Ethics*, Oxford, Oxford University Press, 1967, pp. 50–63.

Gettier, E. L. (1963), 'Is Justified True Belief Knowledge?' *Analysis*, Vol. 23.

Gombrich, E. H. (1951), 'Meditations on a Hobby Horse or the Roots of Artistic Form', in *Meditations on a Hobby Horse and Other Essays on the Theory of Art*, London, Phaidon, second edition, 1973, pp. 1–11.

Goodall, Jane van Lawick (1971), *In the Shadow of Man*, London, Collins.

Green, T. H. (1883), *Prolegomena to Ethics*, third edition, Oxford, Clarendon Press, 1890.

Green, T. H. (1885), *The Works of Thomas Hill Green*, in three volumes, edited by R. L. Nettleship, second edition, London, Longmans Green, 1890.

Grice, H. P. (1957), 'Meaning', in P. F. Strawson, ed., *Philosophical Logic*, Oxford, Oxford University Press, 1967, pp. 39–48.

Harrison, Bernard (1979), *Introduction to the Philosophy of Language*, London, Macmillan.

Hegel, G. W. F. (1807), *The Phenomenology of Spirit*, translated by A. V. Miller, Oxford, Clarendon Press, 1977.

Hempel, Carl (1935), 'On the Logical Positivists' Theory of Truth', *Analysis*, Vol. 2, No. 4, pp. 49–59.

Hodgson, Shadworth (1886), 'Illusory Psychology'. References are to the appearance in E1, pp. xli–lvii.

Hofstadter, D. R. and Dennett D. C., eds (1981), *The Mind's I*, Harmondsworth, Middlesex, Penguin.

Hume, David (1739), *A Treatise of Human Nature*, edited by L. A. Selby-Bigge, Oxford, Clarendon Press, 1975.

James, William (1890), *The Principles of Psychology*, in two volumes, New York, Dover, 1950.

Jardine, N. (1986), *The Fortunes of Inquiry*, Oxford, Clarendon Press.

Kant, Immanuel (1781–7), *Critique of Pure Reason*, translated by Norman Kemp Smith, Macmillan, London, 1978. References are in the customary form of an A/B pair of numbers referring to the pages in the first and second editions.

Kant, Immanuel (1785), *Grundlegung zur Metaphysik der Sitten*, in *Kants Werke*, Vol. IV (Akademie Textausgebe), Berlin, Walter de Gruyter, 1968.

Kenny, Anthony (1964), Introduction to St. Thomas Aquinas, *Summa Theologiae*, Vol. 22, *Dispositions for Human Action (Ia2ae 49–54)*, London, Eyre & Spottiswoode.

Kuhn, Thomas (1973), 'Objectivity, Value Judgment and Theory Choice', in *The Essential Tension*, Chicago, University of Chicago Press, 1977, pp. 320–39.

Lewis, David (1969) *Convention*, Cambridge, Mass., Harvard University Press.

Locke, John (1690), *An Essay Concerning Human Understanding*, in two volumes, London, Dent, 1961. References are given by book, chapter and paragraph.

Lovejoy, A. O. (1920), 'Pragmatism *versus* the Pragmatist'. References are to the appearance in M13, pp. 443–81.

Lovejoy, A. O. (1922), 'Time, Meaning and Transcendence'. References are to the appearance in M15, pp. 349–70.

McGilvary, E. B. (1912), 'Professor Dewey's "Brief Studies in Realism" '. References are to the appearance in M7, pp. 454–61.

Mackie, John (1977), *Ethics, Inventing Right and Wrong*, Harmondsworth, Middlesex, Penguin Books.

Malcolm, Norman (1963), *Knowledge and Certainty*, Ithaca, New York, Cornell University Press.

Mead, George Herbert (1934) *Mind, Self and Society*, edited by Charles W. Morris, Chicago, University of Chicago Press, 1962.

Medawar, P. B. (1969), *Induction and Intuition in Scientific Thought*, London, Methuen.

Mill, J. S. (1843), *A System of Logic*, London, George Routledge, no date.

Morgenbesser, S., ed. (1977), *Dewey and His Critics*, New York, Journal of Philosophy, Inc.

Nagel, Thomas (1979), *Mortal Questions*, Cambridge, Cambridge University Press.

Nagel, Thomas (1986), *The View From Nowhere*, Oxford, Oxford University Press.

Nussbaum, Martha C. (1986), *The Fragility of Goodness*, Cambridge, Cambridge University Press.

Peirce, Charles S. (1931–58), *The Collected Papers of Charles Sanders Peirce* in eight volumes, edited by Charles Hartshorne, Paul Weiss and Arthur W. Burks. References are given by volume and paragraph number.

Perry, R. B. (1917), 'Dewey and Urban on Value Judgments'. References are to the appearance in M11, pp. 361–74.

Plato, *The Dialogues of Plato*, in four volumes translated by B. Jowett, fourth edition, Oxford, Clarendon Press, 1953. References are given by dialogue and Stephanus line number.

Popper, Karl (1972), *Objective Knowledge*, Oxford, Oxford University Press.

Prall, D. W. (1923), 'In Defense of a Worth*less* Theory of Value'. References are to the appearance in M15, pp. 338–48.

Prall, D. W. (1924), 'Value and Thought-Process'. References are to the appearance in Morgenbesser (1977), pp. 621–9.

Putnam, Hilary (1981), *Reason, Truth and History*, Cambridge, Cambridge University Press.

Quine, W. V. (1969), *Ontological Relativity and Other Essays*, New York, Columbia University Press.

Rice, Philip Blaire (1943a), ' "Objectivity" in Value Judgments'. References are to the appearance in Morgenbesser (1977), pp. 630–9.

Rice, Philip Blaire (1943b), 'Types of Value Judgment'. References are to the appearance in Morgenbesser (1977), pp. 649–59.

Rorty, Amelia O., ed. (1980), *Essays on Aristotle's Ethics*, Berkeley, University of California Press.

Rorty, Richard (1982), *Consequences of Pragmatism*, Brighton, Sussex, Harvester Press.

Rorty, Richard (1985), 'Comments on Sleeper and Edel', *Transactions of the Charles S. Peirce Society*, Vol. XXI, No. 1, pp. 39–48.

Russell, Bertrand (1915), *Our Knowledge of the External World*, second (1929) edition, New York, Mentor, 1960.

Russell, Bertrand (1919), 'Professor Dewey's "Essays in Experimental Logic" '. References are to the appearance in Morgenbesser (1977), pp. 231–52.

Russell, Bertrand (1921), *The Analysis of Mind*, London, George Allen & Unwin.

Russell, Bertrand (1940). *An Inquiry in Meaning and Truth*, Harmondsworth, Middlesex, Penguin Books, 1962.

Santayana, George (1923), *Scepticism and Animal Faith*, New York, Dover, 1955.

Schilpp, P. A. (1939), *The Philosophy of John Dewey*, second edition, New York, Tudor Press, 1952.

Sleeper, R. W. (1985), 'Rorty's Pragmatism: Afloat in Neurath's Boat, but Why

Adrift?' *Transactions of the Charles S. Peirce Society*, Vol. XXI, No. 1, pp. 9–20.

Smart, J. J. C. (1986), 'Realm *v.* Idealism', *Philosophy*, Vol. 61, No. 237, pp. 295–312.

Spaulding, Edward Gleason (1911a), 'Realism: A Reply to Professor Dewey and an Exposition'. References are to the appearance in M6, pp. 483–500.

Spaulding, Edward Gleason (1911b), 'A Reply to Professor Dewey's Rejoinder'. References to the appearance in M6, pp. 501–11.

Spaulding, Edward Gleason, and Dewey, John (1911), 'Joint Discussion with Articles of Agreement and Disagreement'. References are to the appearance in M6, pp. 146–52.

Spaulding, Edward Gleason, *et al.* (1911), The Program and First Platform of Six Realists. References are to the appearance in M6, pp 472–82.

Strawson, P. F. (1959), *Individuals*, London, Methuen.

Strawson, P. F. (1970). 'Meaning and Truth,' in *Logico-Linguistic Papers*, London, Methuen, 1971, pp. 170–89.

Tiles, J. E. (1985), 'A "Rationalist" Approach to Dispositional Concepts,' *Theoria*, Vol. LI, Part 1, pp. 1–15.

van Fraassen, Bas C. (1980), *The Scientific Image*, Oxford, Clarendon Press.

Wiggins, David (1975), 'Deliberation and Practical Reason' in Rorty (1980), pp. 221–40).

Williams, Bernard (1978), *Descartes, The Project of Pure Inquiry*, Harmondsworth, Middlesex, Penguin Books.

Wittgenstein, Ludwig (1953), *Philosophical Investigations*, translated by G. E. M. Anscombe, Oxford, Basil Blackwell, 1963.

Index

121, 133; *see* evaluation, prizing, proto-values

verification(s), 105, 110, 130–1, 133, 137, 152; transcendence, 105

Vienna Circle, 6

wants, will, 83, 129, 168, 173–9, 207; incoming/out-going, 33–5; general will, 213; object-determinateness, 170, 173, 221; to

survive, 40; weak-will, 177–9; *see* feeling, desires

Watson, J., 6

Wiggins, D., 241

Williams, Bernard, 53–4, 111, 116, 118–19, 121–4, 127–8, 131, 214, 217, 237, 246

Wittgenstein, L., 3, 4, 5, 6, 24, 77, 98–101

Woodbridge, J. E., 240

worth, 182; judgments of 178–9